MASCULINDIANS

MASCULINDIANS

CONVERSATIONS ABOUT INDIGENOUS MANHOOD

SAM MCKEGNEY

UMP
University of Manitoba Press

CONTENTS

INTO THE FULL GRACE OF THE BLOOD IN MEN

AN INTRODUCTION

I FIRST USED THE TERM MASCULINDIANS a few years back to highlight the construct-edness of popular cultural representations of Indigenous men.[1] Built from a collision between the floating signifiers "masculine" and "Indian," the term draws attention to the settler North American appetite for depictions of Indigenous men that rehearse hypermasculine stereotypes of the noble savage and the bloodthirsty warrior (as well as their ideological progeny—the ecological medicine man, the corrupt band council-lor, and the drunken absentee). As Brian Klopotek argues, "For at least the last cen-tury, hypermasculinity has been one of the foremost attributes of the Indian world that whites have imagined. With squaws and princesses usually playing secondary roles, Indian tribes are populated predominantly by noble or ignoble savages, wise old chiefs, and cunning warriors. These imagined Indian nations comprise an impossibly mascu-line race" (251). Taiaiake Alfred explains the colonizing function of such "impossibl[e] masculin[ity]" later in this volume, arguing that "there's no living with it because it's not meant to be lived with; it's meant to be killed, every single time. They're images to

1. I first used the term in an article called "Warriors, Healers, Lovers, and Leaders: Colonial Impositions on Indigenous Male Roles and Responsibilities" in a collection en-titled *Canadian Perspectives on Men and Masculinities: An Interdisciplin-ary Reader* (2011). I later used it in my title for "Masculindians: The Violence and Voyeurism of Male Sibling Relationships in Recent First Nations Fiction" in a collec-tion entitled *Literature for Our Times: Postcolonial Studies in the Twenty-First Century* (2012).

SAM MCKEGNEY is a settler scholar of Indigenous literatures. He grew up in Anishinaabe territory on the Saugeen Peninsula along the shores of Lake Huron and currently resides with his partner and their two daughters in traditional lands of the Haudenosaunee and Anishinaabe peoples where he is an associate professor at Queen's University. He has written a book entitled *Magic Weapons: Aboriginal Writers Remaking Community after Residential School* (University of Manitoba Press, 2007) and articles on such topics as environmental kinship, masculinity theory, prison writing, Indigenous governance, and Canadian hockey mythologies.

be slain by the white conqueror." The term *Masculindians* acknowledges the ubiquity and influence of this regime of images, while drawing attention to the imbricated nature of race and gender in settler colonial imaginaries.

In Gerald Vizenor's terms, the word "Indian" is, after all, a manifest manner; it is a "simulation" incapable of representing the complexity of Indigenous lived experience, marking instead "the absence of real natives—[the] contrivance of the other in the course of dominance" (vii). Reducing diverse histories, worldviews, and modes of existence to a static constellation of tropes, the concept of the "Indian" both domesticates difference and dilutes specificity. "*Indians*," Vizenor argues, "are immovable simulations, the tragic archives of domination and victimry" (ix–x) that portray a sense of fixity that is anathema to meaningful Indigenous continuance. Like the simulation "Indian," the simulation "masculinity" points more to a "*historical, ideological process*" (Bederman 7) than to particular qualities or discernible identities. Gail Bederman defines "manhood" as "the process which creates 'men' by linking male genital anatomy to a male identity, and linking both anatomy and identity to particular arrangements of authority and power. Logically, this is an entirely arbitrary process. Anatomy, identity, and authority have no intrinsic relationship. Only the process of manhood—of the gender system—allows each to stand in for the others" (7–8). I tend to think of "masculinity" as a tool for describing the qualities, actions, characteristics, and behaviours that accrue meaning within a given historical context and social milieu through their association with maleness, as maleness is normalized, idealized, and even demonized within a web of power-laden interpenetrating discourses. Particularities of culture and history inevitably inform the makeup of the web, and movement among social contexts inevitably causes particular threads of discourse to gain prominence or to recede into the background as masculinity is conceived and expressed differently in kitchens and workplaces, in classrooms, bars, and bedrooms. Yet what comes to be considered masculine within a given context necessarily falls short of capturing the complex experiences of individual men, even as this constellation of meanings continues to influence how men's identities are lived and understood.

The "arbitrary process" of masculinity is, of course, complicated in contemporary Indigenous contexts by the layering of racialized, patriarchal gender systems over preexisting, tribally specific cosmologies of gender—impositions conducted through colonial technologies like the residential and boarding school systems, legislative alterations to Indigenous structures of governance by the Indian Act in Canada and the Bureau of Indian Affairs in the U.S., and the forced removal of Indigenous communities from traditional hunting and fishing grounds to reserves and reservations. As Mark Rifkin illustrates in *When Did Indians Become Straight?*, the attack on "native social formations… conducted in the name of 'civilization'" constituted an "organized effort" to make Eurocentric notions of gender "compulsory as a key part of breaking up indigenous landholdings, 'detribalizing' native peoples, [and] translating native territoriality and governance into the terms of… liberalism and legal geography" (5–6). In other words, the manipulation of Indigenous gender systems constituted a key element of dispossessive colonial policy in both Canada and the U.S. And, as South African writer Njabulo Ndebele asked evocatively after I had presented on some of these issues at a symposium, "If we are unable to see and imagine the land, how can we answer the question, 'what is masculinity?'" Yet, over the past quarter century, Indigenous women's groups, Indigenous men's groups, and Indigenous feminist and queer/Two-Spirit activists and scholars have been struggling to locate, theorize, and affirm traditional nation-specific understandings of gender in order to restore senses of rootedness and balance that might overturn the insidious normalization of settler heteropatriarchy on Turtle Island. As a result, contemporary Indigenous negotiations of gender identity are often conditioned by the interplay among a variety of Indigenous and non-Indigenous discourses (from filmic representations to the news media to what is taught in schools to what is modelled in families to traditional teachings and so on).

Although my use of the term *Masculindians* was initially intended merely to identify and critique simulated settler stereotypes about Indigenous men, I've become increasingly convinced of the term's generative potential. It points to what I see as an urgent need to grapple with both Indianness and masculinity, and it does so via an irreverent neologism that resists the pull of gender essentialism, biological determinism, and what Vizenor calls the "faux science" of "race" (xiv). Like Dana Claxton's brilliant art piece *Daddy's Got a New Ride*, which graces the cover of this volume, the term *Masculindians* plays with expectation, historicity, and stereotype while acknowledging the sensual immediacy of corporeal and territorial realities. It recognizes the representational/discursive as inherently enmeshed with what Ty P. Kāwika Tengan calls "bodies and gender and lands," all of which "need to be thought of in relation to one another." In speaking with the Indigenous men and women I interviewed for this project, I've come to understand the terms "masculine" and "Indian" not only as a means of tracking colonial simulations and technologies of coercion that have served to alienate Indigenous men from tribal specific roles and responsibilities; they also act as tools for imagining and enacting empowered, non-dominative Indigenous male identities that serve the interwoven struggles of communal health, gender complementarity, and Indigenous continuance. Inspired by Craig Womack's axiom "that there *is* such a thing as a Native perspective and that seeking it out is a worthwhile endeavor" (4), this collection is premised on the assumption that there are such things as Indigenous masculinities and that discussing—and even theorizing—them is not only worthwhile but necessary. Richard Van Camp argues later in this collection that what "we're not talking about" is "killing us and it's wounding us and it's harming us." *Masculindians* seeks to get people talking about Indigenous masculinities so that, in Kateri Akiwenzie-Damm's words, "[our] sons are going to be able to find a wider range of depictions of Indigenous men that will inspire them, influence them [and] teach them in the Nanabozho way what to do and what not to do. So they'll have more to draw on than… Indigenous men have in the past."

Thus, although this collection remains shadowed by the ongoing legacies of settler heteropatriarchy and socially engineered hypermasculinity, it maintains a cautious commitment to the ongoing prescience of masculinity as a concept that retains utility while being, of course, fraught. At a recent Indian Residential Schools Truth and Reconciliation Event, Ellen Gabriel declared, "There are men's roles and there are women's roles, in a Haudenosaunee worldview, and there's no need to read more into it than that" (IRS TRC). Barbara Alice Mann agrees, arguing that "gendering entirely permeates Iroquoian culture," and "Women do women's things, while men do men's things,… but, in the final analysis, all the people are fed" (98, 97). In a Cree context, Neal McLeod indicates that although "some people want to radically deconstruct gender," in his experience "there is a clear cluster of things that make up what we might call Cree men, or Cree masculinity." Yet, despite these affirmations, Jessica Danforth cautions against all forms of biologically determinist thinking in which "we're pointing at people's gender parts saying… 'this is' and 'this isn't.'" Demanding that we "interrogat[e] that policing impulse" "by reclaiming roles rather than looking just at body parts," Danforth crafts a vision of Indigenous gender as "a universe" in which "we're all stars." What is necessary is a sense of balance between the need to name and affirm Indigenous maleness, on the one hand, and recognition of contingency, indeterminacy, and gender fluidity, on the other. In their recent efforts to relearn "what it means to be an Indigenous man" through interviews with elders from a variety of tribal backgrounds, Kimberly Anderson, Robert Innes, and Jonathan Swift provide a model of this type of balance. They describe their study as a process of "thinking about how and why patriarchy was introduced to our communities, of considering how it has contributed to violence and social dysfunction among our peoples, and of looking to our traditional cultures to dig up what we can about healthy Indigenous masculinities" (267). Attuned to the complexity of influences on gender over time, these researchers seek not only to "dig up" Indigenous understandings about masculinity that have been obfuscated by colonial history, but also to theorize how those understandings can be mobilized in the service of community well-being and continuance in diverse contemporary contexts. They ask, "What do our men need to move forward in terms of being healthy Indigenous males?" (267). Such investigation and theorization is not strictly reclamatory but indeed creative. The burden of the discussion for Anderson, Innes, and Swift—as in *Masculindians*—therefore, is not on the recovery of a mythic "traditional" or "authentic" Indigenous masculinity; as Brendan Hokowhitu reminds us, "To buy into the notion that [Indigenous] culture can be 'authenticated' is to align with the colonizer" ("Death of Koro Paka" 133). Rather, the emphasis must be on exploring sources of wisdom, strength, and possibility within Indigenous cultures, stories, and lived experiences and creatively mobilizing of that knowledge in processes of empowerment and decolonization. As Hokowhitu argued recently at the 2013 meeting of the Native American and Indigenous Studies Association, "the study of Indigenous masculinity offers an untapped rubric for theorizing decolonization."

The goal of this volume, then, is to honour agency and creativity so that Indigenous masculinities can be theorized as both discursive phenomena and lived clusters of meaning that function in relation to, but are not predetermined by, either the biopolitics of settler colonialism or traditional cosmologies of gender (with "traditional" here meaning the ongoing lived embodiment of culture rather than something static and historically remote). Like identity and kinship, Indigenous masculinity, as it is used here, "isn't a static thing; it's dynamic, ever in motion. It requires attentiveness… [and] is best thought of as a verb rather than a noun, because… [it] is something that's *done* more than something that simply *is*" (Justice, "Go Away, Water!" 150). For this reason, many of those to whom I turn in the interviews that follow are creative artists. As Louis Riel famously prophesied, "My people will sleep for one hundred years, but when they awake, it will be the artists who give them their spirit back" (qtd. in Wyman 85). Vine Deloria Jr. argued along similar lines, "Our poets … are the only ones today who can provide this bridge, this reflective statement of what it means and has meant to live in a present which is continually overwhelmed by the fantasies of others of the meaning of past events" (x). Not only do artists interrogate and explicate the past; they envision, and indeed create, alternative futures. They imagine otherwise, and by awakening and inspiring others they remake the world in time. As Joanne Arnott illustrates later in this volume, "What I vision… [is] something that I can realize, and what I have to honour is the distance… I have to build up earthwork underneath the dream until that dream is resting on the earth and that's the reality."

Within the acknowledgements to his 2009 short story collection *The Moon of Letting Go*, Richard Van Camp dedicates the story "I Count Myself Among Them" to "all the artists" he credits with welcoming him "into the full grace of the blood in men" (213). With these words, Van Camp illuminates a ceremony of becoming that echoes the rites of passage colonial powers have sought to suppress and many in this volume argue need to be (re)imagined, (re)affirmed, and (re)enacted to facilitate conditions of health and balance in Indigenous communities; he also testifies to the resilience of such rites even within contemporary terrain burdened by the legacies of attempted genocide. Too often conversations about Indigenous masculinity begin from a position of presumed deficit that unwittingly accepts the perverse "success" of colonial policies of dispossession while obfuscating the living models of non-dominative and empowered Indigenous manhood that persist in families and communities, in teachings and stories, in minds and in actions. Here Van Camp honours specific men who have informed his sense of self as a male-embodied writer from the Tlicho nation. He locates strength in a community of creative, kind, and supportive men, and he

TO HONOUR AGENCY AND CREATIVITY SO THAT INDIGENOUS MASCULINITIES CAN BE THEORIZED AS BOTH… DISCURSIVE PHENOMENA AND… LIVED CLUSTERS OF MEANING THAT FUNCTION IN RELATION TO, BUT ARE NOT PREDETERMINED BY, EITHER THE BIOPOLITICS OF SETTLER COLONIALISM OR TRADITIONAL COSMOLOGIES OF GENDER

2. A recent report for Indian and Northern Affairs Canada (INAC) by Martin Cooke, Daniel Beavon, and Mindy McHardy applies the United Nations' Human Development Index to gendered populations among Indigenous peoples in Canada. Using adapted criteria employed by the United Nations to measure human rights, development, and well-being, the researchers demonstrate that the conditions of Indigenous men are improving at a much slower pace than those of Indigenous women in Canada. The report identifies growing "gender disparities in the Registered Indian population…, with Registered Indian women having considerably higher educational attainment and life expectancy than their male counterparts" (i). Rates of suicide for Indigenous men in Canada peak at 140 suicides per 100,000 people, while rates of suicide for Indigenous women peak at fifty suicides per 100,000 people, still four times the national average (Centre for Suicide Prevention 1). And it is difficult to speak about the struggles of Indigenous men without mentioning the disproportionate numbers embroiled in the Canadian penal system. According to Corrections Canada, in 2011 Aboriginal men accounted for 25 percent of the male adult prison population in Canada while making up approximately 3 percent of the country's male population (Dauvergne). While these statistics and the Cooke report do not alleviate the deplorable conditions of many Indigenous women, they do suggest a frequently neglected crisis to be unfolding among Indigenous men (one that undoubtedly affects women, families, and communities).

extends the circle of their influence through stories that explore growth, loss, love, power, and responsibility.

The language with which Van Camp celebrates this community of men is rich with intergender fluidity, recognizing a need for manhood to be named but not in a way that postures the discrete autonomy of Western European individuation. Van Camp configures his own absorption into the company of men through a delicate tension between "grace" and "blood" that speaks to the interplay between story and lived experience, between spirit and physicality, between masculinity and femininity, between the ephemeral and the enduring. The image of blood evokes both the latent power to exercise physical violence and the inevitable vulnerability that attends mortal existence, gesturing toward the creative and destructive forms of power described by Daniel Heath Justice in *The Way of Thorn and Thunder* as "moving between the blood of war and the blood of the moon without fear" (18). And while "the blood in men" implies anatomical alertness and attentiveness to the biological realities of physical persistence—ancestry, lineage, and embodied history—"grace" cuts back against biological determinism with its ethereality and its reliance upon external, unpredictable bestowal. "Grace" alludes to the socially constructed idea of *masculinity* while "blood" alludes to *anatomical maleness*, but neither achieves its full meaning in the other's absence. In this way, even as Van Camp acknowledges that "manhood" and "masculinity" are socially ascribed concepts with only refracted relationships to biological maleness, he insists that their exploration, interrogation, and affirmation are ultimately vital. This insistence is one of the many things that make Van Camp's writing so urgent and so valuable.

Bonita Lawrence argues that "empowerment for women means…. we need to talk about empowering our men" (qtd. in Anderson 276). While artists like Van Camp have been exploring these issues for decades, much of the "talk" about empowering Indigenous men—at least in the academy—has yet to occur.[2] While several pathbreaking works of Indigenous feminist theory have been published in the past twenty-five years—including Paula Gunn Allen's *The Sacred Hoop: Recovering the Feminine in American Indian Traditions* (1986), Lee Maracle's *I Am Woman: A Native Perspective on Sociology and Feminism* (1996), Kim Anderson's *A Recognition of Being: Reconstructing Native Womanhood* (2000), Andrea Smith's *Conquest: Sexual Violence and American Indian Genocide* (2005), and Cheryl Suzack, Shari Huhndorf, Jeanne Pearreault, and Jean Barman's *Indigenous Women and Feminism* (2010)—the only book-length study of Indigenous masculinity theory to be published at the time that I write this introduction has been Ty P. Kāwika Tengan's *Native Men Remade: Gender and Nation in Contemporary Hawai'i* (2008). Alongside Tengan's work, Brendan Hokowhitu's seminal articles on Māori masculinity, popular culture, and sport offer the most substantial and sustained scholarship on Indigenous masculinities in a global context. Yet, as both Tengan and Hokowhitu make clear, the conditions of Maoli and Māori communities are contextually unique and collapsible with neither each other nor the conditions of diverse Indigenous communities throughout North America. Despite confronting many of the same technologies of settler colonial dispossession, Maoli and Māori nations claim distinct cultural heritages that inform distinct cosmologies of gender. Furthermore, the gendered valences of their experiences of colonial incursion have been idiosyncratic. As Tengan explores in *Native Men Remade*, the feminization of the Hawaiian islands by the tourist industry has conspired with the economic disenfranchisement of Indigenous Hawaiians to foment experiences of pervasive emasculation for many Maoli men; in New Zealand, conversely, the colonial education system has worked in conjunction with sports media to reify perceptions of the naturally physical Māori male athlete that Hokowhitu argues dangerously sequester notions of Māori masculinity in the realm of the hypermasculine. While each of these situations indeed resonates with some Indigenous experiences on Turtle Island, both Hokowhitu and Tengan caution against simplistic comparative frameworks in their interviews in this volume, arguing that intellectual engagements with Indigenous masculinities require specificity, historical precision, and nuance. "Look for complexity," Hokowhitu charges, "as opposed to the simplistic answers."

In North American Indigenous contexts, critical work focused on masculinity has been limited and is just now emerging with studies like that being conducted by Anderson, Innes, and Swift, and Jessica Ball's ongoing work on Indigenous fatherhood. Discussions of male-specific issues can also be found in texts like Taiaiake Alfred's *Wasáse* (2005) and *Peace, Power, Righteousness* (1999) and in Eduardo Duran and Bonnie Duran's *Native American Postcolonial Psychology* (1995), but these tend to be peripheral to the works' themes. There is also a small body of work predominantly by non-Indigenous critics examining settler representations of Indian manliness in film, literature, and art, but this work generally falls short of making the bridge between popular cultural simulations and the lived realities of Indigenous persistence. Probably the richest source of critical information on North American Indigenous masculinities from Indigenous sources has been non-academic work by knowledge keepers like Basil Johnston in *Ojibway Heritage* (1976) and Tom Porter (*Sakokweniónkwas*) in *And Grandma Said...* (2008), who embed discussions of male roles and responsibilities within broader explorations of tribal specific worldviews. The other corpuses of critical work that have sustained attentiveness to North American Indigenous masculinities have been Indigenous feminist and queer/Two-Spirit theory.

In its analysis of the corrosion of Indigenous women's power in governance and the colonial imposition of heteropatriarchy, Indigenous feminism has demonstrated consistent commitment to tracking the alienation of Indigenous men from traditional roles and responsibilities. Similarly, in its efforts to revitalize non-dualist Indigenous cosmologies of gender, queer/Two-Spirit theory has, of necessity, attended to masculinity, especially in its essentialist, violent, and hegemonic forms. Yet, although Indigenous feminist and queer/Two-Spirit theories have effectively destabilized biological determinism and recovered the fluidity of gender concepts within many Indigenous worldviews, these theories have tended to retain a celebratory posture toward the feminine that has not been shared in their discursive engagements with the masculine. For example, building from the work of Chrystos and Beth Brant, Qwo-Li Driskill identifies "radical Two-Spirit *woman-centred* erotics as tools for healing from colonization" (59). The potential of radical *man-centred* erotics—whether Two-Spirit, queer, straight, or otherwise identified—as tools of decolonization remains unexplored. Such reticence is understandable given the violence perpetrated against Indigenous women and queer/Two-Spirit individuals in the course of heteropatriarchy's spread throughout North America, as Andrea Smith's and Driskill's scholarship attests. The reality of such ongoing trauma perhaps informs the fact that although Driskill's groundbreaking article "Stolen from Our Bodies" charts the author's "journey back to [hir] body" and "the journeys of other First Nations people back to their bodies" (51), it is difficult to find reference to maleness anywhere in the article beyond the vilification of a "white masculinity" that "murders, rapes, and enslaves" (53). Affirmations of biological maleness and celebrations of masculine power always risk trading in biological essentialisms and being conscripted into chauvinism and misogyny, especially when masculinity becomes conflated with strength and dominance. However, as Kateri Akiwenzie-Damm indicates later in this volume, "power's not necessarily a negative thing. We all need to feel empowered. We all need to assert our own power in different ways, but there have been so many negative examples of that being expressed that as soon as you say 'power,' I think for a lot of people that means power *over* something." This, I believe, informs a pervasive reluctance to champion male power in contexts conditioned by settler colonialism wherein systemic oppression, historical trauma, and economic disenfranchisement heighten the potential for lateral, intimate, and gender-based violence.

> **AFFIRMATIONS OF BIOLOGICAL MALENESS AND CELEBRATIONS OF MASCULINE POWER ALWAYS RISK TRADING IN BIOLOGICAL ESSENTIALISMS AND BEING CONSCRIPTED INTO CHAUVINISM AND MISOGYNY, ESPECIALLY WHEN MASCULINITY BECOMES CONFLATED WITH STRENGTH AND DOMINANCE.**

When I asked male writers during a recent roundtable on the subject of Indigenous masculinities where they look for sources of strength, three of the four tellingly responded with tales about women—mothers, aunties, friends. This prompted Warren Cariou to interject: "I guess the question becomes what's a viable model for men to model themselves after now. So should men model themselves after women?" ("Strong Men Stories"). Joseph Boyden implies as much in the extended version of the interview that appears in this collection, arguing that "what it is to be a man is to be a woman. To act like you think a woman would act and then you're going to truly understand what it is to be a male." Yet as Janice Hill *Kanonhsyonni* indicates, there are limitations to pursuing understandings of Indigenous manhood solely as it is refracted through womanhood. "I can teach [my son] to be a good human being to the best of my abilities," she argues, "but I can't teach him how to be a man.... He needs to be going with the men." *Masculindians* pursues conversations that will enliven a more rich and diverse spectrum of possibilities for considering what it means to be an Indigenous man. This collection considers what is at stake in naming and affirming masculinity and maleness in contexts conditioned by ongoing settler colonialism and heteropatriarchy, while staunchly refusing to be pressured into silence by critical anxiety. Spurred on by Van Camp's reminder that "what we're not talking about [is] killing us," this collection deigns to discuss Indigenous manhood in a variety of contexts and from a variety of perspectives. Together these conversations avow the utility—perhaps even the necessity—of analyzing and theorizing Indigenous masculinities, as an emergent field of study that can be braided together with feminist and queer/Two-Spirit modes of analysis in the service of healthy individuals, balanced relationships, and empowered communities. In other words, this collection of interviews asserts the positive social and political potential of Indigenous masculinity theory—built from and dependent on Indigenous men's experiences and functioning in solidarity with (but not subordinated to) Indigenous feminist and queer/Two-Spirit theories—as "an untapped rubric for theorizing decolonization."

Between October 2010 and August 2013, I conducted twenty-three interviews with Indigenous artists, critics, activists, and elders on the subject of Indigenous masculinities, the majority of which appear in the pages that follow. The interviews of between forty minutes and two hours took place in offices, parks, kitchens, coffee shops, restaurants, and bars, a few over the phone or on Skype, and even one in a car driving down Highway 401 in Ontario. The interviews were recorded, then transcribed, then returned to the interviewees who were free to make any alterations, deletions, or additions they desired. Many made small edits for clarity, and some allowed the interviews to stand exactly as transcribed. In order to fit them all in a single volume, I then abbreviated each interview to approximately 5,000 words, ensuring that each interviewee endorsed the material marked for inclusion. The full transcripts of selected interviews can be found on the University of Manitoba Press website along with a handful of audio recordings (http://uofmpress.ca/). The lone exception to this formula is the interview with Basil Johnston, which was conducted on stage at the Gladstone Hotel in Toronto as part of Pages Bookstore's *This Is Not a Reading Series* in 2007 and was published previously in *Studies in Canadian Literature*. Although this interview took place long before I had conceived of the Indigenous masculinities project, its thematic relevance made it a logical fit for this collection.

My hope was that each conversation would develop organically in relation to the interviewee's interests and concerns. Although I had prepared lines of inquiry and specific questions in every case, I encouraged each interviewee to take the conversation in the directions she or he thought would be most productive, while I attempted to adopt a posture of alert responsiveness—with varying degrees of success, as you will see. As a result, the interviews take on lives of their own, ranging from Janice Hill's heartfelt monologue, which required no questions from me whatsoever, to the rapid fire back-and-forth with Brendan Hokowhitu who eventually, by the conversation's close, began to interview me. The texture of the conversations was also influenced by my level of

THESE CONVERSATIONS AVOW THE UTILITY—PERHAPS EVEN THE NECESSITY—OF ANALYZING AND THEORIZING INDIGENOUS MASCULINITIES, AS AN EMERGENT FIELD OF STUDY THAT CAN BE BRAIDED TOGETHER WITH FEMINIST AND QUEER/TWO-SPIRIT MODES OF ANALYSIS IN THE SERVICE OF HEALTHY INDIVIDUALS, BALANCED RELATIONSHIPS, AND EMPOWERED COMMUNITIES.

familiarity with the interviewees. While I took care to be conversant with the work of all interviewees prior to our meetings, I am fortunate to call many of those interviewed for this project my friends, which served the practical function of making it easier to arrange our meetings while also lending the conversations an air of comfort and intimacy. In approaching potential interviewees, I prioritized those whose work I find particularly provocative in its dealings with gender. Beyond that, I wanted to speak with people of diverse cultural backgrounds, from different territories, in different stages of their lives, and of different genders and sexual orientations. I wanted to speak with established and up-and-coming artists, and to poets, playwrights, novelists, performers, and non-fiction writers. And I wanted to speak with scholars who approach Indigenous masculinities from a variety of critical vantage points: feminist, queer/Two-Spirit, sociological, anthropological, literary. The range of voices that appear in the pages that follow suggests that I've had at least some success (although the vast majority of interviewees come from the geographical space commonly referred to as Canada, and there is a slight predominance of interviewees from Cree, Anishinaabe, and Haudenosaunee backgrounds). The organization of the interviews is also somewhat arbitrary, as the interviewees do not fit discretely into the categories of "artist" or "critic" or "elder." The writers are also theorists, the critics are also creative, and the wisdom-keepers employ story to explicate cosmology. I've attempted to signal this interdependence and fluidity by naming each of the collection's three sections "Wisdom, Knowledge, Imagination" and then emboldening one of the three terms to emphasize main themes emerging in conversations housed therein. These move from discussions emphasizing culture, history, and worldview in Part I to those emphasizing the theorization of gender in Part II to those emphasizing artistic interventions in the discourse on Indigenous masculinities in Part III. These emphases are, of course, not mutually exclusive, and subjects emerge and overlap with considerable fluidity.

The discussions that make up *Masculindians: Conversations about Indigenous Manhood* grapple with themes crucial to the generation of masculine self-worth and the fostering of empowered, balanced, and mutually supportive gender relations. They speak of possibility and strength. They speak of beauty and vulnerability. They speak of sensuality and eroticism. They speak of shame, stigma, racism, and violence. They speak of nurturing, mentorship, companionship, and love. And they speak of stories and songs and acts of embodied connection that root Indigenous persistence in interpersonal reciprocity, in relations with other-than-human kin, and in sacred landscapes and waterways. I am grateful to the interviewees for their generosity, their gifts of wisdom, and their intellectual rigour. I am thankful for the time I got to spend with each of them and for the critical work that emerged from those meetings. Some of the "talk" about "empowering... men" that Bonita Lawrence identified as necessary back in the year 2000 emerges in the pages that follow—not final answers, but ideas and insights capable of inspiring further investigation and discussion. It is offered in a spirit of generating dialogue in the hopes that these voices will be joined by those of youth, adults, and elders from throughout Indian Country committed to seeking pathways to balanced and empowered gender relations that will shed the heteropatriarchal impositions of colonialism and invigorate myriad forms of healthy masculinity that honour Indigenous cosmologies of gender while strengthening and nurturing the terrain of Indigenous continuance.

WORKS CITED

ALL UNCITED QUOTATIONS ARE TAKEN FROM INTERVIEWS
WITHIN THE PRESENT COLLECTION.

Alfred, Taiaiake. *Peace, Power, Righteousness: An Indigenous Manifesto*. Toronto: Oxford University Press, 1999.

———. *Wasáse: Indigenous Pathways of Action and Freedom*. Toronto: Broadview Press, 2005.

Anderson, Kim. *A Recognition of Being: Reconstructing Native Womanhood*. Toronto: Second Story Press, 2000.

Anderson, Kim, Robert Alexander Innes, and John Swift. "Indigenous Masculinities: Carrying the Bones of the Ancestors." In *Canadian Men and Masculinities: Historical and Contemporary Perspectives*, ed. Christopher J. Greig and Wayne J. Martino. Toronto: Canadian Scholars' Press Inc., 2012. 266–84.

Ball, Jessica. "Fathering in the Shadows: Indigenous Fathers and Canada's Colonial Legacies." *The Annals of the American Academy of Political and Social Science* 624, 29 (2009): 29–48.

———. "Indigenous Fathers' Involvement in Reconstituting 'Circles of Care.'" *American Journal of Community Psychology*. 45, 1 (2010): 124–138.

Bederman, Gail. *Manliness and Civilization: A Cultural History of Gender and Race in the United States, 1880–1917*. Chicago: University of Chicago Press, 1996.

Centre for Suicide Prevention, The. "Suicide Among Canada's Aboriginal Peoples." *SIEC Alert* 52, September 2003.

Cooke, Martin, Daniel Beavon, and Mindy McHardy. "Measuring the Well-Being of Aboriginal People: An Application of the United Nations' Human Development Index to Registered Indians in Canada, 1981–2001." Ottawa: Indian Affairs and Northern Development Canada, 2004.

Dauvergne, Mia. "Adult correctional statistics in Canada, 2010/2011." 12 October 2012. www.statscan.gc.ca/pub/85-002-x/2012001/article/11715-eng.htm#a7 (acessed 11 November 2013).

Deloria Jr., Vine. "Foreword." *New and Old Voices of Wah'Kon-Tah*, ed. Robert K. Dodge and Joseph B. McCullough. New York: International, 1985. ix–x.

Driskill, Qwo-Li. "Stolen From Our Bodies: First Nations Two-Spirits/Queers and the Journey to a Sovereign Erotic." *Studies in American Indian Literatures* 16, 2 (Summer 2004): 50–64.

Duran, Eduardo, and Bonnie Duran. *Native American Postcolonial Psychology*. Albany, NY: State University of New York Press, 1995.

Gabriel, Ellen (moderator). "Two-Row Wampum and Reconciliation." Quebec National Event of the Indian Residential Schools Truth and Reconciliation Commission, Montreal, Quebec. 25 April 2013.

Hokowhitu, Brendan. "The Death of Koro Paka: 'Traditional' Māori Patriarchy." *The Contemporary Pacific* 20, 1 (2008): 115–41.

Hokowhitu, Brendan, with Kim Anderson. "'Pretty Boy' Trudeau vs. the 'Algonquin

Agitator': Showing the Ropes of Canadian Colonialist Masculinities." Presentation at NAISA 2013 Conference, Saskatoon, Saskatchewan. 13 June 2013.

Johnston, Basil H. *Ojibway Heritage*. Toronto: McClelland and Stewart, 1998 [1976].

Justice, Daniel Heath. "'Go Away, Water!': Kinship Criticism and the Decolonization Imperative." In *Reasoning Together: The Native Critics Collective*, ed. Craig S. Womack, Daniel Heath Justice, and Christopher B. Teuton. Norman: University of Oklahoma Press, 2008. 147–68.

——. *Kynship: The Way of Thorn and Thunder*. Wiarton, ON: Kegedonce Press, 2005.

Klopotek, Brian. "'I Guess Your Warrior Look Doesn't Work Every Time': Challenging Indian Masculinity in the Cinema." In *Across the Great Divide: Cultures of Manhood in the American West*, ed. Matthew Basso, Laura McCall, and Dee Garceau. New York: Routledge, 2001. 251–73.

Mann, Barbara Alice. *Iroquoian Women: The Gantowisas*. New York: Peter Lang, 2000.

Maracle, Lee. *I am Woman: A Native perspective on Sociology and Feminism*. Vancouver: Press Gang Publishers, 1999.

McKegney, Sam. "Masculindians: The Violence and Voyeurism of Male Sibling Relationships in Recent First Nations Fiction." In *Literature for Our Times: Postcolonial Studies in the Twenty-First Century*, ed. Bill Ashcroft, Julie McGonegal, Ranjini Mendis, and Arun Mukherjee. New York: Rodopi Press, 2012. 375–85.

McKegney, Sam (moderator). "Strong Men Stories: A Roundtable Discussion on Indigenous Masculinities with Warren Cariou, Daniel Heath Justice, Gregory Scofield, and Richard Van Camp." Winnipeg, Manitoba: University of Winnipeg, 1 February 2013.

McKegney, Sam. "Warriors, Healers, Lovers, and Leaders: Colonial Impositions on Indigenous Male Roles and Responsibilities." In *Canadian Perspectives on Men and Masculinities: An Interdisciplinary Reader*, ed. Jason A. Laker. Toronto: Oxford University Press, 2011. 241–68.

Ndebele, Njabulo. Personal Comment. "The Art of Critique: Writing, Communal Differences, and Different Communities Symposium." Kingston, ON: Queen's University, 27 Sept. 2011.

Porter, Tom (Sakokweniónkwas). *And Grandma Said… Iroquois Teachings as Passed Down Through the Oral Tradition*. Transcribed by L. Forrester. Bloomington, IL: Xlibris Corp., 2008.

Rifkin, Mark. *When Did Indians Become Straight? Kinship, the History of Sexuality, and Native Sovereignty*. New York: Oxford University Press, 2011.

Smith, Andrea. *Conquest: Sexual Violence and American Indian Genocide*. Cambridge, MA: South End Press, 2005.

Suzack, Cheryl, et al., eds. *Indigenous Women and Feminism: Politics, Activism, Culture*. Vancouver: UBC Press, 2011.

Tengan, Ty. P. Kāwika. *Native Men Remade: Gender and Nation in Contemporary Hawai'i*. Durham: Duke University Press, 2008.

Van Camp, Richard. "Acknowledgements." *The Moon of Letting Go*. Winnipeg: Enfield and Wizenty, 2009.

Vizenor, Gerald. *Manifest Manners: Narratives on Postindian Survivance*. Lincoln: University of Nebraska Press, 1999.

Womack, Craig S. *Red on Red: Native American Literary Separatism*. Minneapolis: University of Minnesota Press, 1999.

Wyman, Max. *The Defiant Imagination: Why Culture Matters*. 2004.

PART ONE

WISDOM

KNOWLEDGE

IMAGINATION

WHERE ARE THE MEN?

A CONVERSATION WITH JANICE C. HILL KANONHSYONNI

I'M STRUGGLING TRYING TO FIND MEN TO TEACH [MY SON] WHAT HE NEEDS TO KNOW. AND I CAN'T TEACH HIM THOSE THINGS, NO MATTER HOW SMART I AM, NO MATTER HOW MUCH I LEARN, I CAN'T TEACH HIM THOSE THINGS AND I CAN'T TEACH HIM TO BE A MAN. I CAN TEACH HIM TO BE A GOOD HUMAN BEING TO THE BEST OF MY ABILITIES, BUT I CAN'T TEACH HIM HOW TO BE A MAN.

16 DECEMBER 2010 Conversation between Janice Hill and Sam McKegney in Jan's office at Four Directions Aboriginal Students' Centre, Queen's University, Kingston, Ontario.

JANICE HILL: The way I have been introducing myself lately is: *Kanonhsyonni yonkiats. Wakenyaton, tanon Kanyenkehaka. Tkiyentanehken (Tyendinaga) tkiteron.* That's how I was taught to introduce myself traditionally and basically what that says is, "My name is *Kanonhsyonni*"—or "*Kanonhsyonni* is what they call me"—and "I'm Turtle Clan from the Mohawk nation and I live in Tyendinaga." My English name is Janice Hill and I'm the director here at the Four Directions Aboriginal Students' Centre.

I've been an educator all my life by vocation and by choice. I'm Turtle Clan, and in our tradition, in our culture, our creation story talks about the fact that the world was created on the back of a turtle. So what I've been taught is that turtle was there at the beginning of time and saw creation as it came into its fruition, and our teaching is that, when you have knowledge, you have a responsibility to share it. It's to be shared, not to be hoarded. And so turtle, being there at the beginning of time and seeing all of that, had a responsibility to share that knowledge. That's how I'm a teacher by birth, I guess. And then I've been trained as a teacher—I have a Bachelor of Education—so, by choice as well. And, really, my whole working career has been spent in education in some form or another.

I'm also the mother of two sons, both of whom I've raised by myself. So I have a lot of thoughts around men and their changing roles, partially because of my sons' absent fathers and also because of my struggle with trying to teach them to be men, being a woman. And my teachings tell me that up until the age of five, children belong to the women, because it's our job to teach them to be loving and nurturing and kind and to teach them about all those emotions and feelings—how to be empathetic and compassionate. That's our role as women to give that to our children, male and female. And, really, their fathers, in our culture traditionally, didn't have a lot to do with the small children, up to age five or six or so, and then they became more involved later. At the time of puberty, or when young boys changed, the mothers didn't have much of a role anymore because those boys were men, and then they had to be passed over to the men to learn man things. And I know I may be really good, but I can't teach my son to be a man because there's things that I don't know and never will know and choose not to know because it's not my responsibility.

The unfortunate thing is that most men in our community don't know those things either, and there's been a whole range of reasons why that's happened. It goes back probably to contact or maybe even before that when our communities were not healthy. More recently, men aren't learning those roles themselves because there's nobody to teach them, or very few people to teach them, which goes back to the residential school era. Our young children were taken away from their families so they didn't learn how to be parents and they didn't learn how to be healthy young men and women because there were no role models for them. The priests and the nuns couldn't teach them how to be good Mohawks or Ojibways or Algonquins, you know? I mean, they didn't want them to learn those things—that's why they were at the residential school, that was the whole point. And, in that way, they succeeded, because here we are all these years later struggling to find our way back to those teachings.

It's not black and white. It's not like the women teach this and the men teach that in isolation of each other because when we're talking about men's roles and responsibilities, it's the responsibility of the women to sit there and listen too, partly because you're going to mother boys and girls that need to know this stuff, but also because you need to know this stuff in terms of having a healthy relationship with a partner. What *is* your responsibility and what *is* his responsibility and where's the line and who does what? To know those separations of responsibility in a respectful way, you know? I know that Mohawk women get a bad rap for being bossy and domineering and perhaps we are— well, we *are*, not "perhaps," we *are* [*Laughter*]. And I think that's been to the detriment of men in our community.

JAN HILL (Turtle Clan, Mohawk Nation) has worked in the field of Indigenous education for more than twenty-five years in such diverse roles as coordinator of adult education programming and principal at the *Ohahase* Education Centre, as adjunct faculty member and co-director of the Aboriginal Teacher Education Program at Queen's University, and as academic dean of First Nations Technical Institute in Tyendinaga. She is currently the director of Four Directions Aboriginal Students' Centre at Queen's University in Kingston, Ontario, in the traditional lands of the Haudenosaunee and Anishinaabe peoples.

In my community, the transition to the twentieth century and the twenty-first century hasn't been as easy for men, I think, as it has for women. Our community is like a circle and everything inside the community is the responsibility of the women (so the social aspect of being a community is the responsibility of the women) and everything outside of the circle (so politics and war and dealing with foreign nations and anything like that) is the responsibility of men. Now, as I said to somebody the other day, we don't have anybody to war with anymore, so that takes away that responsibility. And men don't hunt as much, you know—and there's not the possibility if they're urban or don't have access to hunting grounds or haven't been taught how to hunt and fish—so that takes away that responsibility. And in terms of being political leaders and dealing with outside governments, that one still exists but even that platform has changed so much because of our relationship with the levels of government: municipal and provincial and federal. That's way different than when we were bargaining with the English or the Dutch or the French in nation-to-nation negotiations.

We're the only people in this country who have a legislative act that governs every aspect of our lives. How we interact and where we can live and what we can do and what we can't do and what our status is and what our rights are, these are all governed by the Indian Act. And to my knowledge, there's no other population of people who are affected in that way. And that has changed our relationship, in the eyes of Canada, anyway, from being an equal negotiating nation of people to being subordinate. We're the responsibility of the government instead of being equal to the government. So, our men don't get to negotiate on the same platform as traditionally our men did, which makes that whole political role null and void. So then what? That void has been created and they haven't been taught to change that role in a different way, more positively.

There's so much in our culture that our men are not learning. When a girl becomes a woman, we're taught that it's her aunties who take her away and teach her everything she'll ever need to know about being a woman. Like, we're talking ten years old, you come to the change in your life and you spend the day with your aunts. I've had women say to me that they'll never forget that day and that they were never told anything since that they weren't told on that day about how to care for their own bodies, about how to care for their partners' bodies, about how to have good relationships, about how to care for their children, about what their roles will be in the community, and if we know their gifts at that time, to talk to them about what their gifts are and what kind of responsibilities that will mean. We tell them as much as we can see and know on that day. And men have that same responsibility with boys. These are the things, this is how you take care of yourself, this is how you take care of your woman, and this is how you care for your girl children, and this is how you care for your sisters and your mother and your aunties, and this is what your responsibility is to them from protection to providing to everything you can think of, right?

OUR COMMUNITY IS LIKE A CIRCLE AND EVERYTHING INSIDE THE COMMUNITY IS THE RESPONSIBILITY OF THE WOMEN... AND EVERYTHING OUTSIDE OF THE CIRCLE... IS THE RESPONSIBILITY OF MEN.

And they're also responsible for telling girls, "This is what men are like," and that sometimes you have to be careful of men because if men are not healthy, this is how they can be too, you know? And about carrying yourself with dignity and respect and remembering that the body is a sacred vessel. We've been talking recently about sexuality and how disturbing it is that our children are so young and already exploring those things when they're nine and ten years old, things that, well, people in my generation would never have thought of doing, you know? And so it's telling them to be mindful of who they are and where they come from and to remember what they're playing with. It's to teach those girls how to carry themselves with dignity, but it's also to teach those boys how to treat themselves and how to treat those women with dignity.

If those teachings were being carried on and going forward the way they were supposed to, I don't think we would have domestic violence and rape and abuse because in our law, under the Great Law of Peace, the most heinous crime is a crime committed against a woman or child. You can be killed for hurting women. If you rape a woman, or hurt a woman or a child, you're done, there's no compensating for that because those are the worst crimes you can commit. And the third one down is a crime against your people, if you do something that takes away from the people. And our children aren't learning those things and our men aren't learning those things, and I think that's a big reason why so many men are incarcerated, in trouble with the law, because they just don't know their place.

I look at my own sons and they're very different people. My oldest son is more fortunate than my younger son because he at least had some uncles and older cousins around when he was growing up to help, for him to spend time with, to learn how to work, and to learn how to be responsible. They're not really traditional men so they couldn't teach him a lot of that, but he was raised in the longhouse because I have been involved in the longhouse community for his whole life and so he learned the culture from many people there. My youngest son is not so fortunate because all the men who were there for my oldest son have had families of their own or they've gone on and it's been difficult to find uncles for him to learn from this time. It's very disheartening for me to know that I've been in my community the last year trying to find men who would commit to teaching him the things he needs to learn and our community is not that large and I'm having trouble. I'm struggling trying to find men to teach him what he needs to know. And I can't teach him those things, no matter how smart I am, no matter how much I learn, I can't teach him those things and I can't teach him to be a man. I can teach him to be a good human being to the best of my abilities but I can't teach him how to be a man.

One of the things we talked about recently here at Four Directions is the need for rites of passage, the need to have ceremony and recognition as boys go from one stage of their life to another. You have to end them being a baby so they can pass on into their boyhood, and end them being children so they can pass into their manhood. And if

> **YOU HAVE TO END THEM BEING A BABY SO THEY CAN PASS ON INTO THEIR BOYHOOD, AND END THEM BEING CHILDREN SO THEY CAN PASS INTO THEIR MANHOOD.**

they're not provided with the teachings they need to do those things and if they're not provided with the ceremony and the understanding that it's time for them to move into the next stage of their life, they never move out of that earlier stage. So we have grown men who are really like babies because they've never been taught it's time to leave that behind now and move on.

One of the other women here and I were talking. She has boys, as well. And we see it in our boys. My youngest boy is twelve right now so he's right where he needs to be going with men. I've done all I can for him at this point in his life in terms of teaching him the things that I have to offer, and now is the time that he needs to have the ceremony to understand that he is not a child anymore. He's a young man, and he needs to move into that role and leave this role alone, and understand that our relationship is going to change now. Because I'm his mother, I'll always be his mother, and I'll always love him, but he can't be my baby anymore. He has to learn how to be a man now. And if I don't do this for him, I run the risk of him not growing up as a healthy man. And what Oneida Elder Al Doxtator talked about the other day is that those men are the ones who look for their mother when they're looking for a partner. Because they're still looking for mother's unconditional love and not understanding that the relationship they need to be looking for is an equal relationship—not look for somebody who's going to take care of you and look after you and do everything for you, but someone who's going to walk side-by-side with you and be your equal, you know? Someone who you will care for and will care for you equally, not somebody who's going be your mother because you haven't realized it's time to move away from your mother and move into your own being.

I'm at that place with my youngest son now, and because he's a different kind of boy than my oldest son was, it's glaring me in the face and I know that he really needs this in his life. So my struggle is trying to find someone to do those things with him and for him, to teach him what he needs to know because he is the type of boy who will need the ceremony and need the teaching and need a guide or a mentor to help him so that he can move into it in a healthy way. So that he can be a man, so that he can be a leader, because I believe he has the capacity to be a leader. He can be empathetic. He can be compassionate. I've been told by many people that he's good medicine. I've had friends who are not well and, just being with him, he was able to lift their spirits. So that's one of his gifts is he's good medicine for people. But he needs to learn how to use that in a good way and what his responsibility is going to be with that medicine that he carries.

REPAIRING THE CIRCLE

A CONVERSATION WITH TOMSON HIGHWAY

"MY SON"... "THE WORLD HAS BECOME TOO EVIL. WITH THESE MAGIC WEAPONS, MAKE A NEW WORLD," SAID THE MOTHER OF THE HERO, THE SON OF AYASH.... SO THE SON OF AYASH TOOK THE WEAPONS AND, ON A MAGIC WATER SNAKE, JOURNEYED DOWN INTO THE REALM OF THE HUMAN SOUL, WHERE HE MET.... [E]VIL AFTER EVIL... THE MOST FEARSOME AMONG THEM THE MAN WHO ATE HUMAN FLESH. —TOMSON HIGHWAY, KISS OF THE FUR QUEEN

18 OCTOBER 2012
Conversation between
Tomson Highway
and Sam McKegney
in Sam's office at
Queen's University in
Kingston, Ontario.

SAM MCKEGNEY: Often discussions of Indigenous masculinities start from a deficit model focusing on the negative. And I was wondering if we could begin with discussions of strength. Perhaps you could reflect a bit on positive gender models that emerge from Cree worldview and language.

TOMSON HIGHWAY: Do you have a tablet that I can put on my lap and write on? I'll do some designs for you because there's some visual explaining to do. My native language is Cree. I speak two Native languages because I come from a part of the country where Cree people moved so far north—my father, namely, and four other young men at a time in the 1920s—that they moved into Dene territory. I come from the Manitoba/Nunavut

TOMSON HIGHWAY (Cree) is a playwright, novelist, and pianist/songwriter. Born along his parents' trapline on what would become the Manitoba/Nunavut border, Highway attended Guy Hill Residential School before studying Music and English at the University of Manitoba in Winnipeg and the University of Western Ontario in London. After graduating as a concert pianist, Highway spent several years in the field of Indigenous social work, working with children, prison inmates, and street people, and with various cultural educational programs. He worked in the theatre industry in Toronto for several years, acting as artistic director of Native Earth Performing Arts from 1986 to 1992. He is best known for his award-winning plays *The Rez Sisters* (Fifth House, 1988) and *Dry Lips Oughta Move to Kapuskasing* (Fifth House, 1989), although he's written and produced scores more. He is also the author of the semi-autobiographical novel *Kiss of the Fur Queen* (Doubleday, 1998) and several children's books published in Cree and English.

border, which is actually Dene territory, so we were Cree people living among the Dene. Our village was half Cree and half Dene. There was the non-status side and there was the status—we're status—and in order to go from the status Cree side of the village to the non-status Cree part of the village, you had to pass through a Dene section, a Dene neighbourhood. Dene and Cree come from two totally different linguistic families. So we speak both languages because we had to. We had no choice. We didn't speak English though. English didn't exist back then. So when you speak Dene and Cree, it's like being able to speak English and Mandarin. It's a real gift to have had that as a child because, of course, the other languages came easier. So today I speak fluent French. And I work in English, French, and Cree—I have books published in those languages. So that's where the big difference comes from.

The fact is that the origin of masculinity—the whole issue of gender—comes from linguistic structure. I think one has to understand that... oh, it's a long story. How do I put it? Human behaviour is ruled, the subconscious life of an individual is governed by the subconscious life of his community, his society. And the dream world, so to speak, is defined by the mythology of a people. To simplify the explanation—or *raccourcir*, to shorten it—languages are given birth to by mythologies, by the collective dream world of a society. And they're given birth to and they're given form by that dream world. So the structure of a language depends on the nature of the mythology. And mythology spills into the discipline of theology, but the difference, of course, is that theology is only about "God" whereas mythology is about god and man and nature. It's interesting when you think about it: mythology, in a sense, is a combination of theology, sociology, and biology—the study of gods, men, and nature.

There's mythologies, of course, all over the world. There's as many mythologies as there are languages. And last time I counted, they say there's between 5,000 and 6,000 languages in the world. And each one of them has a superstructure, like I say, given birth to by mythology, so that mythology is what decides the structure of the language. And those mythologies are divided into roughly three different categories: there's monotheism, there's polytheism, and there's pantheism. These are all Greek words: *Theos* is "god." So monotheism is about "one" god. Polytheism is about "many" gods. Pantheism is about god in "all"—pan meaning "all." So the first mythology has one god, the second has many gods, and the third is a society where god has not yet left nature—god is in nature, nature is god; in a sense, biology is god.

So the monotheistic superstructure is Christianity—there's only one god in Christianity—and polytheism is what preceded Christianity in that part of the world, the eastern Mediterranean. The Greek and Roman mythologies are polytheistic systems, just like today in a society like Japan. Shintoism is a polytheistic superstructure, meaning that there are many many gods in Shintoism. And then there's pantheism; that's Native. In monotheism, there's only one god and it's also a phallic superstructure. There's one god and he's male. Male with a capital M. Then there's man with a small m. And there's female with a small f. And finally then there's nature. So there's He, he, she, then it. In that order. One of my students asked me, "Is there a She with a capital S on this superstructure?" There's none. There's no room for it. There's no room for the idea of She with a capital S. And the other thing that you'll notice here is that there's only two genders: male and female. And the male has complete power over the female. God created man first, and woman is an afterthought from his rib bone. It would be very interesting to see a society where, first of all, god was female—imagine the kind of world we would have if god was female and she created woman first and then created man from her rib bone? What an enormous difference that would make in human behaviour.

So polytheism is not a phallic superstructure. It's a semi-circular superstructure, interestingly enough, in the sense that there are many gods and goddesses. In fact, the principal deities, the pantheon of twelve gods among the ancient Greeks atop Mount Olympus, consisted of six gods and six goddesses. So it was evenly divided. And there is historical proof of the time in history when one goddess was replaced by a god, resulting in seven male gods and five female gods, and that was the beginning of the end of the idea of divinity in female form. And those gods, as you probably know, are Zeus, the king of the gods; the queen of the goddesses being Hera, his wife; and then there's Poseidon, god of the sea; there's Hermes the messenger god; there's the god of the intellect, Apollo; and then there's Demeter, the goddess of grain, the goddess of the earth, an earth-based goddess, the goddess of fertility, really; the goddess of war, Athena; and the goddess of love, of human sexuality, Aphrodite, who became Venus in Roman mythology; and so on and so forth. So there's all these gods and goddesses along this semi-circle and there is room in this polytheistic structure for the idea of male and female divinity.

Over here, pantheism is a complete circle. (My weakness here is that I don't speak ancient Greek. That would help me tremendously in my analysis of this situation.) But over here there is no "he" and there is no "she." In the Native languages of North America, so far as I know—certainly Cree, Ojibway, and Dene—there is no "he" and there is no "she." There is no gender. In the monotheistic superstructure, on the other hand, there seems to be an obsession with division of the universe according to gender. There's the part of the universe that is male and then there's the part that is female. And it's even more pronounced in French with *le* and *la*. And it's even more pronounced in German with *der*, *die*, and *das*. In French un bureau is masculine but *une table* is feminine. Very interesting that most of the negative nouns are feminine: *la colère*—anger; *la douleur*—pain; *la tristesse*—sadness. Whereas the positive terms, for the most part, are masculine: *le bonheur*—happiness. And of course there's always exceptions, but that's generally the case. And it's always the man having superior power over the woman because of the creation story that underpins this superstructure.

If the universe in a monotheistic system is divided into genders—that which is male and that which is female—the universe in a pantheistic system is divided into animate and inanimate. There's the animate part of the universe and there's the inanimate part of the universe, meaning that there's that which has a soul and that which has no soul. Anything that has biological life is a living, animate creature. In Cree we'd say, *ana nepêw*, the man. *Ana iskwéw*, the woman. *Ana mistik*, the tree—*ana* being the article. *Ana asinîy*, the rock. They all have a place in the circle. There is no gender difference and one does not have power over the other. The only way that these animate creatures can be made inanimate is if you kill the man and the body becomes *anima mêo*, the corpse. It's no longer a he, it's an it. *Anima*, that's one of the great accidents of linguistics, in that it has nothing to do with the Latin *anima*—which is where the word "animate" comes from, meaning "soul." The only way you can make this living creature inanimate is to remove the life, so she becomes *anima mêo*, a corpse. The only way you can turn the tree into an inanimate creature is to chop it down and turn it into a chair. So that a chair is a tree without a soul. And a rock has a soul, according to this superstructure, and the only way you can make it not have a soul is to kill it, to crush it up into cement, and to make a sidewalk out of that cement. So that sidewalk is a rock without a soul. So the rock is now *anima miskêw*. So the articles change accordingly.

Basically in Cree all of these living creatures have equal status, as do all of these non-living creatures. So that this circle contains two circles: there's the circle with the animate creatures and within that is the circle with the inanimate creatures. When a man dies, he goes to another circle. He undergoes transference. He doesn't go to hell or heaven. He just stays here, which is why we believe that the planet is just filled with our ancestors. They're still here, they never went anywhere. My brother, who died of AIDS twenty-one years ago—tomorrow is the anniversary of his death—he never went anywhere, he's still here, still with me. Even biologically, I have his lips, I have his eyes, I have this, I have that. I even have his voice, apparently.

So there's room on the living circle, the animate circle, there's room for the male and the female, as well as all of these other shades of gender. We have the he/shes, and we have the she/hes. We have room for the idea of men with the souls of women and women with the souls of men. Those are gay people. To put it in blunt terms, the role of men in the circle of our society was to hunt and the role of women was to give birth—my mother had twelve children and my father was a fabulous hunter—but there was also a group who biologically were assigned neither role. Neither the hunt nor giving birth. So our responsibility became the spirit, to take care of the spirit of the community, which is where all the artists are from. This is why so many artists are gay. And that's our job, to create this magic; we're the magicians.

Noticing European life from up close as a Native man, the great arc of European history contains three arcs. First of all, there's war after war after war after war in which human blood has been spilt; I swear to god, there's not a square inch of that continent that hasn't been soaked in human blood. And 97 percent of that is caused by "man." When you look at world wars, where are the women? Why are these men killing each other? Where are the women in all that? When you see these military marches, thousands and thousands and thousands of soldiers… it's just men. Where are the women? Anyway, that's one part, the destruction, the pain, and the agony and the trauma. Europeans are a traumatized people. To this very day, we talk to our friends in France about the Second World War and they start to cry because their parents were prisoners of war. There are Jewish friends who lost parents to the Holocaust, who were incinerated in Auschwitz.

And that's one arc. The other picture you see that astonishes you even more is that they're still there, the Europeans are still there, and they're beautiful. The Italians are beautiful. The Spanish are beautiful. The Germans are beautiful, physically and emotionally. And that beauty was given to us by "woman." She's the one who nurtured those people, who made them survive, who gave birth and rebirth and rebirth. And the third arc of European civilization is the shoes, the hair, the fashion, the theatre, the poetry, the music, the architecture, the film, the pure spectacle of it all, a spectacle for which people pay millions of dollars from all over the world to come and gawk at. And that was given to the planet by these people—the he/shes and the she/hes. And yet in the monotheistic superstructure there's no room for them. There is no room for a third gender here in this phallic superstructure. Nobody crosses the path. Anybody who crosses that dividing line is to be destroyed, and we were destroyed by the thousands.

So on this side of the diagram the idea of god in female form is completely non-existent, and god as male has complete power over us, the male has complete power over the woman, and all have complete power over nature. On the other side of the diagram the power *is* nature. To take this idea of the phallic structure versus the yonic

EVEN THE PENIS HAS NO SOUL. IT'S AN INANIMATE CREATURE BY ITSELF. THE ONLY PARTS OF THE HUMAN BODY THAT HAVE A SOUL BY THEMSELVES ARE THE VAGINA, THE WOMB, AND THE BREASTS—THE FEMALE RECREATIVE PARTS OF THE HUMAN BODY.

structure—meaning "womb-like" structure—the idea of the animate and inanimate dichotomy needs to be made more specific. The parts of the human body are, by themselves, all inanimate. The head by itself doesn't have a soul. The hand by itself doesn't have a soul. The stomach by itself doesn't have a soul. Even the heart by itself doesn't have a soul. On the male side, even the penis has no soul. It's an inanimate creature by itself. The only parts of the human body that have a soul by themselves are the vagina, the womb, and the breasts—the female recreative parts of the human body. Those are the only parts that have a soul. And that is the very centre of the idea of matriarchy and the idea of divinity in female form. Where in one superstructure god is super-male, in the pantheistic superstructure god is super-female. And that's where the She with a capital S belongs. From this other superstructure she's been completely excised, creating the male/female power imbalance.

When 1492 came along and Columbus came along, the most significant item in his baggage was the religion—the theology/mythology. That's when the god met the goddess for the first time and punctured her, and the circle was broken, almost destroyed, to serve the Genesis-to-Revelation straight line. So what we artists are doing right now is trying our very best, especially female artists and feminist thinkers, to bend this straight line back into a circle, to repair the circle. If the principal prayer in the Christian canon says, "Our Father, who art in Heaven," where's our mother? The fourteenth century and the fifteenth century, when the witch-burnings were at their height in Europe, that was the very same period that the monotheistic superstructure arrived in North America. I live in France; I swear to god, when the wind has a certain power, you can hear the women screaming and howling in the middle of the night. It was the thing to do on a Saturday night in villages across Germany and France and Spain and England, to go down to the village square and watch the women scream their tits off through the flames. Wholesale destruction. And as recently as 1945, women in France weren't allowed to vote or own property. And as recently as sixty years ago here on this campus women weren't allowed; they weren't allowed to set foot on campus. They were chained to their wombs and their kitchens. And now, finally, the superstructure that made such horror is being bent back into a curve and the circle is being repaired. And that's what we see right now.

SM: How can even those who identify as heterosexual men learn to recognize that health and power for women is, in fact, a pathway towards their own health and well-being? In other words, how do they not perceive women's power as their own emasculation?

TH: That's the other side of the coin. That's the dark side of the coin, eh? It's easy to trash all men. I mean, god knows, where I come from up north, where Christianity just swept across like a wildfire, up there—I mean the situation is changing now, thank goodness—but when I was growing up, men used their women like punching bags. Wife battery was like… it was like a festival. It was like an art form. And rape happens every day. Even down here in Kingston, a town as civilized as it is, is not free of the battery of women. There are women being beaten right now somewhere in this city.

Let me put it this way, I grew up and went to school with Helen Betty Osborne—you know that name? She's from Norway House in northern Manitoba and I'm from Brochet, Manitoba. We went to the same school and we're about the same age. In fact, she was my younger brother's girlfriend for a short while, like puppy love—fifteen or sixteen, whatever it was. Those four guys who abducted Helen Betty Osborne dragged her off into the forest, and raped her by ramming a screwdriver fixty-six times up her vagina and left her there to bleed to death—it was November in northern Manitoba, that's already winter—those guys are considered "normal." They're just normal healthy guys. There's no taboo against that kind of behaviour. That's just what men do with girls. They were just out, four guys having a good time with a girl on a Saturday night. That's all it was. You know, if those guys had gone into those bushes and made love to each other instead, then and only then would they be considered sick, Where does that thinking come from? It comes from that [points to the phallic, monotheistic superstructure on the diagram]. Just for that one crime alone, it's worth it to take this superstructure apart and have it replaced by a woman-centred superstructure, the pantheistic circle. Just for that one crime alone. Imagine that happened to your daughter, you know?

On the other side, as a gay man, when I look at stories like that and I see all these women being battered across America, I thank my lucky stars every day of my life that I'm not a heterosexual man. I'm so proud to be who I am. For one thing—we're not perfect, we're far from perfect, there's a lot of abuse that happens within the gay community—but we don't treat women like meat. We don't consider women as just a hole to stick your dick into, which is what too many heterosexual men think of women as. There's way too much of that kind of thinking and that kind of behaviour—running through women like pieces of toilet paper. But, on the other hand, there's an awful lot of straight men who are trying their very, very best to reverse that trend, to change their behaviour for the better. And I'm surrounded by them. Some of my best friends are straight men; I just love them. When they're beautiful, they're beautiful. And one of the things that makes them truly beautiful is when they have no fear of their femininity, their feminine sides. Because ultimately, whether we're born into this world biologically male or biologically female, we are either 90 percent female and 10 percent male—eighty-twenty, seventy-thirty, sixty-forty, fifty-fifty. Myself, actually, I'd imagine I'm about forty-sixty. I love women too… just not as much as men, physically. Emotionally, they're equals. It's when you believe that you're 100 percent male that the trouble starts. That simply doesn't exist biologically, spiritually, psychologically. We all have elements of both sexes in us. And so men who are scared of that, who are terrified, and who are trying to prove that they are 100 percent male, those are the men that go around ramming screwdrivers up people's vaginas. They're real men.

IT'S WHEN YOU BELIEVE THAT YOU'RE 100 PERCENT MALE THAT THE TROUBLE STARTS. THAT SIMPLY DOESN'T EXIST BIOLOGICALLY, SPIRITUALLY, PSYCHOLOGICALLY.

And, on the other hand, if those boys had been seen walking down the street holding hands and kissing in public, I think that they'd be much healthier men. And so I'm surrounded by these heterosexual men who are not afraid of holding hands, who are not afraid of hugging. There are even heterosexual men who've gone to bed together—you don't even have to have sex. Sex is so grossly overrated in this society. And there are reasons behind that that go back again to those superstructures. In only one of these superstructures is there a story of eviction from the garden. And guess which one? According to the other ones we're still in the garden. You don't think that tree over there in the garden is a miracle? So I have friends like that whom I absolutely adore. And fascinatingly enough, thank god, those are the men who make the best partners to women, who treat women as equals. And even more importantly, those are usually the men who make the best parents.

SM: You were saying that a lot of violence erupts from male panic around "what if I'm not 100 percent masculine, if I'm not 100 percent male?"—which connects intriguingly to some of the depictions in your work. For instance, Big Joey [in *Dry Lips Oughta Move to Kapuskasing*] dreams of blood spilling out from his groin, which he perceives as an indication of his impotence or emasculation, when it could be seen as the awakening of female power through symbolic menstruation or something…

TH: Absolutely, that's what that scene's all about. The superstructure of mythology is so deeply embedded in the human subconscious that we don't even realize it's working within us. I'll give you a prosaic example. The cereal that we eat comes from the goddess Ceres, who was the Roman version of the goddess Demeter, goddess of grain. And so in eating that cereal, we pay homage to the goddess of grain. Whereas in the monotheistic superstructure, the idea of female divinity is completely forbidden—it's a crime. That moment of orgasm, that moment when the human body is at its peak in terms of the experience of pleasure, that's when you come face-to-face with Aphrodite, the goddess of love, the goddess of orgasm—that joy, that extraordinary physical joy—which is forbidden in this system because Aphrodite doesn't exist here [pointing to monotheism on the diagram]. Which is why sex is so fucked up in this society. You're not supposed to do it. It's forbidden. Nobody does it. It's only for recreative purposes. You have two kids, and that means you've only fucked twice in your life. How sick can you get? When the human body is just so filled with these lovely, lovely, lovely liquids—tears and perspiration being the least of it, you know?

I always dreaded going to heaven. When we were kids and we were being taught by these missionaries and these nuns, the charts showed that all the white people went to heaven and all the brown people went to hell. Ever since then I didn't want to go to heaven. In heaven you can't smoke, you can't drink, and you can't have sex—in hell you can do all of them, all of them. If there's a party anywhere, it's in hell, not up there with the one male god who says all the way through the First Testament, "I am the only God and I'm a jealous God, and anyone who worships another god will be destroyed"—now who else talked like that in 1930s Germany? To me, monotheism is a form of fascism. It's brutal. And too many people have had brutal fathers who've had masculinity beaten into them. The prisons of our country are filled with the victims of that system. The prison system of our country is filled with the products of abusive marriages of that ilk. Anyway, if you do what I say, you'll go to heaven and you'll spend eternity on your knees telling god how perfect he is because, for some reason, even though he's supposed to be omniscient he has to be told a thousand times a day how great he is. Down here in hell you'll spend eternity on your knees doing something one hell of a lot more fun. One hell of a lot more interesting. And that's where I'm going.

But those men who embrace their femininity—who cook, who make cakes for their wives and children, all that kind of stuff—those are the men who are contributing to the elimination of the very dangerous system of monotheism and to the revitalization and the renaissance of female divinity and pantheism. If anything ensures that the planet survives the next century, it'll be pantheism not monotheism, the circle not the phallus. So time is of the essence, in that sense. And Aboriginal literature couldn't have come at a better time.

SM: What do you see as the role of literature and performance and dance and music in this mythological revolution?

TH: The arts, it's a medicine. It's a salve that society needs. Imagine a world without music, without dance, without theatre, without colour, just a black-and-white world of he and she. And who adds the colour? All the colours? The other genders. And you have to have that, or else you just die. Life wouldn't be worth living.

THIS IS A VISION

A CONVERSATION WITH LEE MARACLE

—————————————————————————————————————

I KNOW YOU DON'T KNOW VERY MUCH ABOUT ME BECAUSE I COULD NEVER TELL YOU— YOU WEREN'T THERE TO TELL. OH, I UNDERSTAND YOU TRIED TO BE THERE, DADDY, BUT IT JUST COULDN'T HAPPEN. I KNOW IT WASN'T YOUR FAULT. STILL, I THOUGHT YOU MIGHT WANT THIS LETTER TO HELP YOU SEE THE KIND OF GIRL I HAVE BEEN WITHOUT YOU. —LEE MARACLE, "DEAR DADDY"

17 MARCH 2011
Conversation between
Lee Maracle and
Sam McKegney at
First Nations House,
University of Toronto.

SAM MCKEGNEY: In the opening section of *Daughters Are Forever* you write, "Tensions invade the men as they dig graves for the dead they were unable to protect. The return of the scent of murder becomes shame as the Earth fails to cleanse her of the magnitude of grief. In their tension, the men swallow her shame." Can you explain the role of colonialism in this shaming process? How are both the shame of men and men's complicity in oppression produced?

LEE MARACLE: I think there's a number of sources. The first one is the epidemics. And I was talking to Khahtsahlano when I was a little girl, who was one of the people who organized the digs for the epidemics, and the first thing he said was, "Well, we didn't have ceremony for them. Too many died at once." So that's the first thing. So those dead didn't have ceremony, which means the living didn't release tension. And secondly, the Earth herself, because she's the mother of those children, didn't release that tension either—because we received our instructions on how to grieve the dead from the land itself, originally. So neither the men who have to dig the graves—and you know, I guess some of the women probably helped—but the men who had to dig the graves were sure to swallow the tension of the earth, who is the mother, who had not had her tension released. Then it becomes toxic. And it's toxic emotionality. We say the earth is sacred, but she is female and if she doesn't get a chance to grieve the loss of her dead, then she's gonna be toxic just like any other female. Female wolves go completely mad if they come upon their lair and their children are dead. They go completely nuts and so do we. And so, that is the tension that those men are swallowing.

SM: How does the swallowing of that tension affect the men's sense of their role as protectors?

LM: The only example I get is Eddy [from *Daughters are Forever*]. He hears West Wind, he actually hears the ancestral voices, hears the voice of the Earth but doesn't want to hear it, because he doesn't know what to do about it. So he runs out in front of a truck and kills himself. Then the second voice that I use is Marilyn's voice herself saying "wait" and the stepfather not waiting. Not attending to the young, not attending to the children, not listening to what they need and addressing those needs. So that's the second voice. And the third voice is the stillness of the women, which then informs the men. Because the women are still, the men don't have to move. They become paralyzed.

SM: And that paralysis then is self-defeating or locks them into those positions?

LM: I'm thinking it keeps them locked to a barstool. That's one of the ways. Locks us in position.

SM: The short story, "Charlie," from *Sojourner's Truth*, contains a powerful depiction of a father recognizing his inability to keep the son out of residential school, and it mentions how he "confided none of his self-disgust to his wife. It made him surly but he said nothing." I'm wondering how silence plays in …

LM: It's not silence. Silence is not speaking. It's a choice. But it's part of the paralysis. Keeps us locked in—"in" being the operative word.

SM: So it's then not a decision-making process at all, but rather the way in which one is contained.

LM: It's just locked in. Yeah.

LEE MARACLE
(Wolf Clan, Stó:lo) is a novelist, poet, educator, storyteller and performing artist. First published in the early 1970s, she is an advocate for and teacher of Indigenous writers from around the world and a mentor to young people on personal and cultural reclamation and healing. She currently works as a professor in the Department of Aboriginal Studies at University of Toronto and as a counsellor to students at First Nations House. Among her many published works are the novels *Ravensong* (Press Gang Publishers, 1993), *Daughters are Forever* (Polestar, 2002), and *Will's Garden* (Theytus Books, 2008), the poetry collection *Bent Box* (Theytus Books, 2000), and the non-fiction study *I Am Woman: A Native Perspective on Sociology and Feminism* (Press Gang Publishers, 1988).

SM: Are there pathways to opening up that silence so that the "self-disgust" is not corrosive?

LM: Breaking the locks, you mean.

SM: Yes.

LM: It's not silence. I just said it wasn't silence, so don't call mine silence. It might be silence from your direction, because you're not in it, you're looking from outside. But it's not silence. So, it's breaking the locks. And there's a number of ceremonies that we have for undoing those locks, for pushing through the paralysis, and for giving voice to the unsaid. But I think that each nation has its own ceremonies and its own outcomes and each individual in those nations has to become through the world. [*gets up to use blackboard*]

It goes like this: here's the baby. And if it's abused, it's surrounded by family. But if this baby is traumatized *by* the parents and others in here, it's bounced out of family and it has to go through the world to return. So it has to come through this doorway first, which right now doesn't want them—so it's double-locked. Colonization has to be addressed. And then dis-integration has to be addressed and then restoration of family has to be addressed. I should say restoration and healing of family. Then reintegration is possible.

SM: And because of how that child has been initially bounced out of this circle of family by those...

LM: That's for anyone who's ever been traumatized by their family—it fits the Irish, too. If you take a look around the world, Indigenous people as a whole are locked into this, outside their own worlds.

SM: And is an initial way of attacking the lock through, I guess, a decolonization process that attends to racism?

LM: That's the keys to the lock. The initial way of attacking the lock is madness. And that's what you see in most Indigenous communities throughout the world. Three-hundred-fifty million people locked into madness. You can really see it in southern Africa. So the madness begins. I think Fanon even talks a little bit about it. But this is how I've seen it. It's like doorways to these rings lead to wholeness at the centre. Then you have a whole person and community. But all these things have to be happening. This fellow in my class today did his first feast and had his family and friends there and he was saying it was the first time he invited his entire family into a feast even though he's been a pipe carrier for a long time. And it's because this madness wasn't being dealt with. And we realized that this had to come first before he could do that, and

THE WARRIOR IS RESPONSIBLE FOR MAKING SURE THAT THIS DOESN'T HAPPEN. THE MALES ARE RESPONSIBLE FOR DIRECTION. AND IF PARALYSIS IS THE MODEL, THEN MADNESS ENSUES.

THIS IS a VISION...

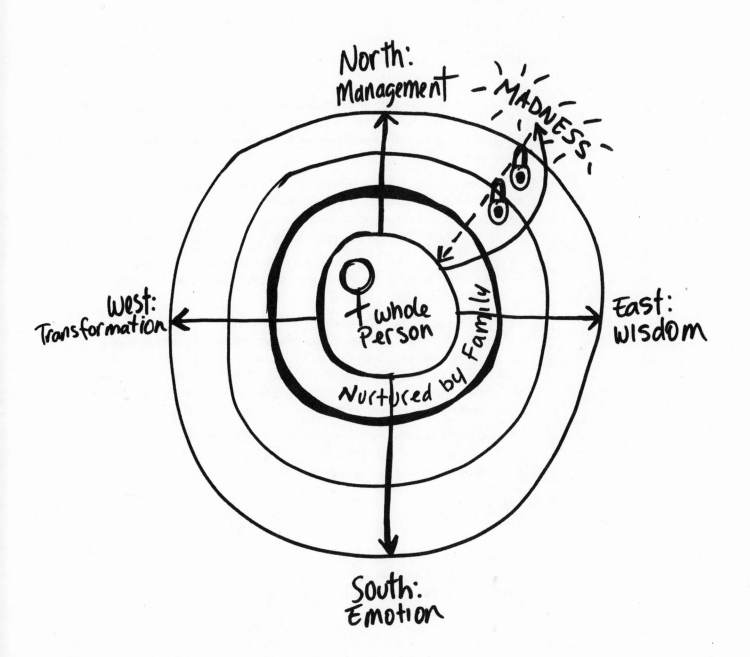

North:
Management

MADNESS

West:
Transformation

whole
Person

Nurtured by Family

East:
Wisdom

South:
Emotion

so then we were able to talk about that. Because the warrior is responsible for making sure that this doesn't happen. The males are responsible for direction. And if paralysis is the model, then madness ensues. And in order to return to family, the child has to go through the world that bounced him out.

SM: How has this been informed by the ways in which colonial governments sought to reform Indigenous family structures—in terms of moving from clan-based kinship structures to imposed nuclear family structures?

LM: I think you're thinking of the government as a little more absolute and powerful than they really are. The nuclear family came about as a result of many many epidemics. We chose it to survive. So it comes out of murder not the state. The state didn't force us to burn our longhouses. But we did. So once they're formed, the state can influence that formation. They can idealize the formation.

SM: We were talking earlier about there being a lot of in-depth work on Indigenous women's issues—I'm thinking of *I Am Woman*, obviously, and Paula Gunn Allen's *The Sacred Hoop* and Kim Anderson's *A Recognition of Being*—but there not being a similar body of literature on men's issues…

LM: I should say there's not a book on it; that doesn't mean there aren't bodies of work. A body is a person. There's lots of men who can speak to this issue. They just haven't been published. [*Laughter*]

SM: I guess the question that I'm moving toward in relation to that is why do you think that there has been such a strong women's voice among Indigenous writers and poets in what is now commonly called Canada? I think back to the Peterborough conference [*Sounding Out: Indigenous Poetics* in November 2010] and there was a lot of discussion among the poets there about the "foremothers" and a connection to really powerful women's voices and ancestries, but there wasn't a similar discussion of "forefathers."

LM: I think it's because the internal world that women have been writing about is female jurisdiction. So you have a lot of Two-Spirit writing and Native women's writing, but the male world outside is this world and if you look around now, there's about as many male writers as there is female, but they're writing about history. You know, *Peace, Power, and Righteousness*…

SM: Taiaiake Alfred …

LM: So they're writing about our relationship to this colonial world, but the internal world has to get straightened out in order for them to go back out and meet that world properly. It's just the way our societies work.

SM: Yeah, yeah. I understand. Well—I don't fully understand but I'm trying. That makes sense to me, is what I meant to say. [*Laughter*]

LM: [*Laughter*]

SM: One thing that I also wanted to ask about is the recognition in a lot of your work of the ways in which male characters have been adversely affected by history, but not in a way that robs them completely of agency. So it's not like they're free of any culpability by virtue of history. How do you balance recognition of the ways in which history has disempowered particular groups with a desire to hold individuals within those groups accountable for damage they may inflict on others?

LM: Yeah, I don't see them as disempowered, and I hope you didn't get that from my work. I don't see them that way. We're always moving. We're either moving this way [*refers to board*] back to wholeness or we're moving around in the hamster cage. We're always moving, whatever it is we're doing. And because we're *communitas*, we're always either looking at the madness or we're walking to the sanity. And I think that's what I'm trying to say in all my work. We're always doing something—we're engaging each other, either in sharing shit or sharing feasts. We're sharing the sacred or we're sharing abuse. But we never stopped sharing, we never stopped our *communitas* way of life. It's particularly true of *Daughters* and *Ravensong* and some of the short stories. But we're never not engaging the community.

Just because you take away the means of making sense of a culture doesn't mean that the culture changes. They took away the things that would make us make sense and continuously reconcile ourselves to ourselves and to the outside world. But it doesn't mean we stopped engaging each other in the same way we've always done it. We're living in nuclear families but we have a *communitas* sensibility. We're living in nuclear families but we still have joint raising of children. We're living in nuclear families, and we're sharing responsibilities, whether it's in madness or it's in wholeness. Whichever direction we're going, it's still the same way. And culture is about the way you do things. So we may not have the words for these things—which is the language—but we definitely do things the way we've always done them. We might be doing different things 'cause we're running around in this hamster cage or we might be doing the same thing our ancestors always did because we've reached wholeness by some miracle. We've gone back to who we always are and who we always will be. That's the saying: *We always are and always will be.* We cannot *not* be ourselves.

SM: This makes me think of *Will's Garden* because although he's seeking ways of negotiating the various circumstances he finds himself in, in high school or wherever, Will is always participating in that community.

> WE'RE SHARING THE SACRED OR WE'RE SHARING ABUSE. BUT WE NEVER STOPPED SHARING, WE NEVER STOPPED OUR COMMUNITAS WAY OF LIFE.

LM: Even when he's silent, he's commentating in his mind. Even in his dreams, he's watching his ancestors. And he does it in English. I remember my son reading it and saying, "I'm so glad you did this because it shows that we can have our culture in English or our language." Because he always felt offended when people said, "You have to know your language or your culture. You can't have culture without a language." Because he always knew he did things differently than everybody else.

I belong to a family of twenty-two siblings, that are now all sober and together, functioning as a unit, building community. So we're all here [*points to the inside of the circle*]— and we were all out here before [*points to the outside of the circle, the realm of madness*]. And you can tell how bad it was out here because my son was friends with my niece and didn't know she was my niece, didn't know it was my sister's daughter. That's how messed up we were thirty-four years ago. And I just made a decision when I was young not to hang out with people who were drunk. I don't care if they were my relatives or not 'cause I'm raising my kids as a sober family. And so they didn't get to know their aunts and uncles until everyone started to sober up, so we were all out here, my kids and I, in what I call a state of madness. Not that I was crazy, but the madness is that we didn't have family here, and therefore you can't actually be whole here. So we're isolated from each other in little pockets of madness [*draws on board*]: There's us quarantined. And that's a very Euro tradition.

SM: Yes, I see. Quarantined!

LM: And there I have quarantined my children away and it took us a long time to make that journey back in. And it took quite a few books. My books have sparked so much re-entry to wholeness in my particular family.

SM: In relation to re-entry and return, what is the role of ritual and initiation in these processes?

LM: Well, if you don't have positive ceremonies, you're going to have negative ceremonies—that's just how humans are. If you watch people that are getting ready to go to the bar, it's really ritualistic. Or go to bingo, it's ritualistic. Or, you know, get into a fight— there's a ritual before a fight. You know how men draw the line in the sand and do the dancing around. You can see it in boxing, you know? It's a terrific ritual, and there has to be a ring. There has to be a public gathered around them. There has to be this, there has to be that… If we don't have positive rituals, which are the ones that keep us going here in the family with a sense of wholeness [*points to board*], then we're going to have mad rituals, rituals that keep the madness running.

SM: I wonder also about the love relationship between Will and Laylanee in *Will's Garden*. Despite their youth, at the novel's end they make a fairly profound commitment to one another…

IF WE DON'T HAVE POSITIVE RITUALS, WHICH ARE THE ONES THAT KEEP US GOING HERE IN THE FAMILY WITH A SENSE OF WHOLENESS, THEN WE'RE GOING TO HAVE MAD RITUALS, RITUALS THAT KEEP THE MADNESS RUNNING.

LM: What's the profound commitment?

SM: Well, I guess it's that they sort of promise to be together when they return to the community after moving away to pursue school and things. I get the sense that they're proclaiming a sort of mutual ownership or belonging.

LM: I don't think that was what I was intending to show. I thought that she said that she wasn't ready, but "when you've gone out in the world, call me." [*Laughter*]

SM: I suppose I read a bit of machismo into Will's framing of it… but that might be my misinterpretation of the novel.

LM: I don't think she said, "I'll be there. [*Laughter*] I'm not gonna wait for ya." But they do make a commitment to contact each other. Nobody knows the end of that relationship, but he's clearly smitten with her. And she clearly is aware of it. But I don't believe I intended to have them commit to each other. He commits to his education and becoming an environmental scientist, which is his role out in the world. He picks up that bundle. And he commits to reading Aboriginal women writers. But the two things he can't commit to right now is reading his mother's diary and his girl. [*Laughter*] 'Cause he's too young! He's not ready, he's not cooked up yet! He's about here, on the edge of wholeness. So, yeah, anyway, that was what I was trying to get to. I'll read it again to make sure I didn't…

SM: I'm the one that needs to go back and read it again!

LM: I might've been mistaken, you know, pushing the envelope just a little bit too far. I did want to point in that direction because it's always a possibility that young people can meet and fall in love. I had a sister who was sixteen, married her sweetheart at sixteen, and is still married to him and they've had a wonderful love together. She was, I think, fourteen when they started dating. But he was in love with her when she was a child and he was sixteen and he just waited for her to grow up enough for him to date her. And I remember him telling the family and I remember my brother saying, "Don't even say that, she's a child, I don't want to hear it. What are you talking about? She's my sister!" But anyway, they still have a very great relationship together. But you never know, you know?

SM: In relation to your criticism—and I'm thinking of *Oratory: Coming to Theory* specifically—you indicate…

LM: Sometimes I wish I hadn't written that one. But go on…

SM: …you recognize, in the Western academy, that the desire for objectivity erroneously erases passion from the equation.

LM: Do I start with theory and evidence and all that sort of stuff?

SM: Yep, you were talking about John Stuart Mill…

LM: Yeah, yeah, yeah.

SM: And what I was interested in relation to that…

LM: I think the thing that I was never able to do in that little piece is say, we can't get away with isolating a part of this text and asking questions because it's a single text, it's a single sentence, really. Think of it as a single sentence. The first part shows the emotionality of this confusion around what theory is.

SM: It also points to my reliance on a particular vantage point, right? My academic training is saying that I need to cut these ideas down to their smallest units of meaning so that I can evaluate and unpack them.

LM: Isolate and quarantine. It's your medicine.[1] It's not your training; it's your medicine. Isolate and quarantine. And I don't know how that began but it's probably got something to do with the plague and the unending fear of epidemic loss, because the only way the plague ended was to isolate and quarantine everybody.

SM: And then, at the same time, it provides an illusion of control when one doesn't have control.

LM: Yeah, exactly. But it became a way of life. So it's part of the way of life. So you look at something and I notice that—sorry, mostly in white men [*Laughter*]—not to belabour this, but white women can generally get a handle on the wholeness of something. Not all of them.

Right in the very centre of Euro-society, your very words cancel out your other words. On one hand, germs, or bacteria, can kill you and yet they're the source of life, you see what I mean? Because you isolate and quarantine, you can't come to understand bacteria from a holistic perspective as the first life. Breathe desire into it, and it keeps replicating, different but the same. And out of it comes all life. It's just the Dene origin story.

So what I'm saying is that you first have to have this view clear in order to see the connection of the whole to the parts. It's about seeing things in their concatenation and in their separation, once you've seen the whole picture. So you're always looking for the whole picture. And we know when we've found it because it's got a northern direction, it's got an eastern direction, it's got a southern direction, it's got a western direction. West is the direction of transformation. North is the direction of organization and management—administration, if you will. East is the direction of wisdom, or life origins, if you will. And South is the direction of the emotion, the heart. The thing is born, it gains life, acquires wholeness, acquires good health, acquires light, is organized

1. Maracle notes that Terry Spanish, a former student of hers who is a language teacher in Michigan, came up with the phrase "isolate and quarantine" to describe these tendencies.

and is managed and administered, and transformed. Then we can know the whole. And now in the light of that, we can look at the centre, because that's the centre of the whole, where all of this has reproduced—or, its culture, if you will—and then we can know the parts in relation to the culture.

SM: Is that the flaw, that people try to understand the parts first?

LM: *Oratory: Coming to Theory* was the whole. There is no way to isolate the parts.

SM: In an interview with Margery Fee and Sneja Ganew, you describe the Wolf Clan as "the backward and forward visionaries for [the] people," who "help [the] people adjust to whatever change occurs." What is the relationship between that role and working as an artist?

LM: Okay, it's not a role. We *are* that. It's not a role. I'm not a role. I'm a Wolf Clan, backward and forward visionary. That is my relationship to the whole. I'm keeper of the backward and forward vision, so if somebody has a vision yesterday, I'm the keeper of it. This diagram is a vision [*marks on board*]. Now, whether it is my vision or my ancestor's vision or a combination of all the visions, or I piece them all together from my experience, that doesn't make any difference. That's what's going to take us from yesterday to tomorrow—this vision. And I keep it. It's my bundle. I'm stuck with it. I mean, a whole lot of minds and wisdom and experience give birth to it. But we naturally are going in that direction. It's not a goal. I think this is why a lot of the young people don't want to be role models, because "role" is the isolated part. And then here's the whole. And your relationship to the whole is distance. No, no, my relationship to the whole is the whole. And every other clan has that same relationship from a different angle, but still it's about the whole. Then in Euro-society everything is about isolating and quarantining, and you get crazy poets like Yeats, who say "The centre cannot hold!" [*Laughter*] Who made you the centre?!

SM: [*Laughter*]

LM: The centre always holds. We might spin and fly off but the centre is gonna be the centre. We may not understand what's going on, but we still have the same responsibility to see it. And whether or not we figure out something from it, it's just a matter of rolling the dice. Things fell into my path when I was very young that contributed to me being able to make some sense of it. Not saying that this is the right way or the wrong way, but it is my vision of the way things are. Someone else might have a different vision and it's equally viable, adequate, and correct. But in Euro-society, only one vision has a place in the universe. Like, how smart is that? We will only use the genius of one individual because the other six billion of you don't count. No, we say everyone has a

IT'S NOT A ROLE. WE ARE THAT. IT'S NOT A ROLE. I'M NOT A ROLE. I'M A WOLF CLAN, BACKWARD AND FORWARD VISIONARY. THAT IS MY RELATIONSHIP TO THE WHOLE.

vision and we have to respect everyone's vision. The saying is that there are an infinite number of pathways to the centre of the circle, so we're always looking for other pathways to consider. And there's six billion people. And gazillions of animals and rocks and ancestors and… it's infinite.

So we're always looking for another pathway to augment our vision but we personally need a vision. And we are always augmenting, clarifying, and substantiating our vision. Mine may never change. Or someone might convince me to isolate and quarantine. [*Laughter*]

SM: [*Laughter*] I don't see that happening in the near future.

YOUNG MEN OF GOOD WILL

A CONVERSATION WITH BASIL H. JOHNSTON

ANIMALS OF FIERCE DISPOSITION, THE BEAR, WOLF, AND LYNX, WERE THE TOTEMS OF WARRIORS. WARRIORS WERE A NECESSARY EVIL. DIRECTLY AND INDIRECTLY THEY CAUSED FIGHTING. FOR THE MOST PART, IT WAS THE YOUTH WHO SOUGHT TO BE COURAGEOUS; AND, THOUGH THERE WERE SEVERAL WAYS OF SO DOING, THERE WAS NO EASIER OR FINER WAY THAN THROUGH PHYSICAL COMBAT. BATTLE WAS A TEST FOR HEART, STRENGTH, AND SKILL. —BASIL H. JOHNSTON, OJIBWAY HERITAGE

4 DECEMBER 2007
A public conversation between Basil H. Johnston and Sam McKegney at the Gladstone Hotel in Toronto, Ontario, as part of Pages Bookstore's "This Is Not A Reading Series." Although this interview was conducted prior to the initiation of this masculinities project, I include it here because it touches on themes integral to the present collection.

SAM MCKEGNEY: In *Indian School Days*, you stress that the experience of residential school was more difficult for the "wee ones" who were ripped from their families and social systems at the ages of five or six and therefore didn't have the foundation of self-worth and culture that older entrants, like you, might have developed. Tell us about your experience of entering the residential school at Spanish and the feelings of dislocation involved.

Throughout his prolific literary career, Anishinaabe elder, orator, and teacher BASIL H. JOHNSTON (Anishinaabe) has advocated passionately for Indigenous cultural revitalization in Canada. Several of his fifteen English-language books, including *Ojibway Heritage* (McClelland and Stewart, 1976), *Ojibway Ceremonies* (McClelland and Stewart, 1982), *The Manitous* (HarperCollins, 1996), and *Honour Earth Mother* (Kegedonce, 2003), participate in the endurance of the Anishinaabe worldview by examining the social, political, and spiritual traditions of the Anishinaabeg. He has published five books in the Ojibway language and developed an audio program for language retention among Anishinaabe youth. His literary works also include the residential school memoir *Indian School Days* (Key Porter Books, 1988) and *Crazy Dave* (Key Porter Books, 1999).

1. The Canadian federal government officially apologized to First Nations, Métis, and Inuit peoples for its part in residential schooling on 11 June 2008, six months after this interview was conducted.

BASIL H. JOHNSTON: The little ones suffered the most, thrown into the schools, as they were, when they were still really babies. They were outcasts—cast out of their communities, families, and homes. And what was worse, they were made to feel unloved and unwanted. They were told, of course, that Jesus loved them, but they were never given the love for which a child's spirit yearns: never hugged, never caressed when they wept, never told "I love you." So when those little ones were released into the world a decade later, they were lost; they were adrift in an alien world that didn't accept them, a world in which they no longer belonged.

I guess, therefore, that I was "lucky"—if you can call it that—to enter the school at ten years of age with some sense of my culture and a sense that my mother loved me. But there was so much pain in that place. I'm talking about students who were violated, students who were raped by their own kind, by older Native students, fifteen or sixteen, and by the priests immediately after mass, by brothers in the various workplaces. And you often wondered what penalties the perpetrators had to undergo. Did they go to Father Superior and say, "This is what I had in mind, and this is what I did thereafter"? Not likely.

I didn't know it then, but when I was raped by two boys and, not long after, I was fellated by a priest immediately after mass, I really was thrown into another world. Abuse is too mild a word. It's a violation of the worst kind. It violates not only the body, the flesh, but also the spirit. And you live with this fear of death and fear of being dispatched to Hell. And I thought, and many of us thought, that we were the only victims.

When I met Lucy, who was my wife and who remained my wife for forty-two years, when I met her and during the... well, thirty-five ensuing years, I never mentioned what happened to me. And when the students at Spanish sued the federal government and the Jesuits, I ended up on the negotiating team. That's when I learned that I was not the only one, that there were hundreds of other youngsters who had suffered the same indignities. And when you become a victim of this, what happens is that you lose whatever sense of integrity that you've got. You are a worthless thing. And it's confirmed in the gospel readings that Jesus had to die for "our" sins.

Anyway, it's hard to get over that. It takes years, years, years. And then I met Lucy who, after a year and a half, well, not quite a year and a half, maybe six months after we started going out, said, "I love you," to me. My sense of integrity and sense of worth escalated.

SM: What do you make of the contrition of church and state representatives regarding their roles in administering this system that enabled your violation and that of so many others? Do you feel that the churches, many of which have officially apologized to Indigenous peoples, and the Canadian government, which will purportedly apologize in the coming months, are sincere in their stated regret?[1]

BJ: When I became part of the negotiating team for the suit against the federal government and the Jesuits, I learned a lot of things. At one of the meetings, they had the Father Superior for the Upper Canada Society of Jesus and his assistant, and one of the members of the team from the girls' school spoke. And there were many, many tears in the audience. And I watched the two Jesuits. There was not a sign of sympathy. Not one.

Two years ago this past Spring, I was invited up to a spiritual centre up on Anderson Lake, just south of Espanola, Ontario. And I was called by the Jesuits and the Anglican Church and the United Church ministries. And I told them, "You know, you talk about sympathy, compassion. You don't have any compassion! It's just a word. And it's supposed to have conveyed a sense of feeling, a sense of pity for your fellow human being. But it isn't there. It's an abstract notion." And that's still my opinion about these institutions.

SM: It's interesting that you identified individual human reactions—or rather, non-re-actions—from the Jesuits at that meeting, but then finished your comments with "these institutions." This suggests that human behaviour can be circumscribed by systems like that of the Jesuits, which you note in *Indian School Days* prevented the brothers from showing the students any form of love. Do you feel that appropriate systems have been put in place to deal with the legacy of residential schools? A system of compensation, for instance, has been set in place with the Common Experience Payments, and such vehicles as the Aboriginal Healing Foundation have been financed and given specific mandates. You mentioned healing circles when you and I were speaking a moment ago; do you care to comment on the relevance of the whole "healing industry"?

BJ: You know, I've found that there's an awful lot of charlatans out there, not only Na-tive, but also psychologists. They have an answer for everything. [*Laughter*] All we need is a healing circle. "Come on in and we'll heal you. We'll take you to a sweat lodge. Brother, come in and be healed!" And even though I'm very cynical about these things, a healing circle is not an instantaneous, miraculous healing. It takes a lot of time. One of the conditions [in our legal suit] that never passed was that we have healing from recognized, registered psychologists. And Wilbur Nadjiwon objected. He said, "I'm not havin' no twenty-two-year-old kid with a psychology degree come and try to heal me, looking inside my soul and my spirit!" And I feel the same way. If I want one, I want one who speaks my language. No. Being healed—the healing has to come from inside, from ourselves. And some don't know it, unfortunately.

I don't think I was able to articulate it, but I used to fight, fight, fight. And each time I fought, there was always some bigger guy, somebody heavier, somebody who knew how to fight a little better, and "pow!" I'd go down. I'd cry. Somebody would say, "Get up!" And I've taken that as a model for life. When you're felled, you don't wallow in self-pity. You get up.

I don't know if the general asking of forgiveness will do much good. I was asked, "Would you forgive?" I don't know. No one has ever asked me, "Will you forgive me?" for what the church has done, for what the government allowed their church to do. The government is just as much at fault. I feel like fighting. [*Laughter*]

SM: I'm glad I'm on this side of the table. If the goal of the Canadian government and the Canadian population is really "truth" and "reconciliation," how can these be attained in the shadow of trauma? After the racist violence of a system of education designed to tear Indian identity from Indigenous students, how can the righteous rage of the Indigenous population not spill out in forms of hatred toward non-Indigenous Canada?

BJ: How? I'm not sure there is one answer. How? Am I a bigot? I don't know. I don't think so. I try not to be. I used to teach high school in North York. I had one rule: be fair in all your dealings. We had some examples of lies, bigotry. I remember there was a grade 10–11 ST&T [Science, Technology, and Trades] class, and one of the boys complained that the boy sitting in front of him always wore the same outfit every single day. And that the boy who wore this outfit smelled. Well, I didn't know quite what to do. But, you know, the boys themselves settled it. They told the complainant that he was a bigot, and they apologized to the boy who was being complained on. That was one way. It was the crowd of maybe twenty-five boys of good will exerting their displeasure. And altogether though, I think, too many people stay silent when we've got incidents or articulations of ill will.

SM: Part of the government's strategy for dealing with the residential school legacy has been to historicize the system by requisitioning historical accounts. Certain church groups have financed such publications as well. In *Indian School Days*, you deliberately took an alternative tack by avoiding sources like government policy statements, federal and church archives, newspapers, et cetera, and focusing on the behaviour of the children—not the typical focus of history. Do you feel that the history of residential schooling in Canada has been adequately accounted for? What are your thoughts on Canadian history as a discipline?

BJ: I was explaining the causes of the razing of Fort Ste. Marie in 1648 by the Iroquois to a group of, I think they were, Mormons. That was in 1968 at the Canadian National Exhibition. And so they went away shaking their heads, you know, wagging their heads, in agreement with this stuff that I had found in history books. After they had gone, Howard Skye (Onondaga from Six Nations) plucked me by the sleeve and said, "Would you like to hear *our* story?" I didn't know that there was another story. The only stories that I knew were those that had been "properly documented." And so he took me aside, and he told me this story:

"When the missionaries settled down in Fort Ste. Marie and Midland, they established a school, and they were teaching the Huron kids and some of the Anishinaabe kids how to read, write, count, and learn all kinds of 'civilized' things that weren't available to the Haudenosaunee youngsters. So the Haudenosaunee or Six Nations asked the missionaries if they could send their boys and girls up to Fort Ste. Marie because this was a good thing.

IT WAS THE CROWD OF MAYBE TWENTY-FIVE BOYS OF GOOD WILL EXERTING THEIR DISPLEASURE... TOO MANY PEOPLE STAY SILENT WHEN WE'VE GOT INCIDENTS OR ARTICULATIONS OF ILL WILL.

"In the Spring, when they went back up to recover their young boys and girls, some of the girls were pregnant and some of the boys had been violated. So the Six Nations issued a warning. The second year, the same results took place.

"Instead of issuing a third warning, they sent eighteen hundred warriors in March of 1648 and torched Fort Ste. Marie."

So that was the story that he told me. And then that also changed the way I look on history today. There are stories that are not recorded. And there are all kinds of stories of events that have been suppressed; it goes a long long way back.

And the [Iraq] war today, it's a war for oil. It has nothing to do with the Taliban, nothing to do with Al Qaeda. Oil. And I'm more inclined to believe that than what the president of the United States says.

SM: What about Indigenous understandings of the past? Have Indigenous communities done a better job grappling with the meaning of this history than, say, mainstream historians or the federal government? What do you feel is needed in this regard?

BJ: My next book will be about that. I am giving back to my heritage what it has given me. That is an understanding of my heritage and my understanding of me. One of the projects is to set down our history from *our* point of view. I'm lucky. I know the stories. I know the words, many of the words. I know how we look on history. And I'm going to make a real good case for the existence of institutions that the United States took up and adopted in its constitution, and that part of which Canada has adopted. I know European history and that they didn't have those institutions until they came over here and found them. We had them. We've got words for them. And I know where they fit in.

SM: In terms of action, we've spoken about external strategies for dealing with legacies of acculturation and violence—strategies like psychotherapy, monetary compensation, and church-run healing circles—but what about strategies emerging within Indigenous communities themselves? What needs to be done throughout Indigenous Canada, and on your reserve specifically, to counteract the corrosive influence of a century of residential schooling?

BJ: In teaching, in schools, we have to get back to the old values. For example, I was talking to Joan Roy in May about the loss of a sense of duty. The whole emphasis is on rights—"My rights are being violated," "My rights are being infringed upon." There's not a word about duties. To us, a right is *debnimzewin*. But each right is also a duty. And we've forgotten to teach those in our Native schools. I've also noticed that they don't teach much in terms of duties to your neighbours in the secular schools and in the public school system of Ontario. And so we have to go back to some of these values: responsibility, duty, right.

And from my readings, I gather that the principal teachers [in Anishinaabe culture] were the grandmothers. They were the holders and keepers of the wisdom. Not so

"MY RIGHTS ARE BEING VIOLATED," "MY RIGHTS ARE BEING INFRINGED UPON." THERE'S NOT A WORD ABOUT DUTIES. TO US, A RIGHT IS DEBNIMZEWIN. BUT EACH RIGHT IS ALSO A DUTY.

much the men, but it was the women. And they were assigned this duty by the community because the males were out and it was the grandmothers who kept the villages together. And they had the primary responsibility of training the youth. And I guess there is need to go back to that system, to have grandmothers taking part in schools, teaching language, teaching the literature of the people. Our literature is rich with stories. I know five or six hundred. It's a matter of putting those in sequence.

SM: Do you consider there to be a role for literature in Indigenous empowerment? I'm thinking of a story from your book *The Manitous* (1995) in which the Anishinaabe Trickster/hero figure Nana'b'oozoo causes the regeneration of the world by breathing life into a tiny ball of mud. You write, "Nana'b'oozoo.... had done what everyone is supposed to do, to quest for that tiny knot of soil, the gift of talent, and to make from it one's being and world" (12). Do you feel that literature and storytelling can be used to create one's "being" and one's "world," or at least to augment one's perceptions of those things? Has storytelling assisted you, for instance, in forms of self-realization?

BJ: Well, it confirmed my worth, my sense of worth, but also the worth of my background. And so that, along with Lucy's love and the love of the Native people who offered me guidance, helped me, I think, restore my sense of integrity and sense of purpose.

SM: The impact of literature—or at least literature that finds an audience—moves beyond the author her-or himself. I've often thought of *Indian School Days* as a story designed to celebrate and consolidate the community that developed among Indigenous students at Spanish, students torn from their families and home communities. In that way, the story is a social act. At the same time, *Indian School Days* reorients historical focus on residential schooling away from administrators and overseers, toward the Indigenous students themselves, thereby recognizing far ahead of most historical accounts the agency retained by Indigenous people throughout situations of acculturation. Do you feel that books like *Indian School Days* facilitate Indigenous empowerment?

BJ: No. I wrote *Indian School Days* with what I knew back in 1979. There were, I think, sixteen of us in Toronto who had attended residential school in Spanish. And we used to talk about the things that amused us when we were there. And I suppose they were little events, silly incidents—that we created—that assisted us in pulling through. And that was the source of *Indian School Days*. It had nothing to do with trying to change or "empower" anyone. It was just to amuse the readers of, at first, *The Ontario Indian*. I had a definite purpose in writing that book: that is to make people smile, chuckle, chortle, guffaw.... There's altogether too little of that human element in any of the books written by the most prominent authors in Canada. A lot of them aren't humorous.

Now, I will write a very different book this time.

THERE IS NEED TO GO BACK TO THAT SYSTEM, TO HAVE GRANDMOTHERS TAKING PART IN SCHOOLS, TEACHING LANGUAGE, TEACHING THE LITERATURE OF THE PEOPLE.

[During the open question period that followed, one audience member noted the age difference between interviewer and interviewee and asked if it had taken a new generation to start dealing with sins of the past like residential school. Johnston responded:]

BJ: I don't think people ever learn. I really don't think they learn from the mistakes of the past. They don't even learn from their own mistakes. They keep repeating them and repeating them and repeating them. I'm not sure that there's any lesson in residential schools that would, you know, enlighten the nation. Maybe it'll get people more sensitive to our situations. I think that much of the situations at home on Indian reserves really cannot be attributed too much to the residential school system but to the Indian agency system. They were our managers. They looked after every single aspect of our lives. They're the guys who held us back.

And now we have professional young people—lawyers, businesspeople—they're the people who are going to make a difference. But I really don't believe that people learn from mistakes that were made in the past.

[Johnston's response apparently chafed against the desire of some in the audience for validation that Canadian society is progressing in terms of human rights and intercultural empathy. Taking offence, a second audience member pressed Johnston to acknowledge progress by asserting that activists and critical thinkers have accomplished a great deal by analyzing the past and seeking out more just and equitable courses of action. To this, Johnston replied:]

BJ: I don't know if I can articulate it clearer than what I've already given voice to. That's my belief, you know, my observation. People don't learn. They make the same stupid mistakes.

SM: Well, does this link back to your unwillingness to simply give up teaching? There are still things to be learned, so you put the ideas out there. You write the books. You want people to read them. You want Anishinaabe children to learn their language, to learn their culture. And just because we don't, I guess, learn the lessons as fully as we should, doesn't mean the teaching should stop.[2]

BJ: No. I never would advocate that.

SM: So maybe there's some learning that still needs to be done.

BJ: There's always hope. *[Laughter]*

2. My leading question here betrays my own unwillingness to heed some of the difficult lessons Johnston had shared during the evening insofar as it seeks to recuperate the author's prior response into the very narrative of progress he had so eloquently repudiated and thereby to placate the generally sympathetic audience.

A CALM SENSUALITY

A CONVERSATION WITH LOUISE BERNICE HALFE, SKYDANCER

I WORK TO BURY YOUR FIST, MY FATHER, MY TONGUE
A WILLOW WHIPPING YOUR CLENCHED HANDS. I CRY
FOR A HUNDRED BLESSINGS TO WASH YOUR GRIMACING
FACE.
—LOUISE BERNICE HALFE, BLUE MARROW

2 FEBRUARY 2011
Telephone conversation between Louise Halfe in Saskatoon, Saskatchewan, and Sam McKegney in Kingston, Ontario.

SAM MCKEGNEY: At the Trent University conference on Indigenous poetics in Peterborough in October 2010, I noticed a profound affirmation by younger poets of those they referred to as their "foremothers." I recall Rosanna Deerchild and Christine Sy and Natasha Beeds and Gregory Scofield all speaking about the earlier generation of women writers who have supported their work and created a lineage that allows them to do what they do. And I was conscious of the conspicuous absence of "forefathers" in their discussion. It made me think of that wonderful section at the beginning of *Blue Marrow*, where prayer is interspersed with the names of hundreds of women. And I guess I want to ask you why there appears to be an absence of male figures in the background of Indigenous poetics in Canada and what the consequences of this absence might be.

LOUISE HALFE: When I wrote *Blue Marrow*, I was very conscious of the absence of historical women in Canadian literature. In particular, Aboriginal women, of course. And if they were mentioned, they were never mentioned by name, they were nameless. It was as if we never played a role in men's lives—the chiefs, the white fur traders, even Governor Simpson with his wife. Also, when I was growing up, my grandmothers made a huge impact in my life. My grandmothers were the matriarchs. The grandfathers hardly said a word. They were very silent, so I never knew them. They worked in the field, they sat with the grandmothers, they looked after the sweat lodges, but they stayed very much in the background.

The other factor is my female chauvinism. This country is celebrated by white men and Native men; where are our Native women in the forefront? They are coming out now, especially in the last five—at the most ten—years where we now are having chiefs, we're having women in Parliament, but it's taken a long time, and frankly I wasn't going to give men the satisfaction of appearing with a larger voice in my print. A part of the reason for that is they have a large voice already in a public forum. They take over our sweat lodges as if they are sole proprietors of spirituality, and there's a lot of chauvinism around that. Women, again, get pushed out of the picture.

SM: Mi'kmaq scholar Bonita Lawrence has discussed in her work the way that spirituality in a lot of Indigenous communities has been claimed as a male right, so things like menstrual taboos around the sweat lodge have been used, not to empower women, but to exclude them. Do you see that at play?

LH: Oh, absolutely. But the exclusion is also valid. And it's not just because of the menstrual cycles themselves. It's because the older men realize the incredible power we possess as women during that period of our lives. And it's not only a spiritual prowess, because we're really creative during that time, we're really fierce. I used to be really fierce during my pre-menstrual cycle. If I didn't have my seclusion where I could meet my creative energies, watch out.

We have the capacity to abuse our sexual powers. It becomes a sick thing. The healthy men know that what is between our legs can devour them. And that's not to say in an unhealthy way, it just is.

SM: I find it so interesting the way that's framed, "to devour." Because having studied a lot of Western philosophy and literary criticism, sexual relations between male and female are all too frequently framed solely as "penetrative." In other words, giving the power to male penis as opposed to an idea of "envelopment" or "devouring," which places power within the female element of copulation.

LH: I have the capacity to abuse my power over my man and others. However, I have too much respect for my husband and I have to answer to my own integrity. That is not to

Born in Two Hills, Alberta, LOUISE HALFE (Cree) was raised on Saddle Lake Indian Reserve and attended Blue Quills Residential School. Leaving residential school of her own volition at the age of sixteen, she completed her studies at St. Paul's regional high school. She is a social worker and counselor and has served as writer in residence at multiple institutions. She was Saskatchewan's Poet Laureate for 2005-2006 and she received an honorary doctoral degree from Wilfrid Laurier University in 2012. Her collections of poetry include *Bear Bones & Feathers* (Coteau Books, 1994), *Blue Marrow* (McClelland & Stewart, 1998), and *The Crooked Good* (Coteau Books, 2007).

say I have always had this awareness. In fact, I didn't much earlier in my life. I abused my sexual prowess and disrespected myself and others.

SM: Your poetry often deals with how shame and stigma can be attached to the body—in particular, the female body, but also the male body. What factors have informed the injection of shame into women's understandings of their physical selves?

LH: In Saskatoon we have a Brown Spoon Club, a bunch of Aboriginal women who get together once a month just to have fun. And it doesn't matter what kind of fun: it can be a movie; it can be a potluck; it can be a cooking spree; it can be an exchange of old jewelry. And the idea of "spoon"—which, to my understanding, runs across Canada among the tribes—we understand it as our vagina because it's shaped like a spoon. The term spoon has often been used in a derogatory way. So, I have used the word "spoon," for myself and in particular in "Valentine Dialogue," to turn it around in my public presentations, and to talk about not only the power of spoon but the community of spoon where people are nurtured from it, where we give feast to the people, they lick it, they eat it, they nurture themselves with it, and they give birth from it.

The other is that—now this is a historical understanding, and I'm not sure how accurate it is, it's just down the line from various people that I've heard it—but before European contact, there was much more sexual freedom among the various tribes. And it was the woman who determined who would stay, if they would accept their husbands. Now in Blackfoot country, they were much more aggressive about an adulterous relationship; they would cut off the nose of the woman, for example. I have no recollection of reading about that in Indian Country. And I also understand that some of my grandmothers had white lovers. A few of them kicked out their husbands for their other lovers. But they had freedom of the mouth, so to speak, which makes me uncomfortable these days, but back then it was a playful thing to have sexual innuendo, joking in talking. These days, among my contemporary peers, they use it to put down and ridicule other women or men. And so that's become a sick way of interaction, where it's a shaming of the person rather than the sharing of a joke in a healthy manner.

SM: In my reading, "Valentine Dialogue" celebrates the community created between the two female speakers, at the same time that these women acknowledge all of the forces that try to make them feel badly about their desires and their physical selves. So the poem takes the reader through the physical ramifications of venereal disease to the potentially derogatory connotations of "brown spoon" and "brown tits," as you just mentioned, through the Christian discourse of shame and contrition, to the father calling one of the women a "cheap tramp" and her mother a "slut." Yet, at the poem's end, there's still an affirmation that desire is inevitable and necessary in the lines, "And my mouth / wants / to feel dair wet lips" (ll. 26–8). How can desire be treated as healthy, as normal, when there are all these different influences seeking to make it seem bad, to make it seem dirty, to make it seem contaminated?

LH: We have to take over ownership of the projection and presentation of our sensuality. And Hollywood doesn't cut it because the observation I've made, and even of women my age, it's like, tits and ass and the belly hanging out and it doesn't matter what shape it is, you know, that Shania Twain belly. It's as if Aboriginal women are being drawn to what they perceive as acceptable and the mainstream is dictating it to them.

I've been trying to find a photographer to do the central photography of Aboriginal women, but they don't get it—nakedness is in itself beautiful. It is how it is projected that can be interpreted as cheap and sluttish. And some of our women still are into that. To me that's just prostitution of the body and the soul and the spirit. One can project their sensuality without even having to expose their flesh. I think if I had an influence, I'd ask APTN to do something that projects healthy Aboriginal sexuality between men and women… You know one of my elders said, "Why do they always show us with our asses up in the air, fucking men in the movies?" It's as if they have to show that degradation of an Aboriginal woman in a sexual act, as if they only know it doggy style. And so, we have to take ownership of that. I don't know how it's to be done; all I know is I carry myself, I hope, with dignity and a calm sensuality that I think I have. And that's all one needs to do.

SM: In Peterborough, you discussed the importance of celebrating your own daughter's coming into womanhood as a significant time in her life. The poem "First Moon" also emphasizes the need for ceremony around that development. Are there ways that awareness of the body can be nurtured in children to foster sexual well-being later in life?

LH: Yeah, well, I've done that with my daughter, in particular. I didn't do it so much with my son because I felt my husband was in charge in that. But he's a white man. So you know, white males don't know how to do it. And now I'm sorry because I should have gone ahead and done it myself. But with my daughter, I started as soon as she was old enough to understand that there's a difference between men and women. And it was a calm and simple and straightforward celebration of the first pubic hair, the first budding of her breasts, on and on until she got her menses, and then I took her home to my home community on the reserve, gathered all the Grandmothers, and we had the first ever Moon Ceremony on the rez. And we made it up because of the loss of the ceremony.

You know, she's thirty years old this month, and she's the most refined young woman I know, and that's not because she's my daughter. It's because she's quite aware of self-respect, and yet knows how to project herself in a sensuous manner. But that has to do with all the rituals that were in place in preparation for where she's at now. And we have to start them young. There can't be any bones about it, of having hang-ups about sexuality. I told my daughter, you don't need a man to give you sexual satisfaction and to feel comfortable in masturbating. I couldn't talk to my son that way because I didn't reach him when he was young. Unfortunately, men have to go out and find their own framework about sexuality.

SM: In mainstream culture, although there are images of male power around sexuality, they seem at times overreactions to anxiety. Anxiety about inadequacy. I'm wondering about the relationship of shame to the male body. In the same poem, so back to "Valentine Dialogue," there's a line about how men "Dink day can hang dair / balls all over da place" (ll. 11–12), which seems connected to ideas of male sexual privilege, but also I think could connect to men's anxieties about their own physical sexuality. And I'm wondering if shame and stigma attach to the male as well as to the female.

LH: Yeah, I suspect that they do just because, I mean, they poke fun at themselves all the time. There's a "bragatory" way of talking when they "score." And it's as if they have notches on their sleeves. And if you're a loose woman, word goes out really fast, and so, what happens with that is they'll take you, regardless of whether or not you consent because you are perceived as a loose woman among men, even if you yourself have a liberal sense of sexuality. So, I mean, how can they feel good about that?

I don't understand this idea of compartmentalization. Having studied it, when two souls come together in their physical form, there's a mutual penetration. It's hard to visualize spirit when it's been abused through sexual violation.

SM: In your poem "Nitotem," there seems to be a connection between suffering in silence at residential school and eruptions of violence back in the community. The young boy in the poem is shown bleeding from his ears after a beating from Sister Superior, unable to hear and isolated by that experience. He is further isolated by sexual abuse depicted in the haunting lines: "inside his chest the breath burst / pain, pleasure, shame. Shame" (ll. 23–4). That shame ultimately seems a catalyst to the grown boy's raping of women "on the reserve" (ll. 25). Would you comment on this relationship among silence, shame, and violence?

LH: Well, they don't know how to love after a while, or their perception of sexuality is so askew that they don't know how to go about it. A kind of sabotage takes place when they are given goodness because they feel that they're undeserving. And that happens to females too. It's so demoralizing to have been on the receiving end of the sexual abuse. I know of men who have been sexually abused by women, and it's horrific. They don't know how to love sexually with the tenderness that is required to have a fulfilling act. So I think that's when the violence is like, "I'll fix you for doing this to me, for fucking up my life." I think the same dynamics happen with women who've been sexually abused by men. Sex becomes a tool for power, which is a form of sexual violence.

I COULDN'T TALK TO MY SON THAT WAY BECAUSE I DIDN'T REACH HIM WHEN HE WAS YOUNG. UNFORTUNATELY, MEN HAVE TO GO OUT AND FIND THEIR OWN FRAMEWORK ABOUT SEXUALITY.

SM: How do you feel the residential school system has changed understandings of gender in Indigenous communities and in Cree communities specifically?

LH: They don't understand it. Priests are still living in skirts and implementing celibacy, which is abnormal. I know there are people who choose celibacy just because they are asexual, they're not interested, but very few people are. So, in my view, they haven't come to terms with it. I mean, the Pope's still preaching about procreation and putting his foot down on abortion. He doesn't understand the woman's physique or the woman's psyche in terms of these choices.

When I was pregnant with my second child—and she taught me lots and lots of lessons—we ended up losing her. My husband and I were happily married, but he was starting medical school the day we lost her. And I struggled with the idea of aborting that child, and I didn't share that with my husband. It was unspeakable, even to me. But in the end, I just decided I had to live with me and I couldn't do it and I would just accept the consequences regardless of how the birth affected me. In the end, she chose to leave us and die shortly after birth. She wasn't full term. But how can a man understand that in a church when he probably hasn't even talked to a woman about those circumstances?

SM: There are many examples of male violence in your poetry, often perpetrated by male parental figures against mothers in front of a female child. Why is it important to recognize the impact such violence has on both the mother *and* the child simultaneously?

LH: Back in my mother's era, they had no resources. They didn't have an Interval House; they weren't taught the cycle of family violence. There was a conspiracy of silence in the community. There was shame attached to it. My mother, in her late nineties, recovered from it. The bitterness simply stayed.

And in terms of the child who's witnessed that, there's post-traumatic stress. The physical violence may not have been subjected to her, but certainly the post-traumatic stress, it almost takes a lifetime to recover from. And some women never do. They go right back into a relationship that subjects them to violence because that's all they know. They don't know how to go and get that clean loving.

And in terms of the men, because of the historical impact of settlement, their livelihood is taken away. The imposition of laws makes it difficult for Aboriginal men to go hunting, especially if you don't have status. So where can they project that rage? They don't have another livelihood or proper education to support their families, which was what happened to my father. And when they were being successful farmers, Indian Affairs took away their implements because they were in competition with white farmers. Again, where do they put that rage and where do they get the money to sustain what they've been trying to do, which is provide for their families and for themselves and to pick up a different lifestyle? So the rage accumulates and the closest place that they have

> **BECAUSE OF THE HISTORICAL IMPACT OF SETTLEMENT, THEIR LIVELIHOOD IS TAKEN AWAY. THE IMPOSITION OF LAWS MAKES IT DIFFICULT FOR ABORIGINAL MEN TO GO HUNTING, ESPECIALLY IF YOU DON'T HAVE STATUS. SO WHERE CAN THEY PROJECT THAT RAGE?**

to expel that rage is within their immediate family. It becomes internalized. That family violence becomes laterally projected within the community.

SM: There's a section of *Blue Marrow* in which the speaker discusses her "Nameless *papa*": "I can not name him. / Will not name him. My poor father. / He is many fathers" (80). The poem speaks from the child's perspective to an elderly father, who has clearly been a source of great violence in the family, yet the grown child seeks to understand that father's actions, working to—in the words of the poem—"bury your fist, my father, my tongue / a willow whipping your clenched hands. I cry / for a hundred blessings to wash your grimacing face" (84). It's so much easier to have a villain figure. But in your poetry, there's such attentiveness to the complex conditions from which violence erupts. In this section from *Blue Marrow*, the speaker has compassion for the father even as that father's sense of dehumanization has informed his acts of violence toward the family.

> PART OF THE UNDOING OF THAT DAMAGE IS TO HONOUR IT AND SAY, "YES, I DID THAT AND I BEG TO BE FORGIVEN." AND SELF-FORGIVENESS HAS TO OCCUR AS WELL AS THE RECIPIENT'S FORGIVENESS.

LH: There needs to be an understanding and people need to differentiate this within themselves. They need to differentiate the person—which is the being, the human being—and the behaviour. Behaviour can be changed and the healthiness of that perception can be taken on. It can be different. And I know so. But it depends on how courageous that psyche is willing to be, to accept that they've already done damage. And part of the undoing of that damage is to honour it and say, "Yes, I did that and I beg to be forgiven." And self-forgiveness has to occur as well as the recipient's forgiveness. They might not get that, but self-forgiveness is ultimately a big thing, and that can only work if they don't repeat that pattern. Hence self-respect is gained.

SM: In the words of acknowledgement and gratitude at the end of *The Crooked Good*, you write that you "offer this story as a way to go inward, so that one may go forward perhaps a little more intact. That is all" (135). How can poetry specifically and art more generally help an audience take an introspective look and thereby become more whole, more balanced, more well?

LH: Well, you study it. You're astute. And this is what I expect good art and good writing to do for me. When I can see myself in a written work, then I say, "Aha, somebody's able to articulate what I've been feeling and what I've been doing. Now that I can see it in print"—whether it's in a photograph or a painting or a song—I say to myself, "Now I recognize the dynamic, what can I do about it?" So the research begins for me, whether it's in book form, whether I'm talking to others, like it's, "How did you do that? I recognize this, how did I do…?" And it's very painful. And really good art is like a portal, where it's an opening for you for recognition in order to take some self-responsibility and go, "Okay, I recognize this and I'm not alone and I know it's happening to others. Now the question is how do I get to refining my own psyche to health?"

SM: Young Indigenous men, at this moment, tend to be a hard audience to reach with poetry. How can the principles of poetic introspection find that particular audience, an audience that is unlikely to gravitate toward a book of written poetry?

LH: One movie that really fine-tuned it for me and really showed how horrific it is and how we could reach people was *Once Were Warriors*. It demonstrated to me the community of violence, what it did to the people. And film can probably do it better than poetry.

Poetry only reaches those who are literate. I go in the community, so I'm able to talk to my poetry and, because of my background in social work and addictions and my own personal work, I can personalize it, and I can teach them how to read it and I can show them the way. But whether or not they choose the way is a different thing. And I just find they're really a tough bunch, in particular on the reserves that I've been to, and it's different from one reserve to another. I may have a respectful adolescent audience on one reserve and a downright degrading one on another. And it's a good thing that I don't internalize it and can give it back to them and show it to them because I know how to do that. I'm a bit of a coyote. But a person who's not prepared for that… I mean, I know a lot of unhealthy poets and a lot of unhealthy artists—it would destroy them because art doesn't heal you. It's your own action and process and insight and willingness that heals you. I mean, there's great artists all over the world and ancient artists that have died of alcoholism or self-inflicted wounds or some sort of suicide. Their art never healed them. It was their process. Like Patrick Lane in his last book, *There is a Season*, it was in the garden, the retrospection, the willingness to face his demons that showed him the recovery back to art. It wasn't art itself that healed him.

SM: That's powerful. And it's almost stopping me in my tracks because that's a central issue that I'm trying to consider in this whole project: what is the connection among the artistic process, the art object, the audience, and ultimately, I guess, healthier ways of being. And what occurs *after* engagement with the art object seems to be key.

LH: I had an excellent psychiatrist and I had an excellent psychologist and I was privileged to work with fine elders. They worked me really hard, and so I expect that of others. Like, don't give me that "I'm healed" bullshit. You know, I hear a lot of that and I'm going, "Oh yeah, yeah." I can say that I am relatively healed, but, boy, I can get suckered too. And so I know that I still have issues, and thank God I do otherwise I'd quit growing.

ART DOESN'T HEAL YOU. IT'S YOUR OWN ACTION AND PROCESS AND INSIGHT AND WILLINGNESS THAT HEALS YOU.

CARRYING THE BURDEN OF PEACE

A CONVERSATION WITH DANIEL DAVID MOSES

*3 NOVEMBER 2010
Conversation between
Daniel David Moses
and Sam McKegney
in Sam's car on
Highway 401 en route
to the "Sounding
Out: Indigenous
Poetics" Symposium
at Trent University
in Peterborough,
Ontario.*

HOW CAN YOU FORGET EVERYTHING AND BE A MAN?
—DANIEL DAVID MOSES, ALMIGHTY VOICE AND HIS WIFE

SAM MCKEGNEY: What was it like growing up on the family farm at Six Nations? What kinds of responsibilities were involved in that type of youth?

DANIEL DAVID MOSES: Well, as soon as I was capable, I helped with the chores. I got up early for years for the morning milking, always aware that my father was up even earlier to get the cows from the field—he was working way harder than I was. It never occurred to me to complain. My perception now is that I contributed to the household as much as I could. And it taught me responsibility.

In contrast I remember being at a friend's house for a meeting. He had kids who were just becoming teenagers, and when they came home for lunch, we had to stop so he could make them sandwiches. I was flabbergasted, thinking (but saying nothing), "These kids are old enough to be doing it themselves. Why are we breaking up our meeting?" I was surprised by how childish they were. I always wanted to grow up as soon as possible.

SM: With the family farm, I'm—what would I be? Three generations removed from the family farm… And it exists for me as almost a mythological space, right? And there seems to come with that image in my head a certain ruggedness that might fall into a category of masculinity. Was there ever a sense for you of the work involved in the farm being decidedly masculine labour?

DDM: I'm not aware of it in that way. It was hard work. We all did the hard work that we were capable of, so there were only a few women who would actually climb onto the backs of the wagons to help with the shovelling. Mostly the men did the stuff requiring physical strength. But the women would be driving the tractors or the trucks or supplying the food. Largely the gender roles were established as you might expect, but it was really just the practicality. The men who had done this work before were stronger and more skilled in doing it. But some of my aunts, when I was younger, before I myself was old enough, they would be up there throwing hay bales onto elevators and shovelling grain. Just caring for livestock, though, anyone can do that. That's how I started out.

The word "matrilineal" still makes sense to me. That's how the family was centred, traditionally, through the women's line. It seems to me that idea is still a functioning thing socially if not legally. My grandfathers passed away and the extended family still gathered for family occasions. It wasn't until the grandmothers went that that family focus disappeared and dispersed, moved to the next generation.

What I was concerned with, in the sense of the word "matriarchal," was that it seemed imprecise as a word to describe that traditional culture. It seemed an effort to contrast the Iroquois with settler assumptions—patriarchy evokes an image of vertical hierarchy—rather than seeing that culture as something more horizontal and balanced between both sexes.

SM: I noticed in one of your author profiles that you mention your distrust of the illusions of prose. Do you still feel that prose obscures by presenting a façade of coherence?

DDM: "A façade of coherence"! I like that phrase. I do think that that's a continuing dilemma, trying to make everything fit into a certain cultural or class set of assumptions about what makes for beauty or clarity or truth. The reality of chaos theory was also supposed to make for a broader understanding of other cultural realities, in my humble opinion. I'm still trying to construct façades of incoherence.

My experience: Simon Ortiz was putting together an anthology[1] and I was contributing an essay about my process. He had some other editor at the press itself doing the final editing of the text, so I sent my piece to this person, this piece I'd written with

DANIEL DAVID MOSES (Delaware) grew up on a farm on Six Nations land along the Grand River near Brantford, Ontario. He created "The Committee to Re-Establish the Trickster" with Tomson Highway and Lenore Keeshig-Tobias, he has served on the boards of the Association for Native Development in the Performing and Visual Arts and the Playwrights Guild of Canada, and he has been involved with Native Earth Performing Arts since the 1980s. He currently teaches in the Department of Drama at Queen's University in Kingston, Ontario. His plays include *Kyotopolis: A Play in Two Acts* (Exile Editions, 2008), *The Indian Medicine Shows: Two One-Act Plays* (Exile Editions, 1995), and *Almighty Voice and His Wife* (Williams-Wallace Publishing, 1992). His books of poetry include *Delicate Bodies* (Nightwood Editions, 1992) and *A Small Essay on the Largeness of Light and Other Poems* (Exile Editions, 2012). He is co-editor with Terry Goldie of *An Anthology of Canadian Native Literature in English* (Oxford University Press, 1992).

1. Daniel David Moses, "How My Ghosts Got Pale Faces," in *Speaking for the Generations: Native Writers on Writing*, ed. Simon Ortiz (Tucson: University of Arizona Press, 1998).

MY RELATIONSHIP TO THE LANGUAGE, BECAUSE I CAME TO CANADA FROM SIX NATIONS, MIGHT BE IN PART LIKE THAT OF AN IMMIGRANT, IF YOU CAN IMMIGRATE OUT TO A COUNTRY THAT'S COME UP AROUND YOU.

my habitual, consciously oral sensibility—lots of air around the words—and suddenly this guy was wanting to collapse all of my small breathy paragraphs into larger block paragraphs. And to top it off, I was writing about my play, *Almighty Voice and His Wife*, and I had used the phrase "bluff of poplars" which is the actual language from that story, that place, that history—I'd done my research. And this editor wanted to change it to "the grove of poplars." So that just broke it for me—Saskatchewan doesn't have "groves"—and I immediately contacted Simon and said something along the lines of, "If these are the sorts of changes you need to make to my piece, I'm going to have to withdraw it because it's preposterous. It's changing what I perceive as the truth I'm telling into clearly something else entirely. I mean, it may be within the conventions of that particular university press, but it's not right as far as I'm concerned and I won't have my name attached to it."

SM: And were you always drawn to poetry? Was that a natural progression for you?

DDM: I only started to be interested in the middle of high school. The paper I've written for the symposium is mostly a memoir—although, I won't be presenting this part of the story of how I came to poetry, because we don't have time. The little moment I'm remembering has me in grade eleven, studying some highly structured poem and my best friend at the time being impressed by it. Whether I was being perverse or actually felt that way, I just said, "That's not amazing, it's just a trick, anybody can do that with a little effort." And he challenged me to do it and put some money on it. So I went home and over the weekend wrote a little poem that was highly structured the way that we'd agreed—and I won the bet. I'm imagining five dollars. It proved my point that that sort of surface characteristic that we're taught to look for as a measure for poetry really could be just a trick, but in the process I had begun to feel there was something else that was going on in poetry that was intriguing to me and I did start paying more attention to it.

SM: So from your very first poem, you were a paid poet.

DDM: I guess so. [*Laughter*]

SM: There's always a collaborative element to writing, in terms of the editing process, as you suggested with Simon's collection, but it's so much more pronounced in theatre. Is there vulnerability in having your work interpreted by actors and directors and set designers and others? Is that always exciting for you or do you have trepidation about it?

DDM: No, it's never been a problem for me. I've always been aware of language as this negotiation. Even though I speak and write in English, I've realized lately that perhaps my relationship to the language, because I came to Canada from Six Nations, might be in part like that of an immigrant, if you can immigrate out to a country that's come up around you. I have warned friends who are basically poets or basically fiction writers that you can't be precious about stuff if you work in the theatre. You're writing for the actors. The actors need something they can work with. You can't leave them dangling too long in the air. They can take a moment or two where you want to use your latest poetic bit, or your nice prose description, but that doesn't work too long on the contemporary stage, so you've always got to come back to your characters, to the actors. It's the reason behind those theatre jokes ("But what's my motivation?"). The actors need their motivation, and they need to be in their emotion, to make the play work. That part of it is a convention and it's a very conservative part of theatre, but that's why people will sit down with it for a couple hours. You need to feel.

Back at the beginning I had rehearsals where actors having difficulties would ask for line changes and revisions. In first productions, I still will listen, and if what they're saying seems reasonable, I'll do it. But by the time I get a play to rehearsal, I'm usually so confident in the piece that, nine times out of ten, I won't change a thing. But what I will do, I've learned from one of my directors, is say, "I'll think about it, let me come back to you." Most of the actors forget about it, they find the sense of the line. Revision isn't necessarily necessary.

SM: And it's acknowledging their desire or their investment in the character... The collaborative element of producing, how does that filter through to the audience? I mean, in theatre you have different audiences every night. It's a totally different dynamic than a movie theatre, or something like that, when you go to a play. Do you think about audience as you're writing or does that come after?

DDM: That comes after, for me. I assume that if I find this interesting and can write about it in a way that is clear and has some beauty, that should be enough to bring the audience along. I think that is the difference, wanting to create art as an expression of an individual's point of view in a particular culture. I find the questions about writing for an audience seem to be based in the capitalist concern for selling a commodity. I'm always trying to *not* be prepackaged. So I'll never write for Disney.

SM: What year would the idea for the Oxford anthology have been originally floated, approximately, and what was the context for that project?

DDM: I guess, almost twenty years ago, now. Early nineties. Oka had happened; Tomson [Highway] had happened, an event. I'm not sure whether *North of 60* had started on television at that point. But I remember, there was a point where it felt like suddenly we Indians were part of what had to be talked about. You could count on one article about Native people being on *Morningside* every week. That lasted for about three or four years, until we fell below the radar again. I mean, The Gap even had one winter where they used Native actors in subway ads. I can remember thinking it was so neat, there was Tantoo [Cardinal]'s picture, there was Tom Jackson and Graham Greene. But it didn't last and you can't go forcing the government to call out the army every five years to keep people's attention.

SM: I've been thinking a lot about *The Indian Medicine Shows* and Jonathan Jones as this hypermasculine violent response to anxiety around effeminacy. I'm interested in your perceptions of that character and what issues you sought to bring forth in his portrayal.

DDM: The play just happened. I had back in my university days written a clown play about Billy the Kid. An interesting experiment, I guess. I put it into a contest, got an honourable mention out of it, but mostly, I wasn't impressed by it, except for one scene, the scene where Billy passes a moment of the day after he's committed his first murder with Jon and his crazy mother. I just thought there was something intriguing about that trio and I would keep that scene in mind. I wanted to explore it at some point. Years later, I was doing a writer-in-residence gig as a poet for the Nakai Theatre in Whitehorse. I was up there for a week—it was winter—just doing a lot of one-on-ones with local writers. But part of the deal was that all the guest writers were supposed to take part in the twenty-four-hour playwriting contest being held at the end of the week.

SM: So you were actually up there mentoring *and* trying to draft a play?

DDM: We were all much younger then. I'd gone up there intending to work on another idea but that morning, when they came to pick me up and drive me over to the college where the contest was taking place, I saw the moon setting over the snowy mountain-scape there and I suddenly remembered this scene. I'll work on that, I thought. And it was ready to happen and it really did come out and appear in maybe twelve hours—*The Moon and Dead Indians*. Everything that's in the play now was there. A bit underwritten but a good draft. But it was also scary to me, so I was thinking of it as a skeleton of a play, as if there was something spooky, uncanny about it, even though it was, I know now, that hypermasculine violence you mentioned that was scaring me. "Where the hell is this coming from?" So I put it away in a drawer for a couple of years because I didn't know what to think of it. I didn't know how to take responsibility for it.

I was still connected with Cahoots Theatre Projects at the time (they'd produced my play *Big Buck City*) and they were doing a development program they wanted me to take part in because I had a bit of a name by then and my participation would ensure them a bit of an audience. And the only thing that I felt I had that might be ready to work on at that moment was that skeleton of a play, so I showed it to Colin [Taylor] and he said, "We have to do this." With his focus I was able to face the material. I found myself reading a psychology book to get the definition of psychopath so I could figure out who the Billy character was. Once I was able to do more historical research—there had been a new book about Billy the Kid—I was able to get more detail into the play and it felt better that way. And then, Lenore [Keeshig-Tobias] around this time also put

AS IF THERE WAS SOMETHING SPOOKY, UNCANNY ABOUT IT, EVEN THOUGH IT WAS, I KNOW NOW, THAT HYPERMASCULINE VIOLENCE YOU MENTIONED THAT WAS SCARING ME. "WHERE THE HELL IS THIS COMING FROM?"

me onto Paula Gunn Allen's *The Sacred Hoop*, which seemed to me to talk about part of the process of the colonization of Native America being the destruction of female spiritual power. I knew I had to answer the question the skeleton play asked and that's where *Angel of the Medicine Show* came from. The two plays gelled and came together into *The Indian Medicine Shows* in a way that I'm really proud of. It's just a really neat piece of theatre.

SM: It seems like in my reading of that play—and other elements of your work—there's sort of a cliff where one drops off into violent response and the person is often pushed that way through fear or anxiety about personal inadequacy or ideas about appropriate behaviour. How do you think that fear is engendered or promoted in contemporary society? The fear that young men can be subject to, which leads them to respond in violent ways. That's just my reading. Where does that fear come from, that anxiety?

DDM: I suspect it's there in the conservative mindset. I'm imagining all these Tea Party people are very sure about just what makes proper behaviour. I could understand, then, that it's kind of scary to see that society has actually been finding ways of commodifying behaviours that they found outrageous and unmentionable, even only ten, twenty years ago. I think things are becoming mainstreamed that were formerly very scary and those Tea Partiers are desperate to go back to this idea they have of what is real, Real Women, et al. But is it really real? Isn't it an image created after the Second World War to get the women to go home and keep house so the men could have the work outside the home? Meanwhile, from what I understand, World War II had already been breaking down gender roles.

SM: Yeah, there's a way in which the nuclear family has been so naturalized through repeated viewings in film and television as the normative social unit that it becomes somewhat unquestioned or something.

DDM: Yeah, people are blind to their own families in front of them and don't realize that so-and-so never had kids and so-and-so are divorced. They see the persistent mirage of the nuclear family. I mean, aren't the recent statistics that the single-parent household is the norm now?

SM: Yeah, exactly. And of course there are other models of social formation and different ways of understanding what kinship means.

DDM: I got mine from my lucky childhood. I lived with my parents and my sister on the farm, but we could, on the way to school—we walked or rode our bikes on the dirt road—we would pass both sets of grandparents' houses and there were also aunts and uncles very close by. My grandmother used to tease me, "You know, you used to run away?" But it was like nobody was worried because I was just running away to Aunt Leona's house.

SM: That's so different, actually, that story, from what we're talking about in terms of fear. Like, there's such anxiety around so many things in contemporary urban society that we don't even allow children to run off and play. To be able to do so in a way that isn't overseen but is connected to the broader idea of the family, it seems so healthy.

DDM: I found it so strange over the last decade how so much of television is about criminal masterminds. I mean most criminals are losers, and on television we turn them into these really scary monsters. I mean, even the reporting of Colonel Williams.[2] He did kill, but it's like all the other details about him are grotesque and pathetic and laughable. I find it strange how people keep talking about him as this incomprehensible monster because I don't think he deserves that amount of respect. There's something very sad about this upstanding life that has fallen into this sad, weird loop in his head.

SM: But then there's also the creation of that figure in the media as something larger-than-life, grandiose almost. By turning it into the monster, it becomes somehow other than us.

DDM: I glanced at a column some woman had written about feeling like the media was using him to put her in her place, to remind her that she was a woman and she was vulnerable. This is one man among millions of people and the actual number of these individuals is so minor. This is such a big complex society and we're actually using these few glitches to define it. The exception makes the rule? How many crime shows are there on in just one evening? How bored are we by our comfort that we need such fantasy? It's one thing for teenagers testing themselves as they grow into adults to feel the need to face horror, but for the society at large? Something's going on...

SM: There's one quotation from *Almighty Voice* that could very well be the title of the project I'm working on right now, and that's "How can you forget everything and be a man?" (*Almighty Voice* 21). I interpret that line as speaking to the difficulty of imagining endorsable Indigenous male identities after hundreds of years of colonization. And not only the ways in which traditional gender roles have been obscured through the violence of dispossession and the Indian Act, but also how simulations of what constitutes Indigenous masculinity emerging in popular culture and the media have muddied the waters. What does that line mean to you, and why is it important for Almighty Voice to articulate that concern in the play?

DDM: I guess the image is in the title of your larger project [*Carrying the Burden of Peace: Imagining Indigenous Masculinities through Story*]. I have that idea in my head that the word from an Iroquois language—which Iroquois language, I'm not sure—that is commonly translated as "warrior" actually evokes the image of someone "carrying the burden of peace," so it has a different emphasis, a different set of values behind it. It's really about someone who is maintaining the good rather than participating in war,

2. Colonel Russell Williams, commander of the Canadian Forces Base Trenton, was convicted of two counts of first-degree murder, sexual assault, breaking and entering, and forcible confinement in October 2010.

HOW BORED ARE WE BY OUR COMFORT THAT WE NEED SUCH FANTASY? IT'S ONE THING FOR TEENAGERS TESTING THEMSELVES AS THEY GROW INTO ADULTS TO FEEL THE NEED TO FACE HORROR, BUT FOR THE SOCIETY AT LARGE? SOMETHING'S GOING ON...

something that by its nature is problematic. It seems to me I was reading somewhere, I guess maybe it was some Cree word that is commonly translated as "warrior" and it also had other implications in the Cree culture that just are lost in the translation to "warrior."[3] So, I guess I'm wondering if that is a way of looking at the traditional languages and seeing what values or wisdoms lurk behind the different translations of them that have more implications for the maintenance of a social fabric.

Just in that moment in the play, the character is questioning his usefulness. He has an image of himself as someone who should be able to take care of his wife, and what is he doing? He's hiding. His mother and his wife are helping him hide. Meanwhile, his father's in prison. He feels he's not doing his job.

SM: To me as reader and audience member, the play juxtaposes in a powerful way those questions from the first act—which point toward somewhat of a tragic trajectory—with the surrealistic second act, which forces the audience to consider the role of representation and semiotics in forcing Indigenous peoples to "forget" what it means and has meant to be a man. How much of writing that play for you was speaking to 1890 and how much was speaking to 1990, you know, in the sense that you were dealing with an historical incident [the pursuit of Almighty Voice—*Kisse-Manitou-Wayou*—by the Northwest Mounted Police in 1895] but also reflecting on how memory and performance and representation affect our ability to understand that history?

DDM: I think I'm always writing from now, from where I am, trying to understand the dilemmas of this life. If investigating how something in the past might have made the present seems useful, I do it. I fell in love with that image of time as a circle or spiral rather than an arrow. It seemed true to my experience. The past can be just off to the side, peripheral instead of far behind. It's easier then to keep its lessons in mind. A student suggested to me, about *Brébeuf's Ghost*, that he thought the play was "Just like Swords and Sorcery, but with Indians!" and I realized that on a certain level, what I've been doing so far is a kind of science fiction imagining, even if it is about the past.

SM: There's a section in *Pursued by a Bear* where you talk about your initial anxiety about the otherworldy or the ghostly or the spiritual—about not truly trusting what you can't feel in your own hands. And I was thinking about that in relation to Craig Womack's recent argument in *Reasoning Together* that "the inability to deal with spiritual reality" limits critical work on Indigenous literatures (364), which implies that attentiveness to the spiritual is a crucial part of ethical Indigenous criticism. And I guess I'm wondering is there a place for secular Indigenous literature? Does it cease to fit that category of literary expression if there's not a spiritual component somewhere embedded within? Does that question even make sense?

DDM: I'm thinking that there isn't such a thing as a secular literature, period. I mean, any literature worth reading has some spirituality, whether it's some conventional idea

3. In the introduction to *Gabriel's Beach*, Cree poet Neal McLeod refers to the *okihcitâwak* or "worthy men" as "hunters, providers, and soldiers" (11).

THE PAST CAN BE JUST OFF TO THE SIDE, PERIPHERAL INSTEAD OF FAR BEHIND. IT'S EASIER THEN TO KEEP ITS LESSONS IN MIND.

of God or some idea of spirits or just the metaphors. You need these metaphors to embody, in an active way, moral values. I just finally read *Crime and Punishment* and I thought it was so neat how it ends up in this spiritual place after dragging us back and forth through the streets of really ugly-looking, very material St. Petersburg.

I feel like it's a responsibility to activate ideals even if you don't have a spiritual experience. I live very much a secular life, I live in the scientifically measurable world. But that scientifically measurable world, while a lot of it can be experienced, a lot of it might as well be magic or spirits. I mean I used the word "X-ray" in a poem, and I worried, would it work, that seems so contemporary. So I looked it up and it's over a hundred years old. We really should be realizing a lot of this knowledge is a mysterious thing. We can't see or feel or smell X-rays. We have to take them for granted. So I think the definition of spiritual needs an adjustment. Certainly, I can see putting the emphasis on Native spirituality just to help maintain a sense of what the cultures and their values are, because we're protecting something, those values that gave them social coherence. In the final analysis, the spiritual is just part of the culture, part of the texture of lived experience.

A MAN BESIDE MY FATHER

A CONVERSATION WITH THOMAS KIMEKSUN THRASHER

PEOPLE LIKE TO COME AROUND AND BELIEVE THEY'RE TOUGH, THAT THEY CAN TAKE ANYTHING THAT CAN HAPPEN ON EARTH. THE DAY THEY LOSE SOMEONE THEY LOVE, THEY'LL FIND OUT HOW HARD IT IS. WE ARE SOFT, YOU KNOW. WE'RE TENDER. IT DON'T TAKE MUCH TO BREAK US. —THOMAS THRASHER

9 JUNE 2011
Conversation among Thomas Thrasher, Keavy Martin, and Sam McKegney in Thrasher's toolshed between the Elder's Residence and the Arctic Ocean, Tuktoyaktuk, Northwest Territories.

THOMAS THRASHER: I became a man very fast. I had to. I'm something like my grandfather. He makes sure he has everything for his family. Everything. When my stepmother began treating my wife meanly—like she tried to treat her like she treated us—but no way she's gonna do that to my wife and my son, eh? So I built a little fourteen-foot by fourteen-foot house by myself. And my dad watched me. You know, he never said nothing—"What is it?" "What is he doing?" He was proud of his son, eh?

SAM MCKEGNEY: And that was when you were just a young man?

THOMAS KIMEKSUN THRASHER is an Inuvialuk hunter, fisherman, trapper, storyteller, and square-dance caller from Tuktoyaktuk in the Northwest Territories. He self-published a memoir entitled *Footprints to the Stars*. At the time of his death in 2011, he was in the midst of co-editing with Sam McKegney and Keavy Martin his brother Anthony Apakark Thrasher's collected prison writings. Some of Anthony Thrasher's writings had been published previously under the title *Thrasher... Skid Row Eskimo* (Griffin House, 1976).

TT: I was seventeen when I got married. I became a man when I was fourteen. When I left the residential school, I became a man beside my dad. I had to become a man. But in a good way, and with him I could do anything. You know, he was my inspiration. And my grandfather. Always helping people. Always. No matter what.

We were like that. We are survivors, eh? Through residential school, I had $19,000 for the years and abuse I went through there. That money didn't mean nothing to me. They think paying us is going to heal us. No. You can't buy pain. You don't give money to pay pain. My brother Tony would be the same, only he tried to get to that place, "I have to go forward." His vision was forward, the future. *I* have to go forward. *I* have to keep going. I'm not going to look back and let that bother me. I'm a man.

When I became free from residential school, I was me. And I have to make my living, no matter what. I've been in jail too before. Just about followed Tony's footsteps, until I met my wife. So I was gifted to have that with my first wife, you know. That's the way we got married years ago. If someone knows you're a good man, you're a good worker, and knows she's a good girl, the two parents agree together: "I give you my girl." "I give you my son. He's a good worker." And her dad says, "She's a good worker. And they'll be a good couple." We became a good couple.

You know, with assimilation... all we hear: "You're gonna go to hell. If you do something wrong, you can't go to heaven." And I was sitting around this morning, and I said, "The beautiful stars up there, that's where my ancestors are." So many of them you can't see them, eh? But they're there somewhere. And we'll all go up there. My brother is up there. My *daduk* is up there. My wife is up there. I know damn sure they're not in heaven. That's where we were assimilated from. And hell, I'll never go there. We were in hell through that, now I'm out of it. I'm free. I'm a star. I'll be up there. I'm not scared to die. I'm going to go where my ancestors are. That's where my footprints will end, with my book. Follow that and you'll be beside me up there too, eh?

A lot of us elders—my parents, my grandparents—they travel by the stars. They're the guidance. They take you where you want to be. And I'm dropped in the middle of Africa or Russia or Edmonton or fifty miles out of here, the stars will show me where I am and where I'm supposed to go. Follow them directions, man. And when the dipper points a certain way, I'm not far from home now. You know, it shows you where you are and where you should be.

My second wife, Linda, she understands very fast my way of thinking. We used to go to church "because," just "because." Where does that go? Nowhere. We quit going to church, because for me going to places like that, I'm a hypocrite. I don't believe in it. I'm not going to believe it. I'm hurting myself if I go there. Only bad memories.

I was an altar boy for fourteen years, man. And every one was... I could make over a million dollars, if I told them what happened to me. But, like I said before, it's behind me. I don't want to get hurt anymore. By doing this over again, I'm going to get hurt again. So I just left it. And the ones who did things to me are never going to be respected as long as they live. No one will love them. No one can say they're good people. And I am a good man. I'm going to carry on through 'cause I have to be. What else could I do? [*Laughter*] What else can we do?

Many times I coulda punched out people. But it's not worth it. You know? I'm only going to hurt his family if I do it. Then they're going to be against me. I don't want anybody against me. It's the best thing to walk away. I won't waste my time. Then they are the ones who get hurt that try to hurt me. Because I walked away. I'm the man that walks away.

Years ago, my grandparents they were home free, so free! When they had leaders like Old Apakark, like your medicine people, through their powers they'd find meat. Through their powers they'd find seals. There was another *anapkuk* in Tuk here, I know him well. It was not long after the missions came. Already there was residential schools along the coast, eh? But this man was still using his power, medicine power, helping people, healing people. A well-respected man. This man's wife is still alive here yet. And this medicine man, he liked this young man because he's a hard-working man and a good hunter. And he wanted to make him an *anapkuk*, pass his—he's getting old now, eh? So he's gonna pass his power to this man to lead his people. The *anapkuk* wanted him to become a leader of his men. So he gave him a chance. He took him, many times, he took him on his shoulder at night flying. He flew with him. Said, "Look what you could do. See, that's where the whales are. That's where the caribou are." He showed him where the good things are to feed and to hunt and look after his people.

"I know you're going to get married soon," he said. "So before I go I want to give you my power," he told him. The young man agreed to take his place, and the *anapkuk* said, "Okay, well, I'll take you around one more time and then, if you accept that you want my name, I'll give it to you." So he took him all over on his back flying around with him, and showed him everything. And his power just about went into the man right then, eh?

So they came home and he told his wife-to-be, "This man wants to give me his power to be like him. A great *anapkuk*." Everybody knew the *anapkuk* in them days. Even other communities, they know who this man is. His woman said, "We're gonna get married in an Anglican Church." And by that time the Anglican Church condemned shamanism because they *were* the religion, you know? And this lady believed so much in that religion but she still loved that guy, eh? And he was in love with her. So he told her, "I'm going to get the power from the *anapkuk* myself and work for our people." "But you cannot marry me," she told him. "You can't. You have to go to church with me. You have to be Anglican like me." He loved her so much, he turned the shamanism down. And after that the *anapkuk* told my uncle that "I tried to change him, but he listened to somebody."

You know, I always wondered, how come there's no more chiefs in Tuk? Modernism took that all away from us. We don't know who's our chief, you know. We've got nothing when we don't got a chief at all in Tuk. I tried to bring it back. I want to bring it back.

But the people that are the leaders now, they never were brought up that way. They were brought up the modern way, eh? They won't accept the fact that an Inuk like me could be their leader because I don't have the education. But look at where the education is. Beyond them. Your degree is who you are: unlimited. Your knowledge is who you are. Your knowledge is: people follow you because you taught them right.

Leadership starts at home, you know. A lot of the things I've learned since I was a little man was by my grandparents, by my uncles, you know, my aunties. Always be kind. Always share what little you have. My dad told me, he said, "When you go to somebody, if he needs a shirt, give him yours." Well, he got that from his grandfather. If someone you see needs a shirt, take yours off and give it to him. And if you have plenty of soup and he has nothing, give it to him. You can get yours later because you're healthy. Never let someone wish for anything. But don't spoil them. Just give them enough. Don't spoil. They'll come too many times! [Laughter]

SM: Did your father used to talk often about his experiences as captain of the ship, *Our Lady of Lourdes*?

TT: Oh yeah. Not too many times he had to struggle, eh? He knew the land so good. Only time that he had some… they travel in ice leads, eh? And then one place there was big ice in between where they were travelling, so they stopped there and tried to figure out how they could get on the other side. They were in about a mile in the ice lead, so they waited and it wouldn't come apart. Instead it was coming in. So what he did, he reversed all the way out of that crack—the ice lead, eh?—and by that time another ice drift is coming. They are surrounded with ice, and the ship was loaded with freight for all the communities along the coast like Holman Island, Paulatuk, and Coppermine, loaded with supplies for all those communities. And they were loaded right down. Even their exhaust was under water.

My dad, he was out of the lead anyway, and there was enough water to travel but he couldn't get out of the ice and he needed to save the ship. And everybody's getting scared. He had to do something, eh? He followed along the edge of the ice and he watched for a place, maybe there might be a place where he could climb up. A smooth place to ramp the ship. And he found one. So what they did, they threw out all the forty-five-gallon drums that are on the ship, on the edge of the ship, threw them out to make the boat lighter. But all the freight, still the food and stuff, was all inside.

So he told them, because he's the boss of the ship, he says, "I'm gonna ram the boat on the ice." They thought he was crazy but they couldn't tell him nothing because he's the captain. They put most of the heavy stuff near the back and the front was high, like this, just enough. He put the engine full blast, and the men was standing right behind by the pilothouse so that the front was up, eh? They came out of the water, right out of the water.

IF SOMEONE YOU SEE NEEDS A SHIRT, TAKE YOURS OFF AND GIVE IT TO HIM. AND IF YOU HAVE PLENTY OF SOUP AND HE HAS NOTHING, GIVE IT TO HIM. YOU CAN GET YOURS LATER BECAUSE YOU'RE HEALTHY.

By the time the ice came in, and after it took off again, they were high and dry. Just about from here to the building—the ship was that far from open water now [*approximately twenty metres*]. So they all got picks and axes, trying to cut it loose. They made a channel into the open water, and they had to get the propeller into the water. Them days people used to load their own shotgun shells. You know you fill your own shotgun with gunpowder? You get gunpowder in kegs them days. And in the freight of the boat was a lot of cases of pickles. Pickle jars, eh? Gallon jars. They had a German engineer there. Good brains. Very good engineer. Professional. He's gonna make bombs. So they cut holes around the side of the ship to put those bombs he made, the gunpowder. He wired it to an engine battery, both sides. [*explosion noise*] Ice blew up, they shoved it out.

Fourteen days they were on that ice floe. Fourteen days. They had a new Hudson's Bay manager from Coppermine. He was an Irishman, eh? He thought he'd never see the world again. He even attempted suicide. My dad took that gun away from him. "You shoot me before you shoot yourself," he told him. So he got scared; he gave that gun to my dad. A few years later he thanked him. That was one of those hardships on that ship.

And, like my dad, you know a ship lasts as long as its captain. He was on that ship for twenty-one years as the pilot captain. On the twenty-first year he was on there he got a heart stroke, eh, a stroke. He was paralyzed one side. And he said, "Sorry. I can't run the ship no more." Because of his health, eh? So there was a priest here who figured he could, well, he travelled many miles with my dad, eh? He figured he's gonna do it. That summer, when he's about two hundred miles from here he ran aground. They had to drag it back. And since that time it's been on land.

I always believe that when a captain dies a ship dies too. That's what happened.

SM: It's a beautiful boat too, eh?

TT: Honestly, it was like a… a cork in the ocean. It wouldn't sink, you know. No matter how much you loaded it. I used to sit up there with my dad, up in the crow's nest. In the pilothouse up on the roof there. Between his legs holding the wheel, eh? Big, big wheel and I was just little.

SM: I loved that story you told us about heading up the river and seeing the trees on the shore when you were little.

TT: That was in 1938. That's when I was sent to school. The year my mom died, eh? I thought it was people, I really thought it was people. "Dad, look at all the people!"

Just before we came that year the bishop bought a plane, one of the first planes in the north in them days, eh? Of course, I was with my dad, everybody's excited—"the bishop's plane is coming!" And we're watching, everybody's watching. They knew which side it was coming. Next thing you know you could hear it, eh? Ooooh, it's coming down. "It's gonna drop!" I was screaming—I ran away. I was scared. I'd never seen nothing like that, eh? Behind this mud house, I was hiding.

I knew a little bit of English by that time because my sisters were already in residential school. My dad was fluent in English, eh? And the bishop was there, and you know they got that long black cassock on with the cross on it, and a big black beard, eh? I was standing beside my dad; he's smoking his pipe, eh, this guy. I told my dad, "Holy, that woman's smoking pipe!" I thought he's a woman, he's got a dress on! And he's got whiskers too. [*Laughter*] He said, "ssshhhh, he'll hear you." Every time we see that bishop after that, my dad push me and give me a look, like "you remember?" That was the time, after that, that I saw all these people here on the banks.

A year later my brother Tony came to school. You know that night when we landed in Aklavik in front of the mission, holy, lots of people on the shore. Lots of kids, school kids. I was scared—so many people, I was frightened. And my dad was walking me up the gangplank. I jumped down and I ran away. I was scared, eh? So they had to look for me. They found me hiding. Brought me back. So my dad just dropped me there and told me he's gotta go and "I'll see you again." That's all he said.

Like, you know, we're family, eh? And when we're at home we all sleep in a little bed, all ten of us kids. And I'm used to that. I grew up like that, eh, keep each other warm. So upstairs in the dorm there it was like these bed rows, beds all over the place. Me, I'm used to having my brothers and sisters sleep with me. And my big brother Peter was there. "We're gonna put you to bed now," he says. "This is your bed now." So I fixed my pillow and I moved way over. I wanted him to sleep with me. He said, "No, we can't." He had to walk away. And I cried myself to sleep.

That's the way we had to... we had no parents left. Lot of time, when I'm writing my book I break down. Like, nobody knows. Don't have to know—I'm a man. [*Laughter*] Lot of times those people like my *anapkuk* say when they failed to raise that person that they tried to save, eh, they cry too. They feel it. But you know, I've got things to do afterward. So it's done. I got other things to do now. It's okay. I won't suffer no more. Like when we lose our child, we cry. We can't keep them forever. But when they go, we have other things to do. We have to look after the others. We cry for a while. We all cry for a while. It doesn't mean we are weak.

You know, come to think of it, I seen my dad cry. It's not hard for me to cry. I guess I was sleeping with my brothers and sisters when my mother passed away. And I was the only one he could confide in. I was the only one with him with the children. So I sat with him at the table. He said, "Tommy, try and wake Mommy up." So I went over. "Mom, get up. Mom." I touched her breast, I said, "Billy, Daddy, her breast is cold." I guess he'd been trying to wake her up too, eh? But he told me to try and wake her. And you know, I looked at him and he cried. I said, "Why are you crying?" He said, "Your mommy will not get up no more." So I cried with him.

I had to look after my brothers and sisters. So I got busy with my brothers and sisters. After, he went to the priest and told him that she died, so he came and he wrapped her up in a blanket and took her away. He came back. "Tommy," he said, "You'll never

I FIXED MY PILLOW AND I MOVED WAY OVER. I WANTED [MY BIG BROTHER] TO SLEEP WITH ME. HE SAID, "NO, WE CAN'T." HE HAD TO WALK AWAY. AND I CRIED MYSELF TO SLEEP.

see your mom again." I said, "Why?' "She's gone," he said. And then life went on. I got to get through for my brothers and sisters. My dad had to do what he had to do. You see, we all cry when we lose our loved ones, but we got to go on. I got work to do. We have to carry on. We have to. But the vision of it is real. It's okay, you have to face it, take it. We will go too, and be ready for it.

This is like when a bottle of Coke is ready to explode? It's coming out now. [*referring to tears*] It's okay. [*lights cigarette*] It's coming out and I won't explode. [*Laughter*]

KEAVY MARTIN: A lady once told me that crying is the first song that we ever sing, when we're born. And I always like to remember that.

TT: You know, people like to come around and believe they're tough, that they can take anything that can happen on earth. The day they lose someone they love, they'll find out how hard it is. We are soft, you know. We're tender. It don't take much to break us when it's with us, especially someone you love. Not even only for someone you love, for your friends. Your buddies, their mother died—you know them, eh? Because you felt it before, you know how they feel, and you can be there to comfort them. Show them, it's okay. We have to go forward and help your family. Show them this.

When I lost my dad, I didn't want to see him die. I couldn't put him down on the ground. I couldn't. When they said, "He's dying. Everybody go up there to pray for him." I don't want to see my dad like that. I want to remember him as who he is. He never left me. He never left me. I won't pray for him. I won't. I couldn't be like that. If I prayed for him the way that I was taught to pray in residential school, I would have sent him to hell. Because I was lying. All prayers are lies. If I was alone, I'd be with him. I would have held him to the end. But my soul was hidden. I didn't want to see him go. I didn't want to see him go. I knew he had to go; I knew he was going. Before. I didn't want to put him away. I want to keep him with me. In me. So he's in me still. I know where he is. It was the first headstone in Inuvik, the first headstone. He was a great man.

There was this old priest. He was the one that did all the artwork in the igloo church in Inuvik. Father Adam, they call him. He was a great guy. He helped a lot of young people that were on the streets, kept them in rectory, they call it. People come sleep there, but they come when they're not, what do you call it, "high," and they don't bring no booze. And he looked after a lot of those people, you know?

But before that, before I got married, in Aklavik I was the one who looked after the boats, eh? You know to make sure they're empty, no more water, bail the water out. I looked after the boats, emptied the boats, the barges. Early in the morning, I do that before everybody goes there that goes shipping for the day. Of course, I'm always running, eh? By this time, I met my first wife. And I'm always running. I'm gonna go there and I'm gonna get it done quick, so it'll be ready before people come. Of course, I was running down there and I seen this father ahead of me walking down. I know him, so I run by him. He said, "Hey, hey! Tommy! Tom!" This was still about from here

ALL PRAYERS ARE LIES. IF I WAS ALONE, I'D BE WITH HIM. I WOULD HAVE HELD HIM TO THE END. BUT MY SOUL WAS HIDDEN.

to the Northern [*approximately 100 metres*]. "Where are you going?" "I'm going down to empty the barges, to check the barge and the boat." "Tommy," he said. "Walk beside me," he said. "Don't walk alone when there's somebody beside you," he said. "Maybe he needs someone to talk to."

And we talked and talked and talked. And after I finished pumping the boat—he was a second pilot, eh, this Father Adam—after we're done there, I gotta go back and have breakfast, eh? "Ah, thank you, Father. I did my work and I'm gonna go have breakfast now." And he said, "Look. Nobody's here yet and you got your work done. You didn't have to run," he said. "You didn't have to run. Take your time. Get things done. Maybe next time you see, you run past like that, maybe he needs help, maybe he needs somebody to talk to. Take your time, stop and talk with him. There's lots of time to do other things. But don't be alone when you see somebody. Stop and walk with him." Take that one word alone to make you change. Stop and talk with someone. He inspired me too, that guy.

You go to that igloo church, he did all of the artwork in there. All on the aluminium, all by hand—pressed flowers in there. Beautiful flower shapes, person too, all by hand. He was a philosopher. Yeah, he was a philosopher. Too bad he was Catholic. [*Laughter*] I'd follow him anywhere.

SM: How long have you and Linda been married?

TT: Going on eleven years now. My first wife died in 1981. Tough years after that, boy. Year I had to go to raise my children, my son. Not to *raise* them; they were old enough. But I had to be there for them, eh? Someone had to. And they all got ladies of their own, so I went on my own.

It's kinda like out of the blue I got married to her, eh? I had a vision of her, you know? Honestly. I know her parents very well. Her dad grew up with me. Wherever we travelled, he travelled with me. With my dad, with us. With our big boat. We took them whaling. We took them back to the trapline. I didn't know her. It's more her mom and dad I knew. But I always seen her—she's always working. Even at a young age at the Hudson's Bay store in them days, cafeteria, the Reindeer Rail. Always providing for herself, eh? Always working. Never home. Just when it's time to go to bed and get up and go to work. I was always out too. I was living in Tuk then, after my first wife died, staying with my niece Jean. I built a house for her. I completed three houses in Tuk. They're still there yet.

And I wanted her, you know, Linda. Like, geeze, me, good woman to have. A hard worker. I never talked to her. Eventually, I brought my accordion there and sit in her parents' room singing, playing accordion and having a great time. You know, inside of me, in me, my heart wanted her. That would be someone to have, someone to live with. I need someone now to carry on.

From here I was called to Fort Good Hope. They had an old-timer hockey team here, eh? And Good Hope was going to have a tournament. So I told her I'm gonna go for a trip. I'm going to be gone for four or five days. When I got to Good Hope in their dance hall, they got lights that can make it bright and dim. Depends. You want it bright, you can make it bright. By a switch, eh? Boy, I got lonesome. All of a sudden.

I knew a lot of my school buddies over there, my school buddies from Aklavik Residential School, eh? I was square dance caller. That's what they wanted me there for. I was sitting there beside my friend, and I looked across the hall and there was a very nice, beautiful, tall girl there. Her hair just beautifully trimmed and tall and well-shaped lady, eh? Well, she looked like Linda. She reminded me of Linda in the way she was happy and laughing, and the way she looked was the way *she* looked. And I said, "Boy, she just reminded me of someone at home," I tell this guy. And the dance went on.

When we came back, I told her, "When I was in Good Hope I saw someone who was just like, honestly, just like you." I had told her before, "I wouldn't mind to be yours." But I dropped the subject, just dropped there. She said, "Yeah, I remember." She remembered when I once said that, eh? And all of a sudden one day we were walking along, and from the store she was coming home. I met her halfway in the bay. She was going home. I told her I was going to go to Hudson's Bay to get some tobacco. She turned around and walked with me. I tell you one thing, in the middle of the bay she took my hand. And the next day said, "Tee, we should get married."[1] Holy smoke! Honestly, I had that vision and it happened. Today we're still together.

1. Tommy's nickname is "Tee."

PART TWO

WISDOM

KNOWLEDGE

IMAGINATION

REIMAGINING WARRIORHOOD

A CONVERSATION WITH TAIAIAKE ALFRED

11 FEBRUARY 2011 The majority of this conversation occurred over the telephone between Taiaiake Alfred in Victoria, British Columbia, and Sam McKegney in Kingston, Ontario. It is supplemented by comments from a discussion between the two in Alfred's office at the University of Victoria on 23 April 2007.

WE NEED TO BECOME WARRIORS AGAIN. WHEN WE THINK OF THOSE PEOPLE WHO TAKE ON THE RESPONSIBILITY TO ACT AGAINST THREATS TO THE PEOPLE, WE THINK OF THE WORD, 'WARRIOR.' BUT, OBVIOUSLY, THE WAY THAT WORD IS UNDERSTOOD IS JUST ONE OF THE MEANINGS OF THE TERM. IT IS EUROPEAN IN ORIGIN AND QUITE A MALE-GENDERED AND SOLDIERLY IMAGE IN MOST PEOPLE'S MINDS; IT DOESN'T REFLECT REAL ONKWEHONWE NOTIONS FROM ANY OF OUR CULTURES, ESPECIALLY THAT OF THE IDEAL WE ARE SEEKING TO UNDERSTAND AND APPLY HERE, OF MEN AND WOMEN INVOLVED IN A SPIRITUALLY ROOTED RESURGENCE TO ONKWEHONWE STRENGTH.
—TAIAIAKE ALFRED, WASÁSE: INDIGENOUS PATHWAYS OF ACTION AND FREEDOM

SAM MCKEGNEY: In my understanding as a settler scholar living in Haudenosaunee Territory, there are ethics in traditional Haudenosaunee society that promote balance in all things, including gender relations. I was wondering if you could reflect upon what sort of political, spiritual, and linguistic foundations create that form of balance?

TAIAIAKE ALFRED: Well, for me it's woven in everything, in all of our ceremonies and songs and dances, and in the Longhouse. And, not only that, but in how the culture has functioned for so long. We've been out of that whole classical, traditional mode for a long time now, but that doesn't mean that everything was wiped out and that patriarchy was imposed outright. I think a lot of stuff in our communities is based on the traditional, pre-contact situation we had. One of those is the role of women, at least in the social and cultural life of the community, if not the political. I mean, you grow up in that kind of environment, and then it gets enforced when you learn more about the traditional teachings, whether it's in governance or any other area. The notion of balance you're talking about is pretty fundamental, and you could pick pretty much any aspect of Iroquoian culture and you'd find it as a central theme in there.

SM: Why was it viewed as crucial to the colonial project to remove that sense of balance from Indigenous communities?

TA: Well, I think there's two main reasons—I guess you'd need to ask a colonizer for the real truth on this—but from our perspective anyways, you look at it in a historical context and there's two reasons. One is that the central objective of colonization, as it was practised in our part of the world, was to impose cultural practices and to impose worldviews that come from Europe on Indigenous peoples. It just so happens that at the time that this project was in full force, doing its business, patriarchy and the subjugation of women were at the forefront of that culture, so I think that was one of the driving forces. It was part of the package of European civilization. So, that's one reason. The other reason is that the particularities of the Haudenosaunee, and a lot of other Indigenous peoples in our part of the world, made it necessary to attack the power of women in the community in terms of decision making—when it came to making war, and making decisions on trade, and economic decisions and so forth—and also the fact that they were the title holders to the land. If you're trying to steal somebody's land, you have to go after the owners, and in the Haudenosaunee community, the owners, it so happened, were the females. So you put those two together, and it's a pretty compelling reason to go after the traditional roles of women in our society.

SM: The way that that was carried out in a political fashion—through the imposition of the Indian Act, and the band council system, and of course residential schools and other forms of dispossession, as well as the encroachment of capitalism—all of this seemed to be going along contemporaneously with cultural production that would reimagine gender relations among Indigenous peoples. I'm thinking about the way that

TAIAIAKE ALFRED (Bear Clan, Mohawk) is a Professor of Indigenous Governance at the University of Victoria. Born in Montreal and raised in the Kahnawake Mohawk Territory, he currently lives in Wsanec Nation Territory on the Saanich peninsula. He is the author of dozens of articles, essays, research reports, and stories, as well as three scholarly books: *Wasáse: Indigenous Pathways of Action and Freedom* (Broadview 2005), *Peace, Power, Righteousness: An Indigenous Manifesto* (Oxford University Press, 1999/2009), and *Heeding the Voices of Our Ancestors* (Oxford University Press, 1995).

first literature and now film—and even newspapers and music—have created simulations of what constitutes Indigenous womanhood and what constitutes Indigenous manhood. And, I'm wondering about your analysis of these, particularly of simulations of hypermasculinity, in film and in literature, about Indigenous men.

TA: Well, the first thing, reflecting on what you just said, is that I think it started much earlier than the Indian Act and all that. The first instance when people changed their worldviews, or rejected their traditional worldviews and took on a Christian perspective of relationships of humans to the universe, you've done the deed then, and the ground is laid, so to speak, for the destruction of our societies. Because it's based on balance, and it is necessary to understand that balance from our teachings, and from the ceremonies and songs and so forth, and if you take on a Christian worldview you forget that. And not only that, you get the implicit bias towards the male that comes from the Bible. So I think it happened pretty early on. The Indian Act and residential schools and all that, to me was kind of the "final solution," so to speak, and it put a capstone on something that had already been laid as a foundation much earlier.

But the other part of your question, about popular culture and its stereotyped images of Natives... I can only say—I haven't studied this as a professional project or anything, that's what you're up to—in my own personal experience and that of my community, I can't really say that the images have fundamentally affected our conceptions of ourselves. At least not me and the people that I know. The images of the buckskin warrior and the hypermasculine images that, like you said, are in film and books and so forth, to me those were there and people were aware of them, but we always thought, "that's the way other Natives are." It's not anyone I know. We had hypermasculine guys and guys who were pretty tough, but they weren't the kind of images that were reflected in movies. There weren't many iron workers and all that in the movies when I was growing up. The images didn't really resonate, and, therefore, they didn't really connect.

I think a lot of it has to do with the fact that the films and movies and the books tend to focus on Plains Indian culture, and we're not Plains Indians, so there was no resonance there either. They were kind of a parody, at least I understood them to be a parody. You know, it's not so much the image that's being portrayed, it's how people react to it. You see something like that on TV or in a movie, and *prima facie*, it's not really insulting to me, because it's not me. But if people are laughing at it, or if people are mistakenly expecting me to be that way, then it's a problem. But to be honest, it wasn't really an issue for me growing up, not so much in the community I come from anyways. I suppose it would be a lot different if you talked to people in the States or on the Plains.

SM: What then have been the influences of the dominant media-informed stereotypes of Indigenous masculinity—for example, the "bloodthirsty warrior," the "noble savage," and the "drunken absentee"?

TA: Well, I think that all of those stereotypes were instrumental to someone else's agenda. For the violence of conquest you needed a violent opponent, so you created this image of the Native as violent warrior, the classic horseback opponent. And then you had all of these other things that were created completely out of context, usually. The way to confront that and to defeat it and to recover something meaningful for Natives is to put the image of the Native male back into its proper context, which is in the family. And so if the image of the Native male is defined in the context of a family with responsibilities to the family—to the parents, to the spouse, to the children (or nephews, nieces, or whatever, or even just youth in general)—if you put the person back into their proper context there are responsibilities that come with that, as opposed to just serving the one responsibility, which is as the foil for white conquest in North America.

So there's no winning in that one for Natives because, firstly, there's just no winning in that kind of power struggle, and secondly, if you construct yourself to serve that role, there may some pride in physicality, and so forth, but there's no living with it because it's not meant to be lived with; it's meant to be killed, every single time. They're images to be slain by the white conqueror. And now that they don't slay them, most of the time, openly, you know, what's the role of the Native male? And they haven't really constructed a role for themselves because they haven't really been put back into the proper context because the communities are still reeling from the conquest.

So the Native family structure, I think, is the most important thing to foster, because then men will recognize that there's just as much pride to be taken in a family role as there is in the Hollywood Indian. So right now a lot of these Natives, they still want to live the Hollywood Indian because it's the only source of pride that they have, the only image that they have. There's no channel, I guess, for productive masculinity in a productive way. You still constantly reproduce the image of all of those four that you talked about—the absentee, the drunk, the tough guy, the warrior—and those are all anti-family messages. They may be good for the man, *maybe*, for a short time, but they're not good overall for the man in the long term. And they're certainly not good for the family. And so I think a focus on rebuilding the foundations of Native communities in terms of looking at responsibility to the community, as opposed to living out someone else's fantasy, is the first thing.

SM: You've included youth voices in much of your work. I'm thinking of some of the interviews from *Wasáse*, for instance, and your co-authorship of the article on the meaning of political participation for Indigenous youth.[1] What factors inform what you describe as the cynicism of a lot of Indigenous youth towards political processes? What creates that sense of disenfranchisement and alienation?

TA: I think first of all, it's a general thing having to do with their age. They tend to be more romantic in their notion of politics, and then they are easily crushed when they find out that politicians lie, and that it's really all about the money and there's no integ-

THE WAY TO CONFRONT THAT AND TO DEFEAT IT AND TO RECOVER SOMETHING MEANINGFUL FOR NATIVES IS TO PUT THE IMAGE OF THE NATIVE MALE BACK INTO ITS PROPER CONTEXT, WHICH IS IN THE FAMILY.

1. Taiaiake Alfred, Brock Pitawanakwat, and Jacki Price, "The Meaning of Political Participation for Indigenous Youth: Charting the Course of Youth Democratic and Political Participation," *Canadian Policy Research Network Research Report*, 2007.

rity in the process, whether it is Native or non-Native. I think that when they start to see the reality—when they get to an age where they can appreciate the reality of what politics is and how it works, and what their elders are doing in the political process—it breeds a cynicism because they have such high ideals given that they're young. I think that's part of it. I think the other part is that they are part of a generation—it's kind of a paradox—our people are getting more and more urbanized, and more and more assimilated, and more and more integrated into technological society, more and more dependent, less and less linguistically and culturally oriented, but at the same time youth are being told that they need to be more Aboriginal, more First Nations. They get on the Internet, or in these seminars, or in counselling or whatever, all these so called "teachings"... so they get these "teachings" and this notion of what it means to be Native in a theoretical sense, and then they turn around and look at the lives that their leaders and their parents and everyone is leading, and they see such a disconnection.

You know, teenagers are always hyper in-tune to hypocrisy to begin with. I don't know if you've experienced it, if you've raised any teenagers, but if you've been in that situation you know that kids from the time they are pre-teens until late-teens, they're looking to catch adults on their hypocrisy every single day. And I think that is a big part of it; it's so easy to see the hypocrisy of what's going on. When you get older, if you enter politics you have to willfully ignore it in order to rationalize your participation in it. Whereas the kids, they don't have any stake in rationalizing it, so they just see it for what it is. And then, sadly, they get turned off by it because they see nothing but hypocrisy. It's very rare, I think, to find a leader that can motivate young people by being a role model in all of the ways that we expect our leaders to be in traditional senses—as a person, being consistent with the philosophy, being strong and courageous, all the things we write about and talk about. It's very, very rare in terms of our leadership in Native communities. There are individuals who have different aspects of all of that, but, I don't know... maybe if you threw some names at me I could respond, but I honestly can't think of an individual who embodies the full spectrum, and is a person who is a leader in the full sense of the word.

SM: I'm thinking about the way in which getting turned off or disenchanted—I guess, what amounts to disappointment in the hypocrisy of the generation before—leads to a need for alternative kinds of communities. I'm thinking specifically of Indigenous male youth, about how gangs function, and what needs or desires are fostered, or can be worked through, with that kind of alternative community. Is that an oversimplification of what leads kids in that direction?

TA: I don't think that is an oversimplification. The only critical response I would have to what you said is the linking of it to this kind of sense of disappointment at the behaviour of leaders because that assumes a foundation for critique where they know and expect some cultural integrity. Whereas, I would say 99 percent of the people involved in gangs, they don't have a cultural background, they don't have any sense of what it is to be Native, or part of a family, or anything. They're just existing in a cultural and social vacuum, and the gang provides some structure in their life and provides an identity which is entirely lacking. So, once you sort of de-link it from culture, and a critique of culture, I think that, yeah, you're right. It does provide something; it provides absolutely essential things. But, unfortunately, that explanation—I'm not saying you're doing this, but I've heard it before—if you go too far with it, it releases gang members from their own responsibility, and it really underplays the significance of the attraction of violence and greed and sheer laziness—intellectual and physical—on their part, to do the hard work to actually make a life. Sure, it operates and it fulfills a function that all humans need, especially these people here who are living the lives they lead, where it's almost entirely absent, that basic family. But on the other hand, they are all acting like greedy pigs, and they're all abusing women and killing and doing violence. So, yeah, they've made those choices. There are a lot of people who need culture who don't go into gangs. It's all about balance. I think that explanation makes sense, but I think it needs to be paired immediately with self-responsibility as well.

SM: In analyzing experiences like that, far too often people find themselves coming down on one or the other side: it's either all the individual's fault or it's all this absence that is political and beyond the individual, when of course they're always interwoven, right? Those things can't function without each other.

TA: Yeah, that's for sure. I think you're absolutely right. Most people pick a side, one or the other, because that's the way most of our learning and most of our policy and most of our law operates, right?

SM: That makes me think—speaking to you from Kingston, the prison capital of Canada—about incarceration, and ways in which masculine identities are moulded in prison settings. I know a few elders in this area who conduct cultural teachings in the different prisons. For many inmates, they haven't had the chance to learn about their cultures until they're in this place, but it's a place that exists as an instrument of ongoing state coercion and violence. So, I guess I'm just asking you to reflect on what these tensions produce or what they can produce.

TA: I don't really know. I don't have any experience, I've never really worked in that context. Of course I know people who have gone into prison and who've gotten out, and who've been involved in trying to learn cultural teachings and doing ceremonies and stuff while they were in prison. But to be honest, I haven't seen it operate in any transformative function… I suppose there are some aspects of traditional Indigenous philosophies and teachings which are personal, which you can take and use to steel yourself, or help yourself survive in that environment. But as for the major thrust of those teachings and so forth, they are all communal and participatory, and they take place either on the land or in the community... It seems to me that what you're getting when you teach in that environment is really one slice of what traditional teachings are—those that are applicable to the kind of environment that those guys are living in. Or women.

It's the same thing—I mean, it's a different environment—but it's a similar problem that you face with trying to teach it in a university, really. You're not out on the land, you're not in a community, and you have kind of a transient population, and so the kinds of things you do in a university tend to be things that are attractive to those people. They tend to be things to just help them maintain themselves while they're here. There's not really a level of commitment to actually living through those teachings, so much as using the teachings in order to make the experiences more palatable or to survive the experience. I suppose it's just that much more heightened for prisoners.

SM: I wanted to ask you also about what Mohawk psychiatrist Clare Brant has called "the ethic of non-interference." I've been thinking lately in some of my work about how traditional ethics of non-interference can become, I guess co-opted might be the right word, by capitalist individualism. In other words, how traditional ethics that support the autonomy of Indigenous individuals can become misconstrued in a capitalist environment that wants the individual to see himself as sort of unmoored from communal responsibility.

TA: Yeah, well, Clare, he was on to something, and I think did a good job of abstracting a key component of Indigenous culture. But, in relation to the question you're asking, there's a big difference between the two because, as it was described by Clare, the ethic of non-interference operates in a larger context of pretty strict rules, and a pretty unified worldview, and a pretty solid sense that is shared among all the people of the community as to what is right and wrong in the end. And, we'll call that a culture, an Indigenous culture and worldview. And, that's a lot different than not giving a damn, and just playing with your iTunes all day long, and not bothering with your neighbour in the context of global capital, where global capitalism seeks to atomize individuals and seeks to communicate with individuals only through advertising—implanted advertising these days, or subliminal advertising—and seeks to control that individual from a corporate perspective, right? They look the same, I guess, when you're walking around.

You could see an individual concerned only with him-or herself, and maybe confuse that with a traditional-minded individual forty years earlier in that community, not judging, or not interfering with what is going on in his neighbour's yard, trusting that either from a spiritual perspective, or that the larger community will right things in the end, that things will be right and balance will come to the community. That's a big difference in terms of the intention and the self-awareness of those two individuals. And, yeah, I just think it's a very precarious state in our communities now, especially since the nineties, or maybe even in the last ten years or fifteen years, with personal technology—omnipresent television, computerization, Facebook, all that kind of stuff—where

TECHNOLOGY HAS REALLY SUPPLANTED THE COMMUNITY AND PEOPLE FEEL LIKE THEY'RE PART OF A LARGER GLOBAL CAPITALISM. THAT'S MUCH MORE REAL TO THEM THAN THEIR LITTLE RESERVE COMMUNITIES WHICH THEY CAN AFFORD TO IGNORE.

there is really no accountability to community anymore. It's increasingly becoming a situation where technology has really supplanted the community and people feel like they're part of a larger global capitalism. That's much more real to them than their little reserve communities which they can afford to ignore.

SM: Yeah, I suppose things like Facebook constitute a form of narcosis, right, if they take people away from recognizing the reality around them. And, of course, that's why they're attractive, because they render what might otherwise be untenable conditions tenable, because they can then be ignored.

TA: That's exactly right. And the way out? I don't know. Most people, sadly, are quite willing to accept a level of gratification that goes only so deep as physicality, or maybe the first layer of psychology, and capitalism gives them that. But, you know, for those individuals who need a level of gratification that goes beyond that to the spiritual, the deeper levels of psychology—whose soul is a bit more attuned to the need for spiritual and psychological fulfillment—then, you know, you have someone you can talk to in terms of being critical of all this, and looking at spirituality and traditional teachings as an alternative. But, to be honest, there are very few individuals who are swayed by that argument.

I find that at the university here we teach the traditional line, and we get people who've been through crisis—either intellectually, psychologically, or sometimes spiritually—they've been part of the capitalist machine and it has harmed them, and they're looking for an alternative. And unfortunately I think our people, at least in Kahnawake where I'm from, they were denied the access to capitalist fulfillment for so long that now they're just tasting it for the first time and they think it's great. But, I already see signs of it cracking. It really is the role of intellectuals and artists and writers to explain for people what it is they're feeling and what's happening to them. There's a lot of people in Kahnawake right now who are in crisis, psychologically and spiritually, because they have too much money. Capitalism is not doing anything for them, it's harming them.

SM: I want to talk a little bit about re-imagining warrior ethics, which you've written about powerfully. To start with, the concept of "carrying the burden of peace"—*rotiskenhrakete*. In Kanien'kehaka society, how do you conceptualize the qualities of men charged with that burden?

TA: First of all, I don't know if that's the actual translation of the word. I know there's debate in our communities as to what that means. I think I've used both... I think I've maybe self-consciously chosen to use that translation a couple of times, because it sounds as compelling as the other one. The other one... are you aware of the other?

SM: I haven't heard it translated differently, so no.

TA: Well, you know, the verb, the central part of the word you're saying is "*skenhra*," *rotiskenhrakete*. But if you look at it from a linguistic perspective, it's not actually right to translate it that way, because it would be *rotiskenhrakete*: "they're carrying the peace." But, when it's pronounced and when it's written it's not *rotiskenhrakete*, it's *rotishrakete*. There's not "*skenhra*" in there, and that literally just means "carrying the burden," or "carrying something heavy," I believe. Some older guys said it could originally be derived from carrying a rifle, because there's a word there, the middle word, might be for iron or steel or something heavy, a burden. So maybe the rust from a rifle or something like that? So there's two different opinions as to what that means, and it's important to make that distinction, because you know, in the territory you live, most of the people there are Handsome Lake followers and they don't really believe in the warrior ethic in the way that it operates in Akwesasne or Kahnawake, so of course they use that translation without question, whereas in Kahnawake they use the other one. It's carrying something, it's carrying a burden, which is good enough for me. Being peaceful is a big enough burden. So I just wanted to make that clarification.

The key characteristic, the key defining characteristic of a warrior is someone who is putting his life at risk, right? It's not so much a set of skills or even traits, it's people who have decided that they're as good as dead, you know? And they are going to go out and do what it takes and fulfill the mandate of that community in terms of defending it, or projecting its power, or going on a spiritual quest. It's a spiritual sense, a spiritually defined role, as opposed to a more political or social role. I think it's not only Indigenous people who have that sense of it. The philosophical—they wouldn't say spiritual there so much as philosophical—the philosophical notion of the role that the Samurai is playing in Japanese society: it's someone who is as good as dead, who is fulfilling the mandate of his retainer, and who is quite willing, and not only willing but savouring, the ability to fulfill that role.

I was in the Marine Corps, and you know, there's a lot of assholes in the Marine Corps, but there's a lot of warriors too who see it as their sacred responsibility to carry on and defend the 236 years of tradition that they are now a part of. It has very little to do with patriotism or anything like that. It's a spiritual role that these guys think they are playing in relation to the Marine Corps and the sacrifices that have been made by previous Marines. And I think in the context of our community, it's a lot better developed in terms of the teachings around it, the ceremonies around it, the history. I think it's a universal thing across cultures where there are segments of the population who, because of their personality or because of their psychological makeup, have been selected and found to be the appropriate person to fulfill that role, serve in that role.

But I want to make a distinction between warrior soldiers or fighters, and having that warrior spirit in everything that you do as an Indigenous person. The essential characteristic is someone who is concerned, who is driven, by the need to satisfy that warrior ethic, and the demands of the warrior ethic, as opposed to someone who is living to satisfy the demands of a value system that is constructed out of capitalism, or Christianity, or anything else. It's clearly for someone who is motivated by something other than success in terms of a mainstream definition. And someone who's willing to sacrifice everything really, someone who's willing to walk away and defend her or his—I don't want to use the word "honour" too flippantly, because I think honour has been misused a lot—but when you think about it, someone who is willing to walk away from success in material terms in order to have respect as a warrior, as someone who has stood up and defended what was right. I think that is a warrior, someone who is embodying that warrior ethic. And, again, not to depress ourselves, but it's a very rare thing these days for someone to want to turn their back on the capitalist rewards system in order to get gratification from the respect that people have for you as someone who is embodying traditional values and defending the truth.

SM: There's a complicated relationship in a lot of your work between the role of the individual in making the decision to live an ethic of struggle, or a warrior ethic, and the need for community recognition and validation of that decision. I'm thinking specifically about a quote from a high-school student named Shana in *Wasáse*, who states, "I think it's important to look at who designates himself as a 'warrior,' or who is designated as a warrior. They serve the people, so they should be chosen by the people. A lot of times, people self-designate themselves, and maybe they're not serving the interests of the main community" (260). How can, at the unit of the individual, a person make the right ethical choices for struggle in positive ways when, of course, that requires a connection and a responsibility beyond the self?

TA: Yeah, well, they have to find a way to create for themselves a relationship, a set of relationships, where it involves them being accountable to respected people in the community they purport to be defending. They have to find a way, if they're not born into that relationship, then they have "Job Number One": put themselves in a position of dependency, so to speak—for their own legitimacy, for their own self-esteem, and their own reward—on people outside of themselves. And, I think in every Native community, fortunately, there are still individuals like that, whether they are elders or not, that are respected people who are happy to mentor younger people in order to teach them and to ensure that they're heading in the right direction. It means putting aside your ego in a fundamental sense, and not being afraid to say, "I'm trusting you with my ego here, and I'm going to take direction from you to build myself up, and to follow through on the path that I've laid out for myself. And, if I go off in a different direction, and you say that that's wrong, I'm going to take that seriously."

In the end it's still the individual. I think it's a truly Native way of doing things because no one is going to come tell you that you're not allowed to take that job, or to do this or say that or write that, but the respect or lack thereof, or mocking or lack thereof that you get from these individuals when you go into that community context is the

...SOMEONE WHO IS WILLING TO WALK AWAY FROM SUCCESS IN MATERIAL TERMS IN ORDER TO HAVE RESPECT AS A WARRIOR, AS SOMEONE WHO HAS STOOD UP AND DEFENDED WHAT WAS RIGHT. I THINK THAT IS A WARRIOR.

EVERY INDIVIDUAL IN THE WORLD THAT WE LIVE IN TODAY HAS TO RECREATE THAT ACCOUNTABILITY STRUCTURE THAT WAS THERE INHERENTLY IN TRADITIONAL COMMUNITIES BEFORE.

end-all and be-all of your rewards system. That's the way I operate. It doesn't really mean anything to me at all what people think of me in an academic context, but it's very important what people think when I go and talk about this stuff in a community, especially among the elders and the people who know the language and the culture, and who have experienced it. They're the ones I look to for criticism or for reward, so to speak. And I think that every individual in the world that we live in today has to recreate that accountability structure that was there inherently in traditional communities before. Everybody operated in that kind of relationship without question a long time ago. Whereas now, you have to do the work of setting yourself up in that relationship yourself.

For me, the sacrifice is in limiting your life choices by that relationship, but the ultimate reward is that you're living in an Indigenous way. And if we say that we want to remain Indigenous, the fundamental thing is being in a respectful relationship to Indigenous communities and being a full and contributing member of a community. You can't do that in an atomized, self-accountable fashion. So there's a price to be paid, but there's also an immense reward.

SM: Do you see a role for art, and literature, and other forms of artistic creation, in creating ethical warrior paths, or ethics of struggle, that are accountable to community? And my other question with relation to that is, how can literature or other forms of art build up gendered roles and responsibilities that are again accountable and can be lived in good ways?

TA: Yeah, I agree. I would go so far as to say, part of the reason that we're in the situation we're in—the problematic situation we're in—is that we don't have enough serious art and literature that is subversive to capitalism and supportive of the worldviews and the senses of identity that are our own: Indigenous. I think most art is capitalist today, and most literature is very mainstream; it's a typical kind of navel-gazing, middle-class, either feminist or politically correct multicultural Canadianism. Even among Native writers, where is the subversion? So I would go as far as to say that it is part of the problem. We don't have that, and it's part of the problem, a big part of the problem.

REMEMBERING THE SACREDNESS OF MEN

A CONVERSATION WITH KIM ANDERSON

WE CAN TALK ABOUT SELF-GOVERNMENT, SOVEREIGNTY, CULTURAL RECOVERY AND THE HEAL-
ING PATH, BUT WE WILL NEVER ACHIEVE ANY OF THESE THINGS UNTIL WE TAKE A SERIOUS
LOOK AT THE DISRESPECT THAT CHARACTERIZES THE LIVES OF SO MANY NATIVE WOMEN.
—KIM ANDERSON, A RECOGNITION OF BEING: RECONSTRUCTING NATIVE WOMANHOOD

*15 SEPTEMBER 2011
Conversation between
Kim Anderson and Sam
McKegney in Ottawa,
Ontario, at the home
of one of Kim's closest
friends. The interview
took place prior to the
Ottawa launch of Life
Stages and Native Women:
Memory, Teachings,
and Story Medicine at
the Wabano Centre for
Aboriginal Health.*

SAM MCKEGNEY: You've dedicated much of your life to investigating women's issues in Indigenous communities. What brought you to those concerns early on, and why have they occupied you so much in your work?

KIM ANDERSON: Well, I've always been interested in social justice. So when I left home to live in Toronto as a young undergraduate student, I started working in Native organizations in the city. I've always been active as a volunteer, and I was working with men when I first started in the community. I worked at the Native Men's Residence as a

KIM ANDERSON (Cree-Métis) is writer, educator, policy analyst, and scholar specializing in community-based research methodologies and gender. She is currently professor of Indigenous Studies at Wilfrid Laurier University in Brantford, Ontario. She has authored two critical books, *A Recognition of Being: Reconstructing Native Womanhood* (Sumach/Canadian Scholars' Press, 2000) and *Life Stages and Native Women: Memory, Teachings, and Story Medicine* (University of Manitoba Press, 2011), and co-edited with Bonita Lawrence an anthology entitled *Strong Women Stories: Native Vision and Community Survival* (Sumach Press, 2003). She is currently co-editing an anthology on Indigenous Masculinities with Robert Innes and Jonathan Swift, to be published by University of Manitoba Press.

literacy tutor when I was in school. And that happened because there were people in that agency who were interested in improving literacy, and I've always been really strong on the value of education. So I worked with men for a number of years as a teacher, literacy helper. I didn't really think about women. Women's issues weren't really on the forefront for me.

I think it really shifted for me when I had my first child, when I went through that experience of being pregnant, giving birth, and then being a mother to this beautiful little boy. I was just so overwhelmed by the sacredness of the experience. And I was also overwhelmed by how the sacred experience of mothering isn't valued or recognized by and large in the mainstream world, how so many women and children suffer from neglect and abuse—and here's this beautiful, sacred medicine and no one's really protecting it or honouring it in the way it should be. And it just so happened that right after I had my son, I was doing research that involved child welfare. I guess I was really hormonal or whatever after giving birth—I had my own newborn baby at home and I was doing research and interviewing people who were involved in the child welfare system and it hit me really hard. It was really hard to go into these situations where I saw women who were struggling with situations of poverty and neglect and abuse and all this kind of thing, and here I was, the mom of this little baby boy. It was hard for me to process all of that. It set off all these alarms bells in my system.

At that point I was doing my master's and I had this research project to do. I was going to do stuff on gender and First Nations politics because I had been working in First Nations politics and I had seen a gender divide there, too, so it intrigued me. But my partner said to me, "Well, why don't you do something for yourself?" So I went out with a desire to learn about resilience, resistance, and recovery of Native women in spite of all the stuff they go through, just to fill myself up with hope. So that's how I started out doing research and writing about Native women. From there, it just became an area where people recognized it as something that I do, so they asked me to work more in it and speak with women's groups, and that's really how I ended up focused on women and women's issues. It was an effort to hold up those things about women that are sacred that got lost in patriarchy and male dominance which results in the violence and crises that we see in our communities today.

SM: When I first read *A Recognition of Being*, I was really struck by how Indigenous women's issues were issues around sovereignty, how seeking out models within the cultures themselves and asserting those models in the face of imposed patriarchy was a means of political resistance at the same time that it was validating the needs of women at particular moments. Did you see that connection as you were writing it? Was it intentionally a political book or was it more about seeking the resources that were actually in the community and seeing where they led you?

KA: I don't know that I had a political intent setting out, but I had come from working in First Nations politics and seeing the fault lines. What I saw, of course, was leadership that was almost exclusively male and people working at the grassroots, community level who were female, and it was like this fault line between the two. I was troubled by the disempowerment that can come when we recognize this group with titles and not this other group who are actually doing the leadership work and the community building. So I had that as a background. And so, in trying to reassert some of the authorities of women, that may have been what was colouring my approach and where I wanted to go with it. But the initial part of it was really about my own healing and sense of hope that I needed. It came directly out of being a mom of a young baby and just feeling so, I don't know, so emotional, but also so moved at what needed to happen. It was so real and immediate to me what had to happen in terms of supporting women and kids. I had this understanding that sovereignty and healing will happen if we reinstate the authorities of women. If we put all of those things back into place, we wouldn't be looking at violence in our communities, was the way I saw it.

SM: And when you say, "put those things back in place", can you give me an example?

KA: Well, I think in our governance structures, we can start there. Finding ways to give women voice and authority. As an example, last weekend I was working with the Women's Secretariat of the Métis Nation of Ontario. They asked me to facilitate a gathering of women from around the province. They brought them in in March (2011) and again recently. And what they said was that women haven't had a place in the official politics or governance of our people for a hundred and fifty years or so. It got knocked out with the Indian Act, with Métis politics, with patriarchy finding its way in, and so on. So, I think that finding ways for women to be engaged in the governance of our nations, in ways in which women do governance—not Indian Act governance or not Métis governance, not those things that are really about male-dominated systems of governance—but governance in which the old ladies truly have a voice. Those types of things. If we can reinstate those types of things in our communities in a real way—not just like, "Oh, we have a Women's Council and we have our Elder Council." But how much authority do they really have in terms of making decisions? So, that's one thing.

I'm thinking about things I learned in writing my latest book (*Life Stages and Native Women*). One of the elders I interviewed, Rene Meshake, grew up in a community that didn't get moved onto a reserve until the 1960s, so he knew more of a traditional homeland territory in northwestern Ontario. He talks about how it was the old ladies who ruled, who governed that community, and how he knew that because of the names they had. So you can read about that. But he also talked about the ceremonies, the rites, the puberty seclusions that women and girls went through. He talked about what it meant to him as a young adolescent male to see these girls come out of their puberty ceremony. They would go away for a while and then they'd come out. And when they

NOT INDIAN ACT GOVERNANCE OR NOT MÉTIS GOVERNANCE, NOT THOSE THINGS THAT ARE REALLY ABOUT MALE-DOMINATED SYSTEMS OF GOVERNANCE—BUT GOVERNANCE IN WHICH THE OLD LADIES TRULY HAVE A VOICE.

came out, they were *kitchi-kwê*, they were the "great woman." His reflection was on the respect that he had for them coming out of there, and what a difference that would make in our communities if we had those kinds of things reinstated—people's sense of the sacredness and the authority, the power that we carried in a good way—how that would shift things. For him, it shifted the way he saw these girls who were now becoming the *kihci-kwê*. He talked about his own identity and the renewed sense of himself as Anishinaabe; how it made him reflect on being closer to the earth, and how *she* is the earth.

So I thought, if we have these things we can start to put into place, it's not just about looking after the well-being and authority that the girls could have. It's about bringing back an understanding of the sacredness of life and how we position ourselves around it as communities on the whole. It would be a totally different world if we worked in that way, right? As it was once, for us. You know, the violence against women is something that's… it's new for us. And so I think it's in part due to the loss of these systems that were in place, governance systems that recognized stages of people's development and systems in which women were in charge of the economies and managing the communities.

SM: So how does that filter into roles and responsibilities? The initiation ceremonies that you're talking about, in many ways, seek not only to encourage a person entering a different stage of her or his life to be self-reflexive and think about her or his own development and identity but also to think through how they connect to others within the family, others within the community, their non-human relations: the responsibilities, then, that they have to the community and that the community has to them. Do you see there being a place for the reinvigoration of those ceremonies, whether it's in a reserve community or in urban spaces or, even more broadly, beyond Indigenous Canada? Are those ceremonies that we're hungering for as a species, that we need in order to be well?

KA: Oh absolutely, yeah. And it's already happening. All along there have been people that have practised these ceremonies underground or have done whatever variations they had to do, which I also write about in the *Life Stages* book. I interviewed people that were going through these things in the 1950s. And, of course, it's making a comeback. Puberty ceremonies are already going on in many places and more and more people are doing them. And I think those are really critical in terms of understanding your roles, your responsibilities, sacrifice, the responsibility community has to you and you to them, all those things that you're talking about. I think it's really critical. And just the reverence for life. Once you go through some of these things, you start to recognize how important they were for reminding you about that sacredness of life.

SM: There's been quite a bit—not enough perhaps, well, certainly not enough—but there's been quite a bit written on Indigenous women's issues in the past fifteen to twenty years and there's been comparatively little written on Indigenous men's issues specifically. Why do you think that's the case?

KA: I'm not sure. Are you talking about scholarly work?

SM: I guess that's what I was thinking of initially.

KA: So if you're talking about scholarly work, I think you can probably just look at the demographic of Native female scholars as opposed to Native men scholars and Native women in university as opposed to Native men, which I'm sure you're aware of, right? I don't know what it is, but the numbers are much higher of Native women in universities than Native men. So that would be one obvious reason. It's just that there's more Native female scholars. I think it also has to do with women being at the forefront of the healing movement in Indian Country, for whatever reason. Maybe women are more apt to work on identity and emotions and all that kind of stuff. They're more apt to organize collectively around these issues. They're more invested in social change, maybe, at the community level because of their investment with children. People will often talk about that—that women are doing healing work because of the kids; their whole motivation comes from trying to make it better for the children. I've written about women chiefs and they all talk about that, about how they're doing it for the kids. So I think because of all those things women have been at the forefront of the healing movement, and therefore we've been more introspective in terms of our identity development, our own needs, where we're going, looking around at what's going on. So out of that, you have more literature, I think.

SM: When you're talking about the interwoven nature of all of those insidious structures—governance structures that are inherently patriarchal, with capitalist economic structures being laid over those, and nuclear family models of social organization being laid over those… and then the colonial pressure to treat those structures as "natural" and "inevitable"—is the foregrounding of Indigenous women's power perhaps a means of struggling against that series of coercive and disabling fictions?

KA: Absolutely, yeah. Yeah, and reconstructing extended family and kinship systems, which also had to be dismantled in order to make colonial inroads. They had to break down those kinship systems and the way in which kinship is connected to the land— that stuff has to be dismantled in order to make colonial inroads. So then, how do we put that back together? Women's authority and power is really a key part of that. It's at the centre of it.

SM: Well, let's bring this into your current research on Indigenous masculinities. What has led you into the research that you're working on currently and where do you see it moving?

KA: Well, as you know, I've been working on women's research and traditional knowledge for twenty years, and over the years people have asked me, "Well, what about the men?" Probably because I talk about the sacredness of women, the power of women, all these things, but what about the men? My response has always been, "Well, that's not really my area and nor do I really see it as something that belongs to me. It's really up to the men to do that and to find their own teachings and do their own work," and so on. But as you know there's been so very little of it—both in this academic world and also at the community level in terms of programming. So in the last four or five years I've started to have young male scholars ask me about that because I work in gender. Some want to work on men's stuff and my response has been, "Yes! I've been waiting for you guys forever." I realized that perhaps it's time for me to work as a facilitator in this. In no way do I want to see myself as *the* scholar, or whatever. But rather somebody who can engage with a whole network of people to try to get the dialogue going forward. And I thought, I'm in a position to do that. I can do that while some of these younger scholars aren't in a position to do that yet. So how about I crack it open and make way for some of these guys to come in and take their positions.

So, that's what started it. And the other part is realizing that we've been working so much with women, but our families are only going to be as healthy as our men are, too. So what really drives me is a vision for healthy families and healthy communities. Perhaps it's time to pay attention to men who haven't had as much of the focus. So that's really just the other side of the equation that I'm working on now.

In terms of my own intellectual interest, I'd like to consider how men find their place in a non-patriarchal society. It's a feminist approach to Indigenous masculinities, which a lot of masculinity studies take. But I've been working as an Indigenous feminist on questions of how to dismantle patriarchy, put women's authority back in our communities, and now I'm wondering, "Where do the men fit in in this? What are their roles? How do we honour them?" And how do we honour them in ways that aren't the ways men are typically "honoured" in Western society, which is around power, authority, money, all those things that make men up there in Western society. If not that, then what? We need to look at that.

So I'm one of many people, including yourself, who are working to open the dialogue and move this forward. I'm inspired from listening to Elders like Danny Musqua, who can talk about living in mid-twentieth-century communities that weren't really patriarchal. Colonialism had these inroads and hooks into our communities, but the grandpas and the uncles were not fully working in a patriarchal system. I'm really fascinated by this and want to continue asking, "Okay, what did this look like, what did it mean, and what was the position of men in those societies? How were they honoured, what kind of authorities did they have, and how did they work in balance with their wives and their female kin?" Because these systems were in place, and the stories are there to tell us how.

OUR FAMILIES ARE ONLY GOING TO BE AS HEALTHY AS OUR MEN ARE, TOO. SO WHAT REALLY DRIVES ME IS A VISION FOR HEALTHY FAMILIES AND HEALTHY COMMUNITIES.

It's a relatively new thing in Indian country, patriarchy. We forget because it's such a dominant system in the world. We forget that it really isn't everything and everywhere. Our people weren't living this way, even in recent history. So that's my interest and where I'm going.

SM: I'm also concerned about shame and stigma as they pertain to the body. There's been quite a bit written on these subjects with relation to Indigenous women and not so much about Indigenous men and the body. And I'm wondering if you have thought at all in your work so far about how Indigenous men are, I guess, taught to view themselves as physical beings (both by the mainstream and culturally).

KA: No, but that's an interesting place to go because of course it brings to mind all the: "You're supposed to look like a buff warrior." So what does that mean, the physical stuff? It goes back to stereotypes that we have to struggle against all the time as Native people. What are the stereotypes of men, in terms of body and body image and what that's supposed to represent—that warrior thing, instead of you're maybe struggling with health and body issues.

SM: We've talked a little bit so far about the institutions that have undermined the connections within Indigenous communities and nations—and we can think about how insidious capitalism has been in separating people from the land and in deconstructing kinship relationships; we can talk about roles of the church; we can talk about the imposition of the Indian Act; we can talk about residential schools. What about institutions as vehicles for positive change? Is there a possibility that education, for instance, can be mobilized to create the kind of balanced gender relations that your work seems to aspire toward? Are there ways that new governance structures can be imposed—not imposed—can organically come into being that will foster that kind of wellness? Or is the whole institutionalized element a danger?

KA: I don't think so. I mean, we could probably have a dialogue about how universities are corporations, white institutions, or whatever. But, I believe in education and postsecondary education. I think, as Bonita [Lawrence] says, for all their colonial logic, universities can be a good place for young Aboriginal people to be. So, it's about those of us who are in the institutions being able to create a space where the shift can happen, either through what we're studying or the way in which we make that happen. So absolutely, absolutely. I think it's opening up more all the time.

As for governance structures, there's no end to what could happen if we allowed a true shift. A number of years ago I was invited to this national Métis governance conference, co-sponsored by several Métis political organizations. It was supposedly about charting a new vision of governance. This was a two-day thing, and Maria Campbell was the only woman. So, at the end, we're sitting there and we looked up at the front—they had all the people that had been teaching the last couple of days lined up at the front, and one of the women in the crowd says, "Well, I respectfully want to thank you for organizing this conference and stuff, but I'd like to ask, where are the women? Where are the artists? Where are the...." If we really want to shift things, we're not going to do it by having only guys sit up there. And Maria yells out, "It looks like the goddamn Vatican up there!"

But what occurred to me when I watched that was: here were all these older men, many of them career politicians. They've been part of a patriarchal governance system for some time. But when they see the old lady get up and remark on the shortcomings of the business, they at least had to listen. I think it's because they grew up in communities where they knew that their grandmothers had power. So even though they've gotten all this other power that Western society has granted—they have nice salaries and cars and things that are in part rewards for buying into some of those systems—they still know about different types of gendered power and governance, and they understand how that works at a certain level. So, I thought, well, what if we did this conference again and we said, okay, let's bring in the old ladies and let's listen to them. Let's try to think about what it meant to have those systems of gender balance in our communities and let's try to reinstate it. Let's bring in the artists and the poets to push us. Let's listen to the youth, the young women and young men. Those things are possibilities. I can't say I see them happening in any big way in terms of Indigenous governance systems yet, but there's talk about it. Maybe there's room. Maybe we're going to be shocked that things will all of a sudden shift and then people will be open to that.

One thing that inspires me is the work I've been doing with the *Kizhaay Anishi-naabe Niin* program at the Ontario Federation of Indian Friendship Centres. This is kind of like a white ribbon campaign; it started out with men working to end violence against women. I went to a training for *Kizhaay* facilitators, and they had a Lakota man named Marlin Mosseau as their trainer. He talked a lot about patriarchy, how it came to our communities and how we all come from matriarchal cultures as Indigenous peoples on Turtle Island. I wouldn't say *matriarchal*, but wording aside, the point was that women's authorities have been lost in our communities. What was interesting to me was how hungry the men were to learn more about this. They wanted to take it in and figure out how they fit in. They seemed happy to embrace being part of societies where women had power. I thought, "I'm seeing something here that I didn't think I'd ever see!" So, you know, things are shifting. And I think that we have to keep up with that or maybe keep ahead of it, I'm not sure, those of us that work in institutions: make space for this shift, recognize it, see it coming, and support it however we can.

SM: How do you maintain attentiveness to the vision of what can be at the same time that you're recognizing that, in a lot of communities, there are desperate day-to-day concerns that are going to take precedence for many within the community? Are there strategies to bring those things together, to be supportive of those day-to-day concerns that are all-encompassing for many and then use that in the service of radical change?

KA: I think one will serve the other; paying attention to one doesn't come at the expense of the other—they serve each other. We need to address the crises around violence against women and kids. Sexual abuse, that kind of stuff, that's going on. But when we do our Indigenous feminist work, we're seeking insight into the gendered issues that underpin the violence against all of our community members, including men. Homophobia, all those things we have to work through in our vision and then frame solutions to the crises from there.

The *Kizhaay* campaign to end violence against women is strengthened and built by talking about patriarchy. In the training I attended, there was lots of talk about patriarchy and what happened and why we become involved in power and control issues, but also how we get back. I was really struck when Marlin Mosseau said, "When the Southern Cavalry invaded our communities, our people were just appalled by what they saw, which was drinking, rape, swearing, rough behavior. They saw these men that were behaving this way and they were just appalled." And then he said, "Over time we've come through this," and—he was talking about his own experiences as a batterer—he said, "So I realized at one point that I had become a Southern Cavalry man and that I needed to get back to being a Lakota man. I needed to find out what that meant." And I was just like, wow! That's really powerful. That's the vision. He's here facilitating this training to end violence against Aboriginal women, but it's the vision that will allow us to shift things much more quickly. It'll happen faster if we work with that, I think.

SM: I think it's difficult for people to recognize the way that violence often comes from a place of weakness and a place of shame. Can the model of combatting shame in oneself be construed as a warrior ethic?

KA: Absolutely.

SM: And so instead of sensitivity being recognized as weakness, it becomes indicative of a form of strength. A lot of people have been talking with me about what imagining the warrior right now means because the warrior is so malleable a concept, even though it's also often imagined in monolithic and overly simplistic ways. So I'm wondering if you might reflect on both the possibilities of fighting against violence as being a warrior ethic and then also different ways in which young men might model a nurturing manhood for themselves and for each other.

KA: I guess it's like: what does courage and bravery mean? Does that mean facing your fears, going down into the deepest parts of yourself, in those dark places that we don't want to work with? That's courage. That is being a warrior. For me, I was thinking about the first time I fasted. It was so hard—not because of going without food or water or any of that stuff. It was that I had to go down to the dark parts of me that I hadn't wanted to face, and a lot of it was related to trauma around my father, who had really a nasty end of life. I had stuffed all that away. So it's pretty terrifying to have to go there,

1. Joe Friesen, "The Ballad of Daniel Wolfe," *Globe and Mail*, 18 June 2011. http://www. theglobeandmail.com/news/ national/the-ballad-of-daniel-wolfe/article1357474/ (accessed 5 September 2013).

and you don't have a choice when you're out in the bush by yourself for four days and nothing else but you, right? So I think those are places of bravery and courage that maybe once we can face those things and go through them, we'll come out triumphant. So people talk about that in terms of coming through their own healing, and all of us as Aboriginal people have to go through that, just as a result of our families and our communities and the states they're in. So I think that's a good way of reframing the warrior ethic. Because there's nothing scarier than facing your own darkest self.

SM: I'm also curious about the attractiveness of gangs as potentially a form of kinship community where one has a role, has a responsibility, has a sense of empowerment, and has a recognizability to those around him. I'm saying it in the masculine but women can be in gangs, too, of course. Could you perhaps reflect on what draws people to gangs and then also consider if there are possibilities for gangs that are not corrosive to their communities but perhaps gangs that can benefit communities?

KA: At one time we had warriors' societies, men's societies, which were responsible for protecting. The attraction to gangs, I think it's all those things that our men lost, which is kinship, community, mentors, older men, older boys and men who they can aspire to work up to, structure, rewards, recognition, all that kind of stuff.

The *Globe and Mail* did this thing on Indian gangs and they talked about the guy who started Indian Posse.[1] He came from a really rough childhood, and they were kind of spinning it like a ballad of Jesse James, this romanticized thing. But this guy basically built a corporation. He ended up in maximum security and actually broke out of maximum security and went on the run for a while. So I was thinking, here's someone who must have some kind of genius that was lost to our communities. He was brave—he had to be brave to do some of the things he did. Courageous. Strong—he had to be physically strong, right? He had to have his wits about him, know how to build teams. Entrepreneurial, all these things. What would happen if we had those kinds of things applied for the good in our communities? What if he had been the leader of some kind of a warrior society to protect the medicine or something like that? What a tremendous amount of potential. Or some kind of an entrepreneur that was able to do something to create economic development. I mean, he was creating economic development—employment, right—but instead of using it all in a way that's so negative and so violent.

So at one time we did have societies. I don't know much about them but maybe it's the historical work we need to dig through and find out, find those avenues for men to belong. I think the military is another one that men have gravitated towards for the same reason. I met a young scholar a few years ago who wanted to talk to me because he'd been in the military and he'd been a cop and he talked about all those things that men look for in those places, part of which is a kinship among other men.

SM: Your work has been quite forceful in its insistence on the need for alliance between men and women. There's that wonderful dialogue you have with Bonita [Lawrence] at the end of *A Recognition of Being*, when one of you stresses that for healthy communities "we need to talk about empowering our men. We need empowered families" (276).

KA: We're all connected.

SM: But I'm wondering if, even in light of that assertion—the integral place of alliance and connection—does the need persist for discrete areas? So you say about the hunger among men for communities of men, is that something that groups and cultures and nations need to build into their societies—places in which women can be together, in which men can be together, or is there a danger then of an exclusionary or sexist ethic being introduced?

KA: We always had that in our traditional societies, right? They're very gendered. There were places for women and places for men. Games, even languages, that men and women used—there was a women's version of the language and a men's version. And, you know, it was all about balance—maintaining harmony and balance and strengthening those two halves of the medicine wheel that we talk about. Absolutely, there's a need for that. And I think we have to create those spaces that can work in a healthy way.

SM: And I guess the danger is when those separate spaces become hierarchized, right? Could you comment on the relationship between individual and collective healing?

KA: Well, the health of the individual *is* the health of the collective. You're only as healthy as the collective, right? You are only as healthy as our Mother Earth, and all our relations.

EMBODIED MASCULINITY AND SPORT

A CONVERSATION WITH BRENDAN HOKOWHITU

▰▰▰▰▰▰▰▰▰▰▰▰▰▰▰▰▰▰▰▰▰▰▰▰▰▰▰▰▰▰▰▰▰▰▰▰▰

MĀORI BOYS ARE LEARNING THAT MASCULINE MĀORI CULTURE IS NOT INHERENTLY STAUNCH, PHYSICAL, AND VIOLENT. MĀORI BOYS AND MEN WHO ARE STEEPED IN THEIR OWN CULTURE REALIZE THE SIGNIFICANCE OF WHANAUNGATANGA (FAMILY), HINENGARO (INTELLECT), WAIRUA (SPIRITUALITY), AROHA (LOVE AND COMPASSION), AND MANAAKI-TANGA (SUPPORT AND CONCERN FOR OTHERS). —BRENDAN HOKOWHITU, "TACKLING MĀORI MASCULINITY: A COLONIAL GENEALOGY OF SAVAGERY AND SPORT"

*2 JUNE 2011
Conversation over
Skype between
Brendan Hokowhitu
in his office at the
University of Otaga,
New Zealand and
Sam McKegney at his
home in Kingston,
Ontario.*

SAM MCKEGNEY: I'd like to begin by asking about the critical value of comparative Indigenous studies, particularly in relation to Indigenous masculinities. What are the potential strengths of comparative Indigenous masculinity studies and what are the dangers?

BRENDAN HOKOWHITU: Firstly, it begins to create—what you're doing and what I've been doing—begins to create dialogue, to start with. That would be the first strength, is that we start talking about things. Contexts are different, but there are also similarities. We've been colonized, and I think the settler/invader histories that were paved have similarities based on discourse more than historical reality. So, the discourse would be authenticity and tradition, and those kinds of things that specifically masculinity is involved with. So I think unpacking ideas of tradition and authenticity is pretty important, comparatively, looking at how those things differ across contexts. It's just like any comparative framework: the differences contain a lot and the similarities contain a lot.

I am currently on sabbatical, and I'm working on an Indigenous masculinities book. I thought about calling it *Māori Masculinities* or *Indigenous Masculinities*, and I guess I want to write a couple of chapters at least that talk to a broader audience. But there are obviously problematics around that—around calling it *Indigenous Masculinities*. It kind of lumps everything in together. The obvious problems or problematics around the idea of Indigenous masculinities comparatively are that we lose context.

SM: Bringing up discourse on traditionalism and authenticity, I've always been impressed at the way that you have resisted in your critical work the draw towards origins, or the specious notion that the only masculinities of value are the masculinities that somehow pre-date corruption by colonialism. I'm wondering if you could just expand on how ideas of authentic masculinity—authentic Māori masculinity—can be problematic, and maybe how they could be useful?

BH: Indigenous peoples have been fooled into believing that we are "traditional" in the unmoving, static, "pre-modern" or anti-modern sense. This is particularly the case for Indigenous masculinity, which is conceived of as patriarchal, backward, sexist, anti-change, et cetera, et cetera. I guess Indigenous masculine formations have been useful in the sense that they have at least built a base—the traditional masculinities have built a base—where communities can understand what it means to be an Indigenous man. Meaning in a strategic essentialist way, where cultural formations can now be used in the postcolonial context to resist. But I think the problems far outweigh the benefits. It has now come to that point where Indigenous communities have to decide what cultural formations are holding us back, and what are still relevant in terms of fighting neo-colonialism.

SM: What technologies of colonialism have been used in the New Zealand context to socially engineer Māori men? What are the real tools of that social engineering process as you've seen them?

BH: Probably the education system, primarily. I think one of the key things was creating an elite Māori masculinity in private boys schools for young men who would go back into their communities and become leaders—an elite Māori masculinity that was very much modelled on a Victorian notion of masculinity, I reckon. So there was kind of a disciplinary function, in the Foucauldian sense, because this process actually involved

BRENDAN HOKOWHITU is Māori of the Pukenga people. Having gained his doctorate from the University of Otago, Aotearoa/New Zealand in 2002, Hokowhitu became associate professor and programme coordinator of the Master of Indigenous Studies at Otago before accepting his current position as dean and professor of the Faculty of Native Studies at the University of Alberta, Canada. He has published extensively on the subject of Māori and popular culture—including masculinity, sport, and film—with articles in such international journals as *The Contemporary Pacific, Cultural Studies Review, International Journal of the History of Sport, Sociology of Sport Journal*, and *Journal of Sport and Social Issues*. He is lead editor of two edited collections and is working on an Indigenous masculinities manuscript. Hokowhitu is a leading expert on Indigenous masculinities internationally.

these guys enacting what it meant to be a modern masculine leader. So I think the education system would be the primary technology in disciplining modern masculinity.

SM: Is the creation of that kind of elite leadership strictly a means of social control insofar as that elite then becomes an authority within individual communities? Or is there a sense that this is a capitalist venture that creates a consumer culture through the fostering of hierarchies within the community? Am I reading into that?

BH: Well, I'm not sure about in your context, but in our context no, I wouldn't think so historically. I'm thinking about the 1930s. See, in New Zealand, and it might be similar in Canada, but in New Zealand those communities were really rurally based, so the hierarchies were less dependent upon capitalism and more dependent upon an amalgam of Indigenous ways of knowing and new formations. However, in more recent times I would agree that some cultural formations are based around a neo-tribal elite, who are typically men, and who have power from brokering deals with, for instance, the state.

SM: In the Canadian context, particularly with the creation of the band council system through the Indian Act, part of that process from a colonial perspective was to displace women's ownership over property, and communal ownership of property and resources, and thereby to create patriarchal, nuclear family households that would then function in the capitalist system.

BH: Prior to the 1970s in New Zealand, it was all about creating this model of the Māori family, moving Māori into the cities and creating nuclear families. But after the 1970s, the New Zealand government tried to figure out, well, if Māori culture is not going to go away, how are we going to work with it? And what they ended up doing was working with Māori masculine elite, basically—the heads of various tribes. The way they tried to interact together was an old-boys network, basically. So, that's how the government state saw itself operating with Māori, was through this kind of elite masculinity, which really cuts a lot of other people out. The state envisions Indigenous leadership to be male and, like in the colonial period, that is who they want to do business with. That is their partner. And, that's financial as well because the monies being dispersed from the Treaty of Waitangi in New Zealand are going to a masculine elite, and they decide where it goes basically.

SM: In terms of the behavioural consequences of creating an elite where a certain type of performed masculinity is valued and validated, do those models permeate throughout the broader community? Or is there a different type of expectation for those who are not within the elite?

BH: I don't think aspiration would be the right word. It's more genealogy-based. It would depend on who you are and where you are. You can rise if you're not genealogically superior, but it's a lot easier if you have genealogical clout, I guess. So, it's

THE STATE ENVISIONS INDIGENOUS LEADERSHIP TO BE MALE AND, LIKE IN THE COLONIAL PERIOD, THAT IS WHO THEY WANT TO DO BUSINESS WITH. THAT IS THEIR PARTNER.

very hard to aspire. It's not like a Western (supposed) meritocracy where individual traits lead to prosperity.

SM: Hybridity often gets mobilized in critical discourse on Indigenous issues as a unidirectional adaptation, where Indigenous communities and individuals take on certain characteristics of colonial societies and therefore become read as hybrid entities. Your work, on the contrary, foregrounds a very dynamic and interactive understanding of hybridity in which codes of masculinity emerge from historically specific cultural interactions between colonizing and Indigenous populations. What is at stake in retaining awareness of adaptation and exchange while thinking of Indigenous masculinities?

BH: It's definitely an interactive process. I think about how rugby developed in New Zealand, and how it's portrayed now by white New Zealanders as—"we came and created this game and you guys joined us"—when in reality it was Māori men who picked up and were real developers of the game in New Zealand, and who ultimately changed the game internationally. These Māori players were very much aware of the way that they were being represented at the time as barbaric savages. So they were thinking about those images, or portrayals, and trying to counteract them by employing a certain amount of mimicry—mimicking English gentlemen. But nonetheless, there was subversion in there as well. It wasn't just, "We're going to copy you guys." It was more, "We're not savages. We're onto it." I think that that rugby example shows how things were, in a broader sense.

SM: Do you see a role for higher education, and education more broadly, in counteracting the kind of social engineering that you critique in your work?

BH: It's probably not related to masculinity, but I think one of the important things is that we're teaching, we're getting various ideas across to rich white kids, you know? So, I think an important part of the decolonizing project is to re-educate non-Indigenous people. And obviously there are problematics about being in an education system that has created what it has created, but, I guess it's about—and I don't want to sound simplistic—taking tools back and trying to use them, trying to work with them. For Indigenous peoples, higher education can help achieve mimicry or it can offer a critical lens to review their histories so that we are more cognizant of what has transpired and hopefully can be more aware of the antecedents of social issues and neo-colonial tactics.

SM: Are you optimistic about what the current education system in New Zealand is offering to Māori youth compared to some of the earlier times that you've analyzed in your work?

BH: By 1969, Native schools in New Zealand were all closed down and Māori were moved into mainstream areas. But by then the damage had really been done. Māori had already begun to think of themselves as physical beings, especially with relation to

BY THEN THE DAMAGE HAD REALLY BEEN DONE. MĀORI HAD ALREADY BEGUN TO THINK OF THEMSELVES AS PHYSICAL BEINGS, ESPECIALLY WITH RELATION TO MĀORI MASCULINITY.

Māori masculinity. Māori men, in particular, had really begun to think of themselves in the physical arena, whether that be sport or manual labour. And then, like all over the world, when the various economic crises happened, it was always Māori who were going to be the worst hit because they were the least educated. So I don't think the education system is doing a good job at all of educating Māori, to be honest. The stats will continue to pathologize Māori. As far as epistemology goes, or teaching different epistemologies goes, you've probably heard of the Kura Kaupapa movement, which is a total Māori immersion system. It is really great, but even then, the education system got ahold of it and has since forced it to align with various education department criteria. So, even there I think the education system has started to control Kura Kaupapa, which is really problematic as far as epistemology goes. So, in answer to your question: no, not really. There are good things happening at universities in relation to ensuring Māori success, but there are a lot of Māori kids who will never make it to university because they essentially come from generations of poverty.

SM: In addition to education as a primary technology of social engineering, I wonder also about popular cultural representations, particularly with relation to Indigenous or Māori masculinities. You've discussed films like *Whale Rider* and *Once Were Warriors* in your writing. How significant are those filmic representations to Māori senses of self?

BH: Especially with *Once Were Warriors*, Māori had never seen themselves on film before, so those representations were really, really key for Māori to begin to talk about dysfunction. The Māori who were in those films were in the centre, as opposed to being on the periphery. This affected not only white New Zealanders, but also non-New Zealanders, and it even affected how Māori themselves began to think about Māori culture and Māori society. So, *Once Were Warriors* was a particularly important film for how Māori began to understand themselves and criticize themselves. Māori critics have really hit it hard for its portrayals, but I think in reality it was a very good, important film, and it brought a lot of the social and political conditions to public light. I grew up in an area where it was very much like *Once Were Warriors*, so seeing that on film I thought was cool and very significant. Although there were certain aspects of the film that were absolutely horrible, like the alignment of violence with Māori culture and that kind of thing.

Whale Rider was more problematic for me because it was a feel-good story which was really a ruse that suggested the plight of Māori in New Zealand society was because of their backward culture, centred on a backward patriarchal system. Now, yes, patriarchy is a problem, but does this stem from "traditional" Māori culture, no. *Whale Rider* was about Māori needing to go through a Western enlightenment, which is pretty sick considering the history of colonization in New Zealand.

SM: Are representations like these working against entrenched stereotypes that have been built up in other films? I'm not really as familiar with the New Zealand context, but in North America in the last fifteen years, films by Indigenous filmmakers have made a big impact, because they're really fighting against a century of very stereotypical and negative Hollywood representations of Indigenous people. Is it a similar scenario in New Zealand? Or are films like *Whale Rider* and *Once Were Warriors* actually addressing more of a vacuum of representation?

BH: I would say a vacuum. *Once Were Warriors* was made by an Indigenous filmmaker—Lee Tamahori—but, of course, *Whale Rider* wasn't. And you would have heard of Taika Waititi. He's kind of the big thing in New Zealand film at the moment. He made the film called *Boy*, which is about Māori—it's a Māori context. It would be a vacuum more than anything else. I certainly don't think *Whale Rider* and *Once Were Warriors* were fighting against stereotypes or anything like that; they were building upon them.

SM: Turning to sport, your work demonstrates how sport has been used in colonial contexts to contain and limit the discourse on Māori masculinity, but also how Māori men have capitalized on the agency offered by sport to struggle against those limitations. Can you speak a bit about the interplay between those two forces: sport as opportunity and sport as colonial tool?

BH: I think in the early days there were lots of opportunities, and I think Māori men were really creative back then. I don't think there are too many opportunities now; it's more about discipline. So, yeah, different historical times. It's become an adage in New Zealand that these Māori guys you see in sport are these great role models and blah blah blah blah blah, but they're not really. They're just reinforcing various stereotypes, I think now. But, historically, there was a subversive aspect to it. Māori men were really trying to demonstrate to the world various things: their creativity, their leadership, and all those kinds of things. Things have changed, definitely. There is still the possibility for subversion in sport, but the days of the impact of Ali, Viv Richards, the black power salute in Mexico are gone. Everything, even resistance, seems to be so quickly commodified and turned in on itself.

SM: Have these changes occurred because of the way that sport has become professionalized? What has caused that shift?

BH: Well, I think professionalization has something to do with it, but we're talking about the 1890s when the Natives toured Europe through until now, so it's like 120 years. So, over that time what sport has done, the way that Māori view sport, and the way that sport uses Māori, have radically changed from that earlier time until now. I don't think it's been just about professionalization. I mean, by the 1990s when rugby became professional—I've been talking about rugby in particular—Māori had been disciplined through sport, and sport was very much a way of assimilating Māori into the dominant society. I think that would have been the case from the 1960s onwards. I can't impress upon you the significance Māori men put on the game of rugby. If you were a good rugby player, you were kind of a god in Māori contexts. I think it's sad because rugby was the one arena where Māori men were given a fair shot, an even playing field, as opposed to an education system that was heavily oppressive. So Māori men gave it a lot of credence.

SM: Is that same kind of esteem available to strong rugby players all throughout their maturation process? Does this apply to youth or is it when one moves to a certain level in the game of rugby that there is that much pride or social esteem attached to it?

BH: Again, I think things have changed. Let's take a period: so from the 1940s through to the 1980s, what I just said would have been very much the case. When you talk about professionalization, I think professionalization has really broken that esteem down. Now you're just a young rugby player. But, back when Māori were predominantly in rural communities, and the game centred on then rural communities, one *hapu* or sub-tribe would go play another sub-tribe in a big game, right? And these players would maybe make their provincial teams, and those players were kind of gods. But now, with the professionalization of the game and the changes in society with most Māori moving into urban areas, that kind of esteem is broken down. It's nothing like it used to be. I don't know about the maturation process, specifically. I think rugby is still really important in New Zealand, but I don't think it's really as esteemed anymore because of the breakdown of the social structure that professionalization, and urbanization, and the modernization of society has created. I wrote a paper with Jay Scherer in *Sociology of Sport* which demonstrates how the professionalization of rugby—and of the Māori All Blacks in particular—is endemic of how things have happened.[1]

SM: In the period where you are discussing esteem in the local rugby pitch, and success in that arena, how does that translate into expectation off the rugby pitch? So, someone who is esteemed in his community as an exceptional rugby player, is he expected to behave any differently off the pitch from those who are not great rugby players?

BH: Yeah, I would say so.

SM: And, is that in terms of greater responsibility, or perhaps a sense of greater—the word that comes to mind because I'm thinking of hockey in the Canadian context is— entitlement. There is a certain degree of, I think, entitlement that exceptional hockey players are encouraged to feel in Canadian communities, that they can do what other people can't do, which can translate into presumptions of deserving greater access to and control over women in the community and things like that. So, I'm wondering, what are the expectations that are attached to that rugby prowess?

1. Brendan Hokowhitu and Jay Scherer, "The Māori All Blacks and the Decentering of the White Subject: Hyperrace, Sport, and the Cultural Logic of Late Capitalism," *Sociology of Sport Journal* 25 (2008): 243–62.

BH: Now? I wouldn't say it's community based. Most successful Māori rugby players would go and play for a school—a respected Māori school, or a respected boys school, or a respected private school. They would just go through grades, and it wouldn't involve much community action. All the Māori players that I see nowadays go back to their communities every now and again, but very seldom so. But, back in the day, back in the time period I was talking about, I'm not sure if it would be different. I don't know about the woman aspect of things, but there would be different kinds of privileges.

SM: I was thinking about the way in which sports writing—on Māori rugby, specifically—has created this idea of the Māori rugby player as "natural athletic body" without the discipline that Euro/colonial, white rugby players might bring or white coaches might bring to the game. How much of that discourse is internalized by Māori men who play rugby, as seeing themselves in terms of their bodies, as opposed to seeing themselves as intellectual, creative individuals who can use their bodies imaginatively in sport.

BH: You know there are again these conflations. The discourse that is most coming to mind is this idea of flair. The Māori All Blacks are quite key to understanding all of this, because when the Māori All Blacks play, they're not just some team that doesn't get any coverage. They get a lot coverage; the news follows them and follows the way they play, and covers their "culture" also, including playing the guitar. When they get on the field they supposedly play like family, and they play with a certain amount of flair. So they do things in a very undisciplined nature, or at least that is the discourse that is being portrayed about Māori rugby, I think. Flair centres on the idea of physical indiscipline. They've got natural flair, so it's not like creative flair, it's inherent flair. The historical genealogy of flair indicates subversion, where Māori men valued the aesthetics of the game, which was counter to the win at all costs of New Zealand rugby. Yet, the idea of "flair" came to subsume this subversion by casting the love of "play" as "indiscipline." Which of course plays into every binary stereotype in the book about the Indigenous savage versus the rational white man.

SM: What about the—etymology is not the right word—but the historical trajectory relating to how the education system sought to create Māori men as physical beings: physical beings in sport, physical beings for the labour force, et cetera? Has that carried on in the discourse of rugby and sport today? Does that conflation of Māori men as predominantly physical—as opposed to intellectual, spiritual, and other facets of human experience—persist?

BH: Yeah, very much so. It's still very present today. I'm thinking about a team that plays rugby league, the New Zealand Warriors, they're called. They play in the Australian league, which is the best in the world. And when I watch their games I listen to the Australian commentators, or the New Zealand commentators; it's very much around

THAT IS THE DISCOURSE THAT IS BEING PORTRAYED ABOUT MĀORI RUGBY, I THINK. FLAIR CENTRES ON THE IDEA OF PHYSICAL INDISCIPLINE. THEY'VE GOT NATURAL FLAIR, SO IT'S NOT LIKE CREATIVE FLAIR, IT'S INHERENT FLAIR.

their physical presence or their natural physical affinity. It has very little to do with their game plan or anything like that. The white guys who are scattered throughout, amongst the team, they give the team structure, et cetera. It's very much so continued on to today.

SM: It makes me think a little bit about your critique, in various places, of Cartesian dualism, of the mind-body split in which the mind is endorsed as primary and treated as the purview of the "civilized." Can sport enable conditions where mind and body become endorsed as integral or inseparable? Are there ways in which, on the rugby pitch, one cannot sever the intellectual from the physical?

BH: Yeah, I mean obviously, yes. But, given the predominant discourses, I would say no. I don't think they challenge that at all. Not in capitalist societies that commodify sport. But it has that potential. And various other sports that are more about aesthetics like skateboarding, or surfing, or other sports that Māori guys have gotten into, or Native guys have gotten into, that are less about winning and more about aesthetics.

SM: The discourse around rugby probably appeals to martial or military themes at times, I imagine, given that it is played on a pitch in a somewhat violent manner with each team trying to invade the other's territory. Is that a fair statement?

BH: Absolutely.

SM: And, you just mentioned a team whose name is the Warriors, right? So, how is the discourse around warriorhood then taken up by the players themselves? Forgetting about the media surrounding the game, how does that become a means of understanding one's place in the game?

BH: I don't know how much it's taken up, but I'm thinking of the nuclear family and the way that Māori guys talk about rugby as an extension of fighting for their communities: "I'm doing this for my community." So, in a way, they position themselves at the front. I think there are interplays there. They don't necessarily say, "Oh, I'm a warrior" or "I'm going to fight that fight" or whatever—they don't use that kind of language. But they see themselves on the sporting field as fighting for their families and communities, and as representing their communities. So it's kind of like war in the sense that the dominant portrayals of war are about going out and then returning, saying, "I did it for my country or my family." So there are links there, I think.

SM: And there's certainly the threat of physical trauma, right? In a sport like rugby you can actually, in various ways, sacrifice your body.

BH: Let me ask you a question: are there many Native guys who play in the NHL?

SM: There is a small handful of Indigenous identified players—Jordin Tootoo, Jordan Nolan, Carey Price, and a few others. So, it's very few, comparatively speaking. I think that's likely to change in the next twenty years or so, just because access to equipment and to travel and things like that is becoming more available for remote communities and Indigenous populations are becoming increasingly urbanized. But it certainly hasn't been commensurate to population statistics, right? Approximately 4 percent of the population is Indigenous, and there's certainly not 4 percent of NHL players who are Native guys.

BH: From what I've been saying and from what you've read in my work, I get the sense that Māori's prominence in sport in New Zealand is just so different.

SM: I think it is. But also, I think the population difference is quite stark. What percentage of the New Zealand population is Māori?

BH: I think in the last census it was something like 13 percent. I would hazard a guess that it's way, way more than that. I think there are a lot of people who don't identify as Māori. So, probably more like 15 percent, and if you include all Pacific Islanders, the number is more like 20 percent.

SM: I think one of the other main factors is the difference between the sports. Hockey requires a lot of equipment, and people who don't have access to resources, they can't play it. Even though the popular mythos has it that hockey is a rural, working-class game, it is increasingly becoming the sport of a wealthy urban elite. And, for a lot of Indigenous communities there's no indoor rink and, as winters become increasingly unpredictable, players can't rely on the outdoor rinks to hone their skills.

BH: So, in New Zealand, back probably from 1900 through to the 1970s, there was a real community element to rugby, especially. You know, one community would travel to another community, and they play a game, and then the communities would mix. Is it the same with Native communities in Canada?

SM: I think there is that intertribal socialization and community building that occurs with Indigenous hockey tournaments these days. Michael Robidoux discusses that in *Stickhandling through the Margins* and it features prominently in Richard Wagamese's recent book *Indian Horse*. That was also the case with lacrosse, historically. As I understand it, lacrosse would often be played over several days, in which two different nations would come together. And, actually, I believe lacrosse was often used as a means of diplomacy. So, the actual game would have consequences in terms of land and fishing rights, and things like that.

Before I let you go, as the leading expert on Indigenous masculinity theory, I wonder if you have any advice for me as I pursue this work?

BH: Well, first I want you to tell me more about your projects. So you're doing this collection of interviews, and you're also writing a critical book, right?

SM: Yeah, the book project is tentatively titled *Carrying the Burden of Peace: Imagining Indigenous Masculinities through Story*, and what I'm examining is how stories by Indigenous authors both analyze the difficulties of Indigenous male subjectivities in contemporary Canada and simultaneously re-imagine and indeed create male roles and responsibilities that can be fruitful in nation-specific settings, in urban settings, and elsewhere. So, how does literature analyze the conditions and the history, how does it work through many of the difficulties and many of the crises, and how does it offer and model various forms of productive and healthy masculinity that can be incorporated and adapted by readers and communities?

There's a lot that can be said about colonialism's coercive work to alienate Indigenous men from what might be construed as traditional roles and responsibilities. I think tracking that is important, but that's not the only concern. Throughout that whole process there have been different ways in which Indigenous men have enacted and lived their masculinity that haven't conformed to what the social engineering has sought to create, right? So, I want to be aware of, and be able to speak about, those processes of social engineering, but then also be very aware throughout the work of the ways in which those models aren't the only models. There are always other things going on. I think literature allows that. In literature you can always see the alternatives, the imaginings otherwise. So, I'm trying to be attentive to that.

BH: Your questions demonstrate to me that you're very much in line with my thinking about how things are complex. You've got the social engineering aspect, but you've also got agency and imagination. Everything's very complex. That would be my only advice—look for complexity, like you're already doing, as opposed to the simplistic answers. The thing to keep in our minds is the risk of pathologizing Indigenous masculinity. It is easy to pick holes at—thinking it's history and we're just the products of that history—but we also need to look for those moments where Māori men, or Indigenous men, are interacting with those discourses and either challenging them or using them for their own purposes. It becomes a much more complex idea than one of dominance or pathology.

THAT WOULD BE MY ONLY ADVICE—LOOK FOR COMPLEXITY...THE THING TO KEEP IN OUR MINDS IS THE RISK OF PATHOLOGIZING INDIGENOUS MASCULINITY.

TALKING STORY, REMAKING COMMUNITY

A CONVERSATION WITH TY P. KĀWIKA TENGAN

THE MEN'S EMBODIED EXPERIENCES SUGGEST THAT THE MOST EFFECTIVE MEANS FOR REFORMING MASCULINITIES DEFINED THROUGH VIOLENCE IS BY REFIGURING WARRIOR AND MASCULINE SUBJECTIVITIES THROUGH BODY-REFLEXIVE PRACTICES.... THROUGH SUCH BODY-REFLEXIVE PRACTICES, MEN COME TO PERFORM AND KNOW THEMSELVES AND THEIR BODIES IN A NEW WAY. —TY P. KĀWIKA TENGAN, NATIVE MEN REMADE: GENDER AND NATION IN CONTEMPORARY HAWAI'I

5 JUNE 2012
Conversation between Ty P. Kāwika Tengan and Sam McKegney at the Mohegan Sun Casino in Uncasville, Connecticut, during the annual conference of the Native American and Indigenous Studies Association.

SAM MCKEGNEY: The sociopolitical context and the history in Hawai'i is unique among colonized spaces and quite different from that of Canada. You speak a lot in *Native Men Remade* about the influence of tourism and its emasculation of culture, for instance. Perhaps you could speak to that history's influence on gender among Kanaka Maoli.[1]

A graduate of Dartmouth College (BA) and the University of Hawai'i (MA and PhD), TY TENGAN ('Ōiwi) is an associate professor of ethnic studies and anthropology at the University of Hawai'i at Mānoa where he is actively engaged as a scholar and community member in the struggles for Hawaiian cultural and political empowerment and self-determination. Tengan's broad interests include Indigenous theory and methodology, nationalism, militarism, identity formation, gender, masculinities, and cultural politics in Hawai'i and the Pacific. He is the author of *Native Men Remade: Gender and Nation in Contemporary Hawai'i* (2008) and numerous articles on masculinity theory, Indigenous ethnography, and Indigenous men's engagements with sport and the military.

1. Kanaka Maoli, like Kanaka 'Ōiwi ("People of the Bone"), is a Hawaiian term for Indigenous Hawaiians. It means the "Real People" (*Native Men Remade*, xii).

2. The separate island chiefdoms were unified through war and treaty by the Hawai'i Island chief Kamehameha, who established the Hawaiian Kingdom in 1810. As a nation-state, Hawai'i received international recognition in 1843 but then suffered an illegal overthrow in 1893 and illegal annexation by the U.S. in 1898.

TY TENGAN: As I noted in the book, that history is very much premised on and continually reproductive of the feminization of the islands and emasculation through representations. Whether that be feminization of men or just a complete erasure from a landscape that's coded as feminine, there's a genealogy or order to practices of gender colonization in the islands. You can find discourses of that—military, explorers, so forth. So the colonial context—whatever we're calling it, "neocolonial" or just colonial straight up—persists and it's gendered in a way that becomes the very context and conditions within which the men that I work with are trying to reimagine, remember, represent themselves against, vis-à-vis the state and these transnational, global tourist industries.

Family structures were also transformed by larger political, economic transformations, which over the course of the nineteenth and twentieth centuries in particular—with the advent of capitalism—created the need for men to be wage earners in a way that removed them from the home for work while women maintained connections to land and to family in ways that had more continuity with pre-colonial gender roles.

SM: How do different understandings of what constitutes "success" in that capitalist paradigm play out in male understandings of selfhood?

TT: This is one of the key issues that contributes to the ways men have been, Hawaiian men in particular, constructed as failures, not achieving—as a group, right?—not achieving the more dominant positions, socio-economically. Although this is kind of complex when we're looking at different points in this history because, during the Kingdom Period,[2] men who are chiefs—who are very "successful," both traditionally and because of their rank—are also working in the context of emergent capitalism. They're not controlling the economy in the kingdom, which comes under the control more quickly of the predominantly white Americans that are missionary descendants or business owners. But as far as control of the polity goes and the legislature, those continued to be dominated primarily by Native Hawaiian men in the Kingdom Period. But after the overthrow, there's a critical disjunction.

After the annexation, in the early years of the Territorial Period, Hawaiians actually continue to dominate the legislature politically because they are the majority of the electorate. The Hawaiian aristocracy forms an alliance with the predominantly white Republican Party—which then becomes a Hawaiian-*haole* (or "white") alliance of the elite—and certain forms of political patronage are established, where many working-class Hawaiians are given government jobs and so are able to have a fair amount of "success." Up until the 1930s really, Hawaiians are still the majority of the vote.

And this starts to change because, at first, other Asian immigrant groups, whose first generation into the territory weren't allowed to vote, are given the full enfranchisement of citizenship when the second generation that is born in Hawai'i comes of age in the '30s and '40s, especially the Japanese Americans. A lot of major changes take place after World War II, when largely Japanese American war veterans and labour leaders help to take control of the government by voting in the Democratic Party, which is seen as more representative of the working people than the Republican Party.

So at that point, and especially during the so-called Democratic Revolution of 1954, you really start to see a major disenfranchisement of Native Hawaiians, who under the old regime of Republican rule were benefitting from the alliance of Hawaiian elites and other *haole* elites. And so as they increasingly did not get those sorts of government positions, and with the rapid transformation to agriculture then tourism, Hawaiians are less able to access the sources of salaries and wages than ever before.

So it's kind of a critical period in the '50s and '60s especially, and you see some dramatic changes in their status, which in part has led to the whole Hawaiian renaissance and other forms of early nationalism in response to increasing marginalization. That's another way in which, materially rather than representationally, the shift in tourism and then also militarism worked against Hawaiian men—against which they in turn had to struggle in material ways.

As far as the question of how this may or may not apply elsewhere, I see it applying to two levels of representation—representation in terms of discourse and images, but also representation in bodies that govern and make decisions. The extent that men are or are not in these positions to represent the people and to control representations of the people in both senses, I think those become key points to focus on anywhere.

SM: In terms of history, that massive change is relatively recent. And the men of the Hale Mua with whom you worked for the book were, if I'm remembering correctly, from their thirties to their fifties—mid-adulthood. The fact that these changes occurred within a single generational memory must have a profound effect.

TT: I think there are clear distinctions between them and some of the older generation of elders who I interviewed for my current project on the military who were not worried about issues of masculinity and representation. They grew up in a very different time, in a territory where Hawaiians weren't as marginalized as they became in early statehood. In the Hale Mua, guys are struggling with these issues in a different way than some of that older generation. And yeah, I think you're right; the majority of the guys who are Hale Mua, this is the reality that they grew up in.

SM: The imagined colonial relationship to territory is constructed very differently in Canadian popular culture with the erasure of Indigenous presence in the urban spaces clustered along Canada's southern border and the representation of northern and remote territories as vast empty expanses of resources to be exploited for the national economy. Thus Indigenous territories that are urbanized are broadly perceived as somehow inauthentically Indigenous and, more conspicuously, Indigenous territories to the north are generally outside the terrain that most settler Canadians will ever experience. This is quite different from the way continental Americans tend to view Indigenous Hawaiian territories as spaces that exist to be occupied briefly in an economy of pleasure and then vacated in the retreat back to a "daily grind." How do these differences affect colonial stereotypes and simulations of Indigenous Hawaiians? For example, are Maoli men affected by colonial tropes like the noble savage, the bloodthirsty warrior, and their progeny via the corrupt band council leader—all of which maintain currency in Canadian popular culture?

TT: That's a pretty familiar trope of Indigenous people unable to govern themselves, right? We certainly had that on our part as well. Although the noble versus the ignoble savage, I think, is an important distinction. Within the Pacific there's a kind of comparison between the noble Polynesian, within which Hawai'i would be seen, versus the nasty or ignoble Melanesian, the Black people of the southwestern Pacific, which get figured vis-à-vis one another. Because of tourism and these earlier forms of representation, Hawai'i is constructed as this welcoming place of "aloha," of paradise and women, and that comes to the tourist as, "What kind of savages do you want to meet? Or not?"

SM: My colleague Bob Lovelace, who's an Algonquin scholar and former chief of the Ardoch nation, reminds me regularly that Canada has a self-perception as a white nation, and yet the white settler population is basically sequestered along the Canada-U.S. border, and as you move northward through the landscape, the Indigenous population increases and increases until, as he says, "the land is ours"—it's predominantly occupied by Indigenous identified people. And that's so radically different than the self-perception of most settler Canadians.

TT: Yeah, you see that in Hawai'i in a different fashion, where marginal lands and communities are more predominantly Hawaiian in terms of percentage of the population. One of my colleagues, Davianna Pōmaika'i McGregor, has looked at that phenomenon. When sugar became the major industry after the 1850s, those lands that were deemed least valuable for sugar tended to remain the most Hawaiian, to put it bluntly. And if you look at Kēhaulani Kauanui's work on the Hawaiian homesteading project, it's those same marginal lands that are set aside for Hawaiian homes. People weren't always making those kinds of connections between representation and other kinds of transformations of the value of land and resources, so that's why I like some of the things that you're doing, really trying to be clear on how these connections with bodies and gender and lands always need to be thought of in relation to one another.[3] And that's something I haven't done myself so I'm now trying to think that through in more direct ways than I did with the book.

SM: There are so many parts in the book, though, that point in that direction. Even when speaking about the fighting arts and the physical experience of disciplined action in relation to other men, which involves occupying space in a really tactile way, right? And, I think, one of the things I was trying to get at in my paper is just how much the

3. Just prior to our interview, Tengan had watched me present a draft of the paper that would become "'Pain, pleasure, shame. Shame: Masculine Embodiment, Kinship, and Indigenous Reterritorialization," *Canadian Literature* 216 (2013): 12–33.

physical experience of embodied practice within particular places enacts a process of reclaiming. Ownership's the wrong word because it places it in capitalist terms, but it's about occupying territory in a respectful, meaningful way.

TT: So it's a repossession, not necessarily legal ownership, but possession and occupancy as a way of reconnecting to self and territory.

SM: In *Native Men Remade*, Rick Bissen frames warriorhood not as the ability to wield violence but rather as the capacity to be courageous, and the example he provides is wearing the malo[4] in public and being unashamed. I think framing warriorhood as both opposition to shame about the male body *and* resistance to shame about culture is so provocative and profound.

TT: There are different kinds of shame visited upon the communities based on their specific histories, and how one deals with that is going to require knowledge of those specific histories and lands and the regimes of shame that are still in many ways maintained and reproduced, often as depictions in media and statistics. Even to this day, they continue to pathologize Hawaiians and Hawaiian men in particular ways, even as there's a concerted effort to work against those representations.

I think the other part of that question, too, is what is a healthy pride, right? There's a lot of ways in which pride can take you to the other extreme in which it becomes chauvinism and leads people to be overly assertive and aggressive, taking them into those spaces of warriorhood that are less productive. Aggressive, pot-stirring expressions of pride that respond to the history of shame can be equally exaggerated, which would also be a really bad place for us to be. When does pride go too far? When does it start to become its own problematic? When do other forms of oppression, particularly within the Hawaiian community, become enacted in the name of pride?

On the one hand, pride is this important aspect that people are always talking about. It's overcoming historic shame, finding pride again in culture and identity. But, in particular, with the Hawaiian men's movement and the warrior movement, I've seen a number of instances where this profound pride will take certain men—not all, but a minority—to the level of asserting "we're the ones, we're gonna be the leaders, and this is how it's gonna be now." They have this fullness of self, which I think is too full in some ways; it's not embracing those other elements of community and family that are still core aspects of who we are as Hawaiians. Because it's that source of pride, the emergent identity, that becomes the focus and starts to reframe the ways in which they interact with others. I don't see this a lot, but I've seen a couple folks where the warriorhood is everything and that's just how they are with everybody. This is their first sense of positive self-worth and that pride evolves into something else and it starts to fuel a different kind of warriorhood than what Rick was trying to articulate.

4. The malo is the basic garment worn by Hawaiian men in precolonial times. According to Tengan, most of the men in the Hale Mua with whom he conducted his participatory anthropology "had never worn a malo before they joined the group, and they struggled to overcome both bodily inhibitions and historical ignorance as they learned to wrap a single strip of cloth ten to twelve inches in width and four to five yards in length over their genitals, between their buttocks, and around their waist to end with a short flap extending to just above the knee" (*Native Men Remade* 17–18).

SM: In an article on the Oka Crisis that occurred back in 1990, Gail Guthrie Valaskakis discusses the need for traditional warriorhood in order to protect the community and protect the landscape and protect the ancestors. However, because Indigenous men—and particularly Indigenous male youth—were able to access ideas of Indigenous warriorhood primarily through the settler media, which was portraying a specific kind of military masculinity that wasn't tempered by community decision making, an individualistic military machismo emerged. So it was the self-proclaimed warrior as opposed to one who is acting on behalf of the will of the people.

TT: This is where some of the pride stuff is tricky. Hawaiian soldiers demonstrate aspects of courage and warriorhood that are part of a traditional, cultural notion of the warrior. And there are many personal, cultural, and material connections between family and community members and these soldiers, which informs a kind of suspension of really important critiques of the military. That affective connection makes it hard for people who are trying to articulate these critiques of the military without getting some backlash.

There's a reputation of Hawaiians in the military for being among the best soldiers. They're the hardest working and best fighters and always putting their fellow soldiers ahead of themselves—a discourse in many ways related to older discourses of Hawaiians being recruited at first for sailors and the fur trade and later on the whaling ships: "They make great sailors! They're always going to jump in the water and save anyone else before themselves. And strong." This discourse speaks to their capacity as compliant, hard-working labourers for these different militarized projects, which is an interesting, very problematic genealogy to the ways in which Hawaiian soldiers are currently *re*-representing that reputation that they've heard in the military. We're known as being the best soldiers because of this, this, and this. So there's a huge amount of pride in that, especially in the face of historic shame.

We're also touching on one of the few ways of economic, social mobility for many Hawaiians. But aside from that—not even aside from, attached to that—there's an emotional investment and valorization because it does something to the sense of self in relation to a broader understanding of "Hawaiian warrior" as it operates in the military, which is connected to a particular kind of Hawaiian masculinity that is accomplished there that isn't always accomplished in other realms. Hawaiian men are not getting the managerial positions. There are always exceptions, but as a group that doesn't quite happen. These continue to be the conditions for structuring the discourse on Hawaiian masculinity and manhood.

There is a cultural way of being that a lot of Hawaiian military men are affirming. There's a way in which the military fulfills a cultural role, which was imagined to have been lost—structures of rank and authority that are very Hawaiian. These pre-colonial structures of rank and authority get dismembered by colonialism: places for warriors, and ways of relating as men among men, with the kind of deep bonds of kin that are

THERE'S A WAY IN WHICH THE MILITARY FULFILLS A CULTURAL ROLE, WHICH WAS IMAGINED TO HAVE BEEN LOST—STRUCTURES OF RANK AND AUTHORITY THAT ARE VERY HAWAIIAN.

formed between men who are not of the same family but are nonetheless able to reconnect in these spaces.

That's what the Hale Mua is trying to do, recreate some of these spaces that were part of the traditional forms of being. They tended to be amongst men who were all related in the pre-colonial period, so it's a little bit different than how it's being articulated now, but still you have these institutions that enable a kind of *communitas*, with the discussion of ritual and spiritual communion. So not only for how it functions but also how it's valorized and coded and invested with emotion and then pride, the Hale Mua takes us back to that.

SM: The Hale Mua provides a particularly safe environment for Maoli men to share and to seek validation of their identities because it's not only a culturally homogeneous space but a homosocial space. I'm wondering about other environments in which Indigenous men gather and the utility of these places in fostering well-being—for instance, you've spoken about the military and we've talked elsewhere about the American football dressing room and we could consider hunting and fishing activities and I'm even thinking about the pub or bar as a place where men will congregate and potentially share with each other in ways that could be generative. The bar is a tricky one because of how it has been characterized as inherently negative or a consequence of colonialism. However, in that social setting, some might say that men have a few beers, we open up, we talk about things we wouldn't otherwise talk about, and that process can feed into other forms of growth that might be positive. But because alcohol has been so attached to the pathologization of Indigeneity, there seems to be a de-linkage. I wonder if you have any thoughts about that.

TT: I've tended to elaborate more on the negative side of that space in my work, but I think what you were saying is important too, to not code it solely as negative. I hadn't thought about that too much before. I mean, those people in the bar, they're us, too. This is not an "Other Hawaiian." These are our uncles and brothers and cousins. And sometimes we're joining them too.

There used to be an ʻawa [kava] bar in Honolulu in the early 2000s called Hale Noa that was part of the revival of ʻawa as an important Hawaiian social and cultural practice.[5] It was never exclusively for men, but it was almost always men that you'd find in the ʻawa bar. There might be women there, too, but I think that men in particular found this a really important gendered space. These spaces are important to our rituals and also for sharing stories around the ʻawa bowl. It's productive of this kind of talk that we're having now. For better or worse, some social lubricant can facilitate it.

SM: I think that really connects to how men are socially conditioned to be uncomfortable with any kind of vulnerability, so it doesn't have to be alcohol but if we're sitting at a

5. ʻAwa is a traditional Hawaiian drink used in ceremony. It has mild intoxicating properties that are far less severe than those of alcohol. ʻAwa generates a feeling of physical relaxation while the mind remains alert.

coffee bar and we're having a coffee, there's a tactile and physical diversion that can potentially guide one to a space of comfort and then perhaps he shares more. I don't know.

TT: There will be guys now who have ʻawa circles in their own homes, rather than going to a bar. Certain Hawaiian men, not all of course, but certain men have found comfort in those spaces in ways like you're pointing to but without the alcohol, which is significant in part because of the ways in which our Hawaiian community continues to see alcohol as a pretty major problem. When you associate alcohol with family violence, working to not succumb to some of those behaviours and tendencies by avoiding alcohol but still seeking out those homosocial spaces becomes important, and I think ʻawa circles provide that in a culturally significant way. It's important for creating safe spaces where people are connecting on a deeper level and feeling and sharing moʻolelo, those stories, having talk stories that are happening there in ways that probably wouldn't otherwise happen.

There are other spaces—fishing is actually a good one. Even today it's the guys that do most of the fishing on these small boats, which is very much in line with the traditional roles of Hawaiian men who fish in the deeper oceans. In the shallower parts, you had women as well who would gather from the shoreline and do some of the shoreline fishing. But the deepwater fishing, that was really the province of Hawaiian men in traditional times. Hunting is another one.

And there are other activities like the *imu*—the underground ovens that are made primarily by the men—where the traditional cooking of the pig and other foodstuffs is done. There are important continuities with pre-colonial roles of men cooking the food. That's what the Hale Mua was historically; it was the men's eating house. It was the men's responsibility to feed the family. They're the ones who cooked. Being in that particular kind of space that is involving this work and gathering and feeding, gives a lot of men a traditional sense of masculinity.

SM: Can I ask you about talk story? I find the idea of narrating one's own experience in a safe context and in a manner that interweaves with and extends a group or communal narrative enormously compelling. So what exactly do you mean by "talk story," and why is it an important tool for individual affirmation and community continuance?

TT: There are different levels of talk story. There's the kind where you're not doing it for purposes of collecting information for the academy, which I was doing in *Native Men Remade*, so I want to distinguish what I was doing from what is more naturally occurring—we're just going to sit around, we're just gonna talk all night or we're just gonna enjoy our company, this connection, this reciprocity. It's as much an emotional connection as it is a transfer of knowledge—more so really. There are a lot of other aspects that one could get into in the aid of what constitutes talk story, but at the core,

THAT'S WHAT THE HALE MUA WAS HISTORICALLY; IT WAS THE MEN'S EATING HOUSE. IT WAS THE MEN'S RESPONSIBILITY TO FEED THE FAMILY.

it's sitting together and connecting on an emotional level, which helps bring us closer as we're engaging in this back-and-forth dialogue.

And in trying to incorporate that into what I see as important for methodology, for interviews, it's to say it's not just me trying to get answers to questions, right? Our ability to have an exchange is crucially at the base of it—an emotional exchange, one that is not just a one-way thing, but one that we both get something out of that's positive. In the larger context of the group, when it's happening on its own, without me recording or anything, this is what creates these bonds. It creates this sense of a shared identity because you're having and engaging in this communicative event, this modelling of personal stories after collective stories. Making these emotional, personal, and collective connections, that's what solidifies a sense of community.

In considering the mode of talk that I think is important to maintain in the interviews I do, I essentially take this form that we're doing right now. It's not just me talking to you. You're talking to me. We're giving each other ideas and we're commenting on each other, enjoying this time. I think part of it is you have to have a certain kind of relationship in order for this to work to begin with. I don't think we could have necessarily had this kind of exchange last year. But, you know, we got to hear each other speak, and we ended up partying two nights ago, and I think there's a different kind of connection now that enables this kind of talk story. At the core of it, you talk story so you can have fun and feel good about it. It's less about figuring this or that out, or remembering that or this story. It's someone you want to catch up with, someone with whom you want to have that good feeling again. That's why you're talking story and that's why talking story isn't completely commensurate with an interview.

IT CREATES THIS SENSE OF A SHARED IDENTITY BECAUSE YOU'RE HAVING AND ENGAGING IN THIS COMMUNICATIVE EVENT, THIS MODELLING OF PERSONAL STORIES AFTER COLLECTIVE STORIES. MAKING THESE EMOTIONAL, PERSONAL, AND COLLECTIVE CONNECTIONS, THAT'S WHAT SOLIDIFIES A SENSE OF COMMUNITY.

OUR BODIES, OUR NATIONS

A CONVERSATION WITH JESSICA DANFORTH

20 OCTOBER 2011
Conversation between
Jessica Danforth and
Sam McKegney at J.M.'s
Restaurant and Lounge in
the Ambassador Hotel in
Kingston, Ontario. Jessica
had been invited by Sam's
daughter Caitlyn to speak
on social justice at the
high school leadership
gathering she was co-
organizing.

WE ARE NOT EQUAL WHEN INITIATIVES TO SUPPORT GENDER EQUALITY HAVE REVERTED YET AGAIN TO "SAVING" PEOPLE AND MAKING DECISIONS FOR THEM, RATHER THAN SUPPORTING THEIR RIGHT TO SELF-DETERMINATION... —JESSICA DANFORTH, FEMINISM FOR REAL: DECONSTRUCTING THE ACADEMIC INDUSTRIAL COMPLEX OF FEMINISM

SAM MCKEGNEY: What drew you to the issue of sexual health for Indigenous people as a crucial element of both sovereignty and community well-being? Why is sexual health so important?

JESSICA DANFORTH: I think that "sexual health," firstly, seems a very clinicized, medicalized term. Sexual health to me inherently means rights over body and space and how integral and crucial those rights are to our very existence, not just as Indigenous peoples but peoples in general. Often people see sexual health as something to do with a problem, as disease control—like HIV prevention, for example, or other sexually transmitted, blood-borne infections—but I would say it's more "sexuality." And to me the way of life that we are creating, or that we're working on, in terms of sexuality and sexual health, is a reclamation. Not only is it foundational to our existence as Indigenous peoples, but that's really where we all came from, you know? In the broadest of senses, that's what unites humanity. Everybody got here because of that.

But I think even more than that, a lot of my worldview and a lot of the information that I receive comes from midwifery knowledge. Traditional forms of medicine and health all centre around people's sexuality, which is really their bodies and their bodily rights, their bodily sovereignty. And autonomy, really, because when we lose control of our bodies, we lose control of our nations. There's a saying that we need land for the people. We need people for the land, as well.

Sexuality is not just having sex. It's people's identities. It's their bodies. It's so many things. A lot of elders that I work with say that you can actually tell how colonized we are as a people by the knowledge about our bodies that we've lost. The fact that we need systems and institutions and books to tell us things about our own bodies is a real problem. If we don't have control over our bodies, then what do we have? If something like body knowledge no longer belongs to community and is institutionalized, then what does that really mean? If we have young people, for example, who are getting educated about sexuality and their parents can't teach them that same knowledge for many crucial reasons, that's a strong indication of colonialism. These are the implications of not having sexual health and sexuality knowledge as an integral place where nations can be strong and centred.

SM: What are the implications of that disjuncture you're referring to—where forms of colonial education have actually limited the knowledge of a generation and then that same colonial system takes ownership over the education of the subsequent generation and their understanding?

JD: It's a complex relationship. If we look at the context of residential, mission, boarding, and industrial schools, in North America and in Australia and New Zealand, then we know that the very thought of sexuality was purposely taught as shameful. And, certainly, the incidence of sexual abuse was so rampant and purposeful. So coming from that generation and then you have this generation who, if they are getting sexual education—and that's a big *if*—they get it in schools. It's a complex relationship because there is that forbidden era. Even if parents or caregivers didn't go through residential schools, there's many other things that they could have been involved in. Whether it's the sixties scoop, whether it was being apprehended by child welfare, whether it was just living in Western society. Western society is not an open society for sexuality. Western settler society brought over sexual shaming. If you look at all laws related to people's bodies: those were colonial impositions. There were no colonial laws related to abortion or

JESSICA DANFORTH is the founder and executive director of the Native Youth Sexual Health Network, a grassroots organization run for and by Indigenous youth that is dedicated to bodily, reproductive, gender, and sexual justice in the face of ongoing colonialism on Turtle Island. Danforth has spent more than half her life mobilizing individuals, families, and communities to reclaim their ancestral rights to self-determine decisions over their bodies and spaces. She has authored numerous articles, blogs, and monologues on activism and sexual health, and she is the editor of two books: *Sex Ed and Youth: Colonization, Sexuality and Communities of Colour* (Canadian Centre for Policy Alternatives, 2009) and *Feminism For Real: Deconstructing the Academic Industrial Complex of Feminism* (Canadian Centre for Policy Alternatives, 2011).

who could marry whom or birth control or anything until settlement and creation of the Confederation of Canada and the Constitution of the United States.

But at the same time, there's the reality of what youth experience. There's the reality that we didn't have things like HIV in our communities fifty or one hundred years ago. It's very recent. I just came from Alberta and there's a huge so-called "outbreak" of syphilis again, but that's not something that's "Indigenous" to the area. And the reality also is that Indigenous peoples—and most acutely Indigenous youth and Indigenous women—experience those statistics at much higher rates. Throughout the world, incidence of not just HIV, but gonorrhea, chlamydia, and other STIs are going down, but in the Indigenous population in North America, it's rising. And doctors have been comparing HIV "epidemics" in Africa to what's going on here in provinces like Saskatchewan and the Northwest Territories and Nunavut. So, that's what makes that relationship complex.

Underlying this issue is the fact that the knowledge is often no longer community-based because it's been taken away from communities and families. One of the slides that we often use at the Native Youth Sexual Health Network when we do education with service providers calls the ABC method of prevention *colonial*. Because the ABC method of prevention for sexual health says, "All your problems should be solved ABC." So, A: Be abstinent. So that's just supposed to work. B: Be faithful. So you should only have one partner. It has to be a heterosexual, monogamous partner. And there's all kinds of public health campaigns in North America that say, "You are less at risk for something if you only sleep with one person," which is so misleading, especially when you consider the amount of rape and sexual assault and violence in our communities. It's such a false portrayal of reality. You could be with one person your entire life and be at risk or not be safe. So that's ridiculous. Then the C is buy a condom. If A and B don't work, everything can be fixed with a condom. And I would say that that ABC method is further colonialism. That's the recipe for prevention from the state—that's the federal government's version of sexuality education, of sexuality knowledge. And we are always—I don't want to say at war—but we are always struggling, we are always butting heads with public health because that's their party line.

Even if they say, "Well, we know that in the case of sexual violence, being faithful isn't going to work," or that "just saying no" isn't actually effective, their materials and education practices keep forwarding that ABC agenda. The reality is that at any point, somebody could pick up that material and it's colonial, it's imperial, it's really an imperial form of prevention. And it's obviously not working. Not just with the rates and the statistics, but even through the direct feedback that we hear from young people around sexual health.

SM: What do you see as alternatives to that colonial model?

JD: I see a bunch of things. The crux of our work is to decolonize from that model. We call a lot of our work reclamation because we don't think that we're actually doing anything revolutionary. We always joke that we didn't wait for Christopher Columbus to come teach us about sex. We absolutely believe that our ancestors were intelligent and had body knowledge. At the very minimum. And there's so much evidence, especially with midwifery knowledge. Midwifery knowledge is really tokenized as being only about birthing babies when traditionally midwives—Indigenous and non-Indigenous—will tell you, it's about the full circle of life. Midwives are only legally allowed to birth babies, but midwifery knowledge is really about centering community knowledge. Because woman is the first environment, as Katsi Cook often says.

When we say "woman" as Indigenous peoples, I don't think that translates properly in English. I think that we get very body-focused—or what I call "underwear policing"—around, "That must mean vagina, breasts, whatever," and it doesn't. In so many Indigenous languages, there are no gender pronouns. There are only two genders in English, which really limits understandings. So I want to make that very clear that even when we say "woman," it's not just tied to body parts or underwear policing.

But, let's say, the uterus is the first environment. Even with the advancement of reproductive health technology, a uterus still has to be involved at some point to carry a pregnancy to term. The limiting of midwives to the birthing of babies and the eradication of midwifery knowledge was strategic and premeditated. Midwives also carried knowledge about "abortion." Abortion, I think, is a very harsh word in English rather than it being about reproductive control, spacing out families, stopping pregnancies at different times when there was rape or famine or drought or war. And midwives have that knowledge. Midwives are also there to intervene in families, so you have midwifery knowledge around if there was a complication in the home, for example. There's a really awesome quote that I heard recently from Nastiq Kango. She's an Inuk midwife from Iqaluit. I was working with her recently and she was saying, "A midwife births a nation." So in Inuktitut, "midwife" translates to "nation-maker." And so-called "leaders" cannot tell midwives what to do. If a midwife births the leader, then the leader can't tell her what to do.

To place sexual health over here and land rights over there is a very colonial, imperial way of thinking. Environmental justice is over here, reproductive justice is over there. We have really paid the price for that. And our work seeks to indigenize by making full cycles tangible so that people can directly see the violence against the land and the violence against our bodies and the different roles that we have to play. Which is why the area of Indigenous masculinities is so important because everybody has a specific role to play, and when we lose one area or one person or one gender in the gendered universe, it creates problems for other things.

Residential schools, boarding schools: not only did they kill the Indian and save the man, but they also deemed Aboriginal women unfit for child rearing. If that's not a clear eradication of midwifery knowledge, I don't know what is. Saying that our ways of child rearing and child bearing are not valid or credible or safe? It also instituted patriarchal gender roles, saying, "You will learn to become a man this way. And you

TO PLACE SEXUAL HEALTH OVER HERE AND LAND RIGHTS OVER THERE IS A VERY COLONIAL, IMPERIAL WAY OF THINKING. ENVIRONMENTAL JUSTICE IS OVER HERE, REPRODUCTIVE JUSTICE IS OVER THERE.

will learn to become a woman this way." And I don't know that that's been interrogated enough. Yes, everyone knows residential school was bad, but what about its effect specifically on gender roles. Where did Two-Spirited children go when they went to residential school? There was only a girls' and a boys' dorm. Youth from different nations—where did they go? So they learned Eurocentric gender roles: "You'll learn to sew to be a good Canadian or American woman. And you'll learn to farm to be a good man." And that's further exacerbated by the sixties scoop, but also, the child welfare system today. We do a lot of work with Cindy Blackstock and the First Nations Child Caring Society of Canada on the number of Indigenous children who are in care. And there are currently more Indigenous children who are in state child welfare than were ever in residential schools at their height in the 1950s. In 2011, it's almost three times that number. I mean, the list just goes on. It's ridiculous.

But what it means, though, is that the eradication of midwifery knowledge and sexuality knowledge was a purposeful nation-state creation that is tied to the existence of Canada and the U.S. What better way to colonize a people than to make them ashamed of their bodies? Which is why the decolonizing project is so important and why gender justice, for example, has to be incorporated. To decolonize and nation-build with each other, we need to acknowledge and understand culturally- and community-based principles of harm reduction. For example, a lot of our elders tell us stories, but in the stories, they're not telling us what to do; they're not saying, "Okay, by the end of the story, you should only do this or that." They're giving us information and knowledge so we can make our own decisions. And that is the ultimate form of non-interference and, really, harm reduction. Reducing harm in any situation is dependent on the wellness of an entire community.

We have to stop referring to ourselves as in the past. There's been this revitalization of rites of passage and coming of age ceremonies. A lot of where my centering comes from is seeing that this is possible. Another alternative is language revitalization, which I see happening in a lot of different communities. But that's why it's important to know that language revitalization isn't just about learning cool words in a language. It's literally about the survival and the sovereignty of a people. To not have to rely just on English, and the fact that English is tied to the state and it's tied to colonialism. It's even about sexuality. One of the things we make sure of is that during processes of language revitalization sexuality knowledge isn't exempted. Making sure that words for people's bodies are part of the revitalization, which hasn't always been the case for different reasons in different places. And sometimes having to make new words. We've had to make new words for things like a condom or a dental dam. We've had to make new words for that, but it can be done. And it is done.

SM: And all languages are adaptive, right? All languages are constantly in process.

JD: And evolving. Not only are Indigenous people constantly referred to as bound to the past but there seems to be a presumption that we were never going to evolve, which is false. We are constantly evolving. Things were always going to change, which is why I think it's important, especially for young people, to look at creating new traditions. I know a lot of people are very: "If it's not broke, don't fix it," but the word "traditional"— even in language and even when it comes to masculinities—I've seen everything from tradition being used to oppress to tradition being used to empower. So the language of tradition is really important because what does "traditional" mean? And who decides? Is everything pre-Christopher Columbus traditional? Or is last week traditional? Is it elders who decide?

By traditions, I don't mean totally changing ways of thinking—it might be that for some people—but I also mean songs. If we don't create songs about our time, who's going to sing about us in the future? Who's going to know about us if we're not doing these things of our time? We've been forced to change and things have come into our communities without our permission. So, I've heard things like, it's not traditional for a man to be x, y, z. And then I always wonder, what does a man even mean? And who decides what tradition is? And when it's hurtful or harmful to somebody, how can it then be traditional? That internalized colonialism that we deal with, that internalized racism and oppression is such a huge issue. We still don't know how to deal with it, if you will. You can't really go up to someone and say, "Okay, you've internalized a little bit of colonialism there." And we can get into the lateral violence, especially when it comes to so-called traditions, because it often involves a policing of traditions, especially around masculinity or what it means to be a man. Or was the definition of a "man" only really started with European invasion, and if that is the tradition of roles and responsibilities, is such manhood really traditional?

SM: Is there a need to reclaim maleness that is not just defined biologically? And connected to that, is there a way to validate those who want to say, "I'm a man and manliness means a specific spectrum of things," while at the same time protecting fluid notions of gender?

JD: Well, I would say that that's like resisting policing, right? There's been so much internalization of policing, and I don't just mean the RCMP. Policing comes from "policy." As regimented or imperial schools of thought are created, people police them. And that type of policing has grown to the point where we're pointing at people's gender parts, biological parts saying, "this is" and "this isn't." I think that a way to resist that is by reclaiming roles rather than looking just at body parts or underwear policing. And really, interrogating that policing impulse. And that's where being Indigenous is so awesome because I understand that gender is a universe and that we're all stars in the universe. That's how infinite it is.

That image of being a star in the universe of gender means that you shine, but it also means that people can look at you knowing that there's infinite other possibilities. You're still shining and bright and awesome, but you're not by yourself up there, right?

IF WE DON'T CREATE SONGS ABOUT OUR TIME, WHO'S GOING TO SING ABOUT US IN THE FUTURE? WHO'S GOING TO KNOW ABOUT US IF WE'RE NOT DOING THESE THINGS OF OUR TIME?

Which is why explaining gender in English is one of the hardest things to do. Even the word "trans" in English—and I want to make it clear: we are very supportive of trans-gendered communities and gender non-conforming communities and peoples—but many friends and family that I know in trans communities also say that even "trans" is a difficult word because it assumes that you're only transitioning from one gender to another rather than being neither, or both, or several, and again, it being so biologically and medically focused. So I think we need to really understand that many teachings are about roles. For example, people often say that midwifery knowledge comes from so-called women, but that doesn't mean that so-called men didn't prepare certain things for birthing to happen, that they didn't, in some communities, help support the woman in a fetal position while she was literally in labour. Whatever role was needed, people had to take it up. You might have a more masculine role or a more feminine role, and the awesome thing about being Indigenous is that I don't get confused. I really am not confused if I think Indigenously about gender and sexuality. I think it makes so much sense.

Every time I hear people say things like, "Gender fluidity or the Kinsey scale of sexuality is so revolutionary," I get really frustrated. Not that I think everyone should go, "Indigenous people, you guys are awesome," but that erasure has direct influences on not just the mainstream population but Indigenous people ourselves. The more we call that "other people's stuff," or we don't own it as our own, the more we become alienated from ourselves. I'm not knocking Kinsey, but that so-called revolutionary first sex anatomy book actually erased so many pre-existing and less complicated and problematic ways of understanding gender and sexuality.

SM: The ongoing erasure of Indigenous knowledge…

JD: …which has real-life impacts. Even to this issue of Indigenous masculinities: If people are made to think that being trans or being Two-Spirited or being gender non-conforming is not Indigenous, then where did that come from? If our versions or our understandings of gender and sexuality aren't credible, then we're losing it. That's appropriation, that's stealing. Do I expect Kinsey to have quoted every Indigenous person in the first book on male sexuality? No. But I think what that did was just—I don't want to say rendered us invisible—it invalidated ways of knowing beyond itself. And it made it harder for us to see ourselves. I'm not confused about Indigenous sexuality or gender at all. I think it makes so much sense. The attempt to understand Indigenous masculinities in a Western theory, such as this, is hard because the measures, or the tools, still don't do it justice.

CHANGING THE SCRIPT

A CONVERSATION WITH WARREN CARIOU AND ALISON CALDER

HE WAS PARTICULARLY SKILLFUL AT PLAYING THIS ROLE WHEN HE HAD AN AUDIENCE
OF NEWS REPORTERS, WHO LOVED TO THINK OF HIM AS A NOBLE SAVAGE.... IT ALWAYS
AMAZED ME THAT THOSE SAME REPORTERS ASSUMED I MUST BE WHITE, JUST BECAUSE
I WORE SUITS AND DROVE A NEW CAR. MAYBE IT'S LIKE VINCE USED TO SAY, PERCEPTION
IS REALITY. WHATEVER THE PEOPLE THINK YOU ARE, THAT'S WHAT YOU BECOME.
—WARREN CARIOU, "THE SHRINE OF BADGER KING"

*13 OCTOBER 2010
Conversation among
Warren Cariou, Alison
Calder, and Sam
McKegney at the Wykham
House Pub at Mount
Royal University, where
Warren, Alison, and
Sam were all presenting
as part of the Under
Western Skies: Climate,
Culture, and Change in
Western North America
conference.*

SAM MCKEGNEY: In *Lake of the Prairies* you reflect on being a writer as a way of continuing your father's stories in written form. Do you perceive there to have been a gendered element of that instruction process?

WARREN CARIOU: Yeah. Certainly, very early on, I pretended to write down his stories as if I was some scribe, even before I knew how to write. And so, I was always really con-

WARREN CARIOU (Métis) and ALISON CALDER (English Canadian) are writers and professors of English at University of Manitoba in Winnipeg. Warren was born and raised in Meadow Lake, Saskatchewan, which features prominently in his memoir *Lake of the Prairies: A Story of Belonging* (Anchor Canada, 2003). He is also author of *The Exalted Company of Roadside Martyrs: Two Novellas* (Coteau Books, 1999) and writer/director of the film *Land of Oil and Water* (2009). He has written numerous articles on the study of Indigenous literatures and holds a Canada Research Chair in Narrative, Community, and Indigenous Cultures. Alison was born in England and grew up in Saskatoon. In collaboration with Jeanette Lynes, she published *Ghost Works: Improvisation in Letters and Poems* (Jackpine Press, 2007). Her poetry collection *Wolf Tree* (Coteau Books, 2008) was a finalist for the Gerald Lampert Memorial Award and won the Aqua Books Lansdowne Prize for Poetry.

1. One of two novellas in *The Exalted Company of Roadside Martyrs.*

scious of the wonder, the power of stories, but also how evanescent they are, how transient they are, so that was my focus. I wanted to preserve these. Part of it was because I felt like I was not the same kind of personality as my dad. I wasn't that larger-than-life, very social character. I always felt more withdrawn. And I still wanted to be like that, but I thought the only way I could manage being that gregarious was I could write, so it was like second-best, you know? At times I would think about it consciously as trying to carry on Dad's legacy in some way. So I don't know if I think about it as a gendered thing, per se, but as a very personal carrying on of what I learned from him. Not just the information I learned, but the ways of telling stories.

ALISON CALDER: But you are the oldest as well, so it may not necessarily be a gendered thing but just the fact that you were the first, and more sophisticated than your younger siblings, who also got the stories but didn't become writers.

WC: Certainly some of my aunts were very good storytellers, but it was more of a male thing to do in the family. It was kind of a pastime with all the many brothers my dad had. Fourteen kids in the family, I think nine brothers, so their male bonding was actually storytelling. But the women would be there, at times, tossing in their versions, as well.

AC: But the bullshitting is really a male thing in your family.

SM: [*Laughter*] I love the scenes of the competitiveness, the good-natured ribbing that goes along with storytelling. Because storytelling isn't always a way of ensuring the belonging of others, it's also a way of potentially excluding others.

WC: Teasing was certainly a major part of my relationship with my aunts and uncles on that side of the family, as well—with them and with each other. There is a certain othering element to teasing, but I think it's actually a performance of, not welcoming exactly, but sort of bringing a person in. I know when I'm in an Aboriginal community, if I'm not being teased, I think there's a problem. Once you're being teased, you've been welcomed in a certain way.

SM: Let's talk about "The Shrine of Badger King"[1] then for a second, which speaks to the desire for forms of male behaviour that can be acknowledged as legitimate by others. I think of Kenny and the Badger King as going in very different directions but each seeking validation of his manhood. Were those concerns you were intentionally exploring or did they just come out organically in the story?

WC: Yeah, that's a good point. I guess one of the things that I was thinking about when I was writing that story was the sort of rough-and-tumble place I grew up. It was a violent place in a lot of ways. It was a place that you had to either—especially if you were visibly Aboriginal—you had to be tough to survive that. And so the story has this one character, the politician, Kenny, who is tough in a certain way, right? And he is also a big guy and can defend himself, but he can pass. He's Métis, but he can pass as white. I wanted to explore that relationship to violence, and so Badger King becomes more a rebel, violent character but Kenny, there's a violence about him that becomes more sublimated but in fact becomes more serious—in a way, it's almost murderous. Whereas Badger, I think, he's not been co-opted into that colonial system as Kenny has. And so, he's a rebel, but he's not murderous in the same way that Kenny is. That's my take on it from a very great distance now. Anyway, so just to get back to your question, I was just thinking about the place of violence in a town like mine, if those guys grew up in a town like Meadow Lake, then they would have had to come to terms with a certain kind of masculine violence and sort of perform in order to survive.

SM: At one point in the story, Vince claims that perception creates reality: "Whatever the people think you are, that's what you become" (18–19). How do outsider expectations of Indigenous men inform the spectrum of possibilities for self-identifying?

WC: Yeah, I think that statement was one of the germs of the story. When I actually worked in government for a couple years, the "perception is reality" thing was something that politicians talked about. But I started thinking about that in much more personal terms, as well. Certainly, self-perception is hugely important: how we think about how we interact with the world. But what that story is about is our perceptions about how other people perceive us. How we *think* other people perceive us. That has a huge impact on how we interact with the world. So Badger King, when he is talking to reporters, he thinks that they want a particular kind of guy, and he performs that and then he gets the benefits from it. Kenny performs a different kind of identity and gets benefits from that, too.

So I guess in terms of masculinity, very often I think the violent exchanges between men that I witnessed growing up are not about the two guys, but it's about the people around them—it's about performing for what people expect, "Hey, this is what I'm supposed to do." So the sense that they are all sort of actors, that is certainly something that I saw growing up. It's about the performance of expectations and playing out a kind of script because you don't really know what else to do in the situation.

SM: And the question that arises, of course, becomes how does one change the script?

WC: That story, "The Shrine of Badger King," it doesn't really break out. The two remain enemies even beyond the grave. Kenny can never let go of that. And if he could, maybe he would be able to be a better person. So I think in a way the story really is an allegory of that inability to let go of the revenge fantasy that is part of his childhood, his initiation into manhood, in a way. But how to change the script? Well, I like to think there are ways of imaginatively reconstructing interactions so that the expectation that everyone has of young men—especially young Aboriginal men—is no longer that they're supposed to beat the hell out of each other. I don't know if some imaginative literature is going to do that, or whether people just being asked to examine the implications of what the script does in people's lives, maybe that's enough to start making change. I'm not entirely sure. I still see some of the same stuff back home when I go there, although it's not as directly racialized now. It isn't white kids against Native kids. But I think there's still as sense of—whether it's Indigenous or not—masculine need to prove oneself through violence. I definitely still see that there.

AC: Do you think these scripts of masculinity are very specific to particular places? You and Sam appear to be having a rational discussion here and not likely to break into fisticuffs. (You never know!) We were talking before about how when we go back to Meadow Lake and see guys that Warren went to high school with who stayed in Meadow Lake and never left, they look like they're about twenty years older than Warren; just physiologically, they're altered. And they've obviously been living very different lives and fulfilling very different trajectories that mark themselves on them. I guess what I was saying was, are scripts different in different places?

WC: Certainly in the world that I inhabit in the university, that's different for sure. I think that there are definitely going to be places in Winnipeg, say, where that script is pretty much the same. Whether that's class inflected or race inflected, it may well be. But yes, I think to a certain degree, it is place dependent, but the places are also marked by class and race in ways that affect the dynamic too.

SM: You note in your critical work that despite the complex and conflicted nature of most people's histories, society pressures us to efface that complexity. What's at stake in that erasure?

WC: No one likes to feel that they have been pigeonholed. We all want everyone else's identity to be simple, and we want our own to be complex. A lot of the work that I've done is about examining—whether it's my own ancestry in particular, or Métis ancestry in general—the ways in which it's important to maintain a sense of the complexity of it. Not only because that's important to the understanding of Métis identity, but it's actually important to the understanding of all identities. The fact of Métis hybridity, in a sense, points to the constructedness of all racialized identities. We're all hybrid in some ways, and we just have these labels attached to an identity that then start to take on validity and normalcy, or a normalizing quality. So I think acknowledging the complexity of my own ancestry, or of another Métis writer's ancestry that I'm talking about, is important for thinking about what race actually is and how it's constructed. So, something that I'm interested in is how your identity is not even fully present to you at any point in time, and is maybe never fully present to you. It's something that could be contingent on discoveries you make in the future.

We take other people's word for it, where we come from. We weren't there! So all our identities are malleable in that way. We are a product of our ancestors obviously, but they're a product of us too, because of how we think about them and accept stories about them, and what they are and what they are not. All racialized identities are a product of self-invention and contingency much more than we like to admit.

SM: Why can't we stomach that fluidity in others that we desire for ourselves?

WC: I think that comes back to changing the script of the story of male masculinity, and masculinity and violence. When I went into a bar as a young guy, I expected all the other guys to be ready for a fight, and they all expected me and everybody else to be as well. We didn't necessarily want to be the one doing the fighting, but we expected everyone else was going to be. It's all so much about what other people are thinking: not what you think, but what you think other people think.

SM: Do you consider identity to affected substantially by mobility? Moving from a small place like Meadow Lake to an urban centre, do you see yourself as belonging in Winnipeg in a way that is similar to the way you feel about Meadow Lake?

WC: No. It's a bit strange for me now, because I've been away from Meadow Lake for so long that I don't exactly feel like I belong there either. But I feel it a lot more there than I do in Winnipeg. I could never live in Meadow Lake, and I know that I never would. Socially I don't think it would ever work. But somehow I still feel much more connected there than I do to Winnipeg, or to any place I've ever lived. Alison's horrified.

AC: I'm not moving to Meadow Lake, I can tell you that much. But you're probably more at home at the cabin than you are in town now.

WC: My mom has moved away from the farm. I had a very, very powerful connection to the farm. But now when we go back, she's living in a condo in town. It's fine, I don't mind going there, but I don't have the same connection to it, because it's a place I didn't know when I was growing up. But we still have our cabin. It's about thirty or forty miles north of town. So that's the place I connect to more now. But I go back, and it's interesting. They teach *Lake of the Prairies* in the high school there now. So people know me, but I don't know them. This younger generation knows me as a writer from Meadow Lake who now lives in the city. So, it's not like I can go back there and fit in and fully belong there either. But, in my own imagination I guess, that is still the place I am most connected to.

SM: How does it feel to have your work read by high school students? Can a book like that actually encourage youth to think critically about the scripts they've inherited?

WC: I never thought that the book would ever be taught in a high school, because I thought there was too much violence and too much swearing, but I guess times have changed. On one hand, knowing how kids feel about books they're required to read, there's going to be a whole generation of kids in Meadow Lake who are going to hate

IT'S ALL SO MUCH ABOUT WHAT OTHER PEOPLE ARE THINKING: NOT WHAT YOU THINK, BUT WHAT YOU THINK OTHER PEOPLE THINK.

me now. [*Laughter*] But thinking about changing the script, I'm hoping that maybe the book will help people to negotiate that really difficult divide that I saw in town when I was growing up. I think the divide is not as strong as it was when I was growing up, that sense of racial division. I think also maybe some of the things about masculinity, but there's not a lot of that in the book. One scene where I talk about this is the stampede, and it's sort of interesting for me to imagine the kids reading that. Not only was Meadow Lake a very racist community when I was growing up, but it was also a very homophobic community. And at that time—it would have been the late nineties—I was sort of an insider and an outsider at the same time. I went out to the stampede and I recognized everything and I knew a lot of people, but they didn't know me. That was the first time that had happened. And as I was leaving I heard some kids laughing, and I didn't know what it was all about. And then I heard one of them say, "Oh, he's a fag anyways." I didn't even know if it was about me. But when I got to my car, I found out that they had sprayed BBQ sauce all over it. So they were stomping on packages of BBQ sauce, and then they had said "He's a fag anyways." That was their word for outsider.

AC: I'm sure it didn't have anything to do with gayness, really.

WC: No, in a way it doesn't. But that was their default term for a person who doesn't fit in. So there was a deep homophobia embedded in that. It was so embedded that people didn't even really think of it as a sexual term. It was just for somebody who's an outsider. So for me, thinking about kids reading that, hopefully it will make them think about that.

AC: I'm thinking about masculinity and economics, or masculinity and money. Different practices of masculinity are permitted by the money you have. Like when Bron [Taylor][2] asked his question at the talk this evening about why aren't there blockades up in Fort Chip [Fort Chipewyan]? Well, there's nothing to blockade, there's no main highway there. And people in Fort Chip can't afford to do that. They would have to go somewhere else to put up a blockade.

WC: It costs like $400 to fly there, right?

AC: They would have to pay a huge amount of money to get out of the community and support themselves when they're away to engage in that kind of warrior behaviour, and it's just not possible for them to do that, so they can't follow that model. I'm also thinking about means of production governing expressions of masculinity. So masculinity in traditional cultures is different than masculinity in post-capitalist culture. If you're out on the land working a trapping line, you're not getting into fights in bars; ideas of masculine power are different—power and expertise. So what's of value is not your ability to beat people up or make money, but your ability to trap and fish and survive, and engage in a kind of subsistence.

2. Bron Taylor, author of *Dark Green Religion: Nature Spirituality and the Planetary Future* (University of California Press, 2010), was among the keynote speakers at the conference we were attending. He had attended the film screening of *Land of Oil and Water* and had asked a series of questions of Warren during the Q & A that followed, including a question about what he saw as a lack of activist responses to invasive resource extraction in northern Indigenous communities.

WC: Some of the culture of violence in Indigenous masculinity has to do with a sense of powerlessness among the men. It's certainly something Maria Campbell writes about in *Halfbreed*. The men get into fights because the people they really want to fight—the colonial powers—they can't get at them. They're not there.

AC: And it also leads, of course, to violence against women and children.

WC: Yeah, exactly. I think that's a pretty clear part of the script. There's a sense of powerlessness and a sense that your life is dictated in so many ways. And the only way to fight that is to fight against another guy who is equally trapped.

While you were getting drinks, Alison was saying that—in her version of psychoanalyzing me—that I was working through versions of Aboriginal masculinity, or Métis masculinity anyways, in "The Shrine of Badger King" story. Near the end, you get this figure of Kenny who is the so-called successful Métis man, but he's a sellout. He's become a suit. And there are so many representations of that that you see in Aboriginal communities. There are people, and they are mostly men, who are profitting from the system, and basically, in a sense, enacting a form of colonialism on their own people. And I think Kenny represents that in some ways in the story. Whereas Badger represents a more, sort of...

AC: Primal? For lack of a better word.

WC: Yeah. Uncontrollable anyway. An irrepressible version that is not necessarily that pretty, but for me, as a writer trying not to identify too much with one character or another, you still have to sort of cheer for him, because he represents something that is not that smooth or sort of colonized version of Aboriginal masculine identity.

AC: It's interesting, in Warren's family, his dad had thirteen brothers and sisters, and his dad was one of the younger ones. The men in the family, and possibly the women, seemed to have particular roles. It was the job of the older male siblings to be labourers, to get money to improve the lot of the younger ones. They worked at generally low-paying or very dangerous jobs.

WC: One of them was killed actually, working on a construction site.

AC: I didn't know that.

WC: Jules.

AC: So they gave at least a part of their wages to support Warren's dad going to university, and then when Warren's dad became a lawyer, members of the family would often—this is my interpretation, anyways—come back asking for money or asking for support in various ways. Ray was always financing various things, and invariably losing his shirt in various ways. The interpretation of Widdowson and Howard[3] would be that

THE CULTURE OF VIOLENCE IN INDIGENOUS MASCULINITY HAS TO DO WITH A SENSE OF POWERLESSNESS AMONG THE MEN.... THE MEN GET INTO FIGHTS BECAUSE THE PEOPLE THEY REALLY WANT TO FIGHT— THE COLONIAL POWERS—THEY CAN'T GET AT THEM.

3. In the paper I delivered earlier that day at the conference, entitled "'*below the poverty line but... above the Arctic Circle*': Carceral Composition, Inuit Critical Autobiography, and the Environmental Decimation of the North," I had sought to deconstruct some of the arguments made in Frances Widdowson and Albert Howard's *Disrobing the Aboriginal Industry: The Deception Behind Indigenous Cultural Preservation* (Montreal: McGill-Queen's University Press, 2008).

that's a problem. The problem is that greedy relatives are coming for handouts all the time, rather than seeing it in terms of kinship structure, which is sort of a cooperative exercise where people contribute various amounts to the pool, and then that pool is redistributed as need be, I guess. Like, your uncle supporting your dad going to university is like an investment, which then pays back to him.

WC: Yeah, seeing it as a reciprocal generosity rather than a hapless idea of investment, would be more appropriate in a way. Certainly you see that in Aboriginal communities all the time, in families all the time. The Aboriginal scholars that I know, they are supporting huge families in a way that non-Native scholars definitely aren't normally doing.

AC: Which also re-conceptualizes the idea of masculinity, at least in this case. As the provider: how do you provide for your family? Well, I provide for my family by supporting you to go to university, so that you will then provide for me in the future, as opposed to providing for your wife and kids in that narrow way, acquiring individual wealth. It's more familial.

SM: And even the idea of accumulation as somehow part and parcel of what progress entails—that human societies are hard-wired to want to accumulate—I think we should interrogate that. And ultimately if you think of the reciprocal generosity that we've been talking about, that's a way of facilitating the well-being of a large group, which in an evolutionary perspective makes the most sense. What doesn't make sense in an evolutionary perspective is for me to carry as much as I can, so that everyone else is screwed.

WC: This reminds me—and I write about this a little bit in *Lake of the Prairies*—the sort of male bonding of going hunting when I was growing up. I was a terrible hunter, and my dad had great patience with me. I have very little desire to go hunting now, but there was something about that activity that was... it was a collective thing, even though each person has their own gun. But, especially when you're hunting deer, you can't pick up on your own very well. So there was this idea that this was something that we were all doing. If we went out hunting geese and got six geese, those were divided among everyone, they were a communal accomplishment, even if one person shot all six of those geese.

As I've said, my father was not a violent person, and I think he provided a good model of how you can be in the world. And he dealt with conflict all the time. Because he was a small-town lawyer, people hated him and people loved him. He had either sent someone to jail or saved someone from jail, so he evoked strong reactions all the time. He spoke his mind about things and would not back down, and he was not physically violent at all in any way that I ever saw. So I think he provided a very good example of how you could be in this place, which was at the time a violent community, and not partake of violence. He was threatened many times, and I didn't know at that time, but I was also part of these threats sometimes. Someone mailed him a photo of me with a

IF WE WENT OUT HUNTING GEESE AND GOT SIX GEESE, THOSE WERE DIVIDED AMONG EVERYONE, THEY WERE A COMMUNAL ACCOMPLISHMENT, EVEN IF ONE PERSON SHOT ALL SIX OF THOSE GEESE.

bullet hole through my head. Crazy things like that! As a result of his position in the community, those kinds of things happened. He was much more prone to using humour than violence, and I think that was something that I learned from him. Growing up I was always aware of the threat of violence, but I wasn't thrilled about it, and there were ways to defuse it.

AC: Do you want to talk about religion in relation to masculinity? Your dad was originally supposed to be a priest, then he "fell" and became a lawyer instead. He went profane rather than sacred. [*Laughter*] But I was wondering how religion, whether it's traditional Aboriginal religions, or Catholicism, or Buddhism, or whatever, might feature into ideas of what it is to be an Indian man.

WC: My dad was very Catholic, I would say, and as a young man, as Alison said. The reason that all the siblings devoted their energy and money to him going to university wasn't because they thought he was going to become a lawyer, but because he was supposed to be a priest. Their mother was incredibly Catholic and that was something I think she felt: one of her children had to become a priest and that's the way it was. Dad was sort of nominated, and I think he wanted to be as well. And obviously the role of a priest is a very different kind of masculinity as well, right? I don't know what changed Dad's mind exactly, because by the time he met Mum he was already in law school, so it wasn't like she tempted him away from the priesthood or anything.

The Catholic religion is very strict and the roles are very rigidly assigned, and I think probably my uncles and aunts grew up with a sense, a very strong sense, that there was a destiny for them, that they were expected to do certain things. My grandmother, she was an amazing woman, but one of her shortcomings was that she judged her children very much, especially the females. I think some of my aunts had real problems coming to terms with that. One of my aunts, who has now passed away, was sort of nominated, I think by their mother, to be the one who would take care of my grandma when she got old. That was to be her destiny. My grandmother was an incredible matriarch, and she really did lay down the law. She raised fourteen kids by herself, so she had to be a strong personality. So on the one hand, she portrayed this role, this incredibly powerful feminine figure; at the same time, she was, I think, dictating roles in a lot of ways. I don't think any of them really rebelled against that until after she was gone. Maybe I'm exaggerating that, but I think there was a sense that her word was law. I guess her role was, in a sense, a more traditionally masculine one in some ways.

SM: Intriguingly, in the way you're representing it, it kept a very traditional notion of the masculine and feminine intact, and at the same it was portraying a very powerful feminine voice, an oversight that militated against the roles that were being delineated for others.

WC: Yeah. It was almost like Queen Elizabeth I. Sort of female, except in so far as she was ruling. In that way she was male. [*Laughter*]

FIGHTING SHAME THROUGH LOVE

A CONVERSATION WITH DANIEL HEATH JUSTICE

14 FEBRUARY 2011 Conversation between Daniel Heath Justice and Sam McKegney in Sam's office at Queen's University in Kingston, Ontario.

INDIGENOUS NATIONHOOD IS MORE THAN SIMPLE POLITICAL INDEPENDENCE OR THE EXERCISE OF A DISTINCTIVE CULTURAL IDENTITY; IT'S ALSO AN UNDERSTANDING OF A COMMON SOCIAL INTER-DEPENDENCE WITHIN THE COMMUNITY, THE TRIBAL WEB OF KINSHIP RIGHTS AND RESPONSIBILITIES THAT LINK THE PEOPLE, THE LAND, AND THE COSMOS TOGETHER IN AN ONGOING AND DYNAMIC SYSTEM OF MUTUALLY AFFECTING RELATIONSHIPS. —DANIEL HEATH JUSTICE, "GO AWAY, WATER!"

SAM MCKEGNEY: What influences were most significant to your maturation and development as a Cherokee man, and how have those influences informed your critical sensibilities as a scholar and a creative writer?

DANIEL HEATH JUSTICE: Really, it was my parents more than anything and then radiating circles of influence beyond that. But I grew up as my dad's youngest child and my mom's only. My mom's his fourth wife. They've been together forty-two years now, forty-three years—a long time. And they had been married seven years before they had me, so I'm my mom's only, my dad's baby, and so I have all of the flawed personality traits of an only child and the youngest child.

SM: [*Laughter*]

DHJ: I was very spoiled. I like to say I was spoiled with love. And I was, I really had a pretty Edenic childhood—with my parents. Outside of that, I didn't have much of a social circle in school, and I was bullied quite a bit. But my folks were and continue to be wonderful and completely supportive. Doesn't mean that there weren't issues—my dad was a very heavy alcoholic until I was six, when he quit drinking, and then we had mortgaged our house so my mom could have a restaurant. Four years later we lost the restaurant and lost the house, so we kind of bounced from house to house for a while and it caused a lot of strain in my parents' relationship. And I kind of became my mom's emotional support because my dad was not a particularly supportive husband at the time. He's since become very sweet and loving. So it was a vexed relationship in that way, but my folks were always really loving and supportive to me—there was never a time when I didn't feel loved at home.

And they were very encouraging of my nerdiness and my love of books. I would go hunting with my dad and I'd lean up against a tree with a novel and read, and he was good with that. You know, I had my rifle; I'd know if there was an elk coming, and being part of the hunt was my responsibility. So we adapted; we adapted some of these masculinist pursuits for my nerdy fantasies. And I spent a lot of time outdoors with my dad and then indoors with my mom. My mom's not a very physically active kind of person. So I had a really nice mix of two different spheres. Out in the woods with my dad, domestically with my mom. But my mom is the dominant personality in the household. She's a tough woman. I learned very early about the strength of women and sometimes what that costs them. My mom had to always be strong even when she didn't necessarily want to be because my dad wouldn't necessarily...he wasn't always emotionally available to her. My dad is a very good man but he worked only when he wanted to, which wasn't all the time, so she supported him a lot. Now his memory is that he was this great provider, but my mom and me, we have a different memory. He'd spend his money on his own stuff and mom would spend her money on groceries and food, or groceries and clothes, and medical bills and whatever. So in terms of coming to a sense of self, there were a lot of things I admired about both of my folks. There were also things I didn't want to replicate about both of them. And my mom at the time—it wasn't diagnosed—but my mom has depressive tendencies, and after we lost the house and restaurant, she really spiralled into deep depression, which caused a lot of anxiety for me because I was her primary emotional support. I was a pre-teen trying to be supportive of a very depressed and very unhappy mother, who I'm very close to.

DANIEL HEATH JUSTICE is a Colorado-born Canadian citizen of the Cherokee Nation. He is the author of *Our Fire Survives the Storm: A Cherokee Literary History* (University of Minnesota Press, 2006) and numerous critical essays in the field of Indigenous literary studies. With James Cox, he is the co-editor of *The Oxford Handbook of Indigenous American Literature* (Oxford, 2013). He's also the author of the Indigenous epic fantasy novel *The Way of Thorn and Thunder: The Kynship Chronicles* (University of New Mexico Press, 2011). He is currently chair of First Nations Studies at University of British Columbia.

But I always—*always*—felt loved at home. My folks were so supportive of all my idiosyncrasies and my fantasy worlds. And although we didn't have very much, I never went without, not really. Had I been my oldest half brother, who was raised when my dad was very much an alcoholic, it would have been a very different situation. He had a very different childhood than I did. My dad was the town drunk when my brother Gifford was being raised. And he remembers coming to the bar to collect Dad, and Dad just really not doing well. And my dad was a binge drinker, so he wouldn't drink for a while, but when he would he would be drinking until he was heaving blood. So at twelve years old, Gifford had to start fending for himself and looking after both himself and our dad. Dad raised him, while his ex-wife, his first wife, raised the other two kids. So, when I was coming along, my brother, who was an officer in the U.S. Navy at the time, thought that I was not the kind of man I should be. So, actually the only judgment I had in terms of my masculinity was my brother. And I always thought that my dad loved Gifford more than me, because Gifford would come home once or twice a year and it was always a big production and everything would be put on hold for Gifford's week and then he was gone. So for a long time I thought that Gifford was the kind of man Dad wanted me to be. Well, Dad never said that, Dad never implied that. But he didn't see Gifford much and he has a lot of guilt about the kind of life Gifford had as a child. So I tried to kind of be a cool guy when Gifford was home but it just didn't work. And so Gifford and I have always had a very vexed relationship. I mean, he insisted that Mom was going to turn me into a fag [*Laughter*], being so close to my mom. Well, you know. With my folks it was great but beyond that I was always facing kind of a critical audience about how I wasn't masculine enough…

So, my sense of self came from having a really good home foundation but also a critical and forthright home foundation. We've always been a bluntly honest family about most things. So Mom would say, "I love your daddy a lot, but I don't want you to be like him in this way." And I could kind of see that on her side, too. Like I would see how depressed she was and I didn't want to be so worked up and hyper-obsessed about things. You always inherit things from your folks even when you're trying not to, and I tend to worry about things like she does and I wish I didn't.

And when I came out, that was probably the hardest time for me and my mom. I was twenty-four, I think, when I actually came out to her. It was hard. But even then, I never felt like she didn't love me. We spent a lot of time crying; she was very angry. She had just lost her dad not too long before then, and then I came out in a not particularly thoughtful way, and so I didn't know until a while afterwards that she was a little suicidal over this, which of course was a burden, but we worked through it. My dad and I have never talked about me being gay. We've never said the word. Although he knows that Kent and I are married. Kent comes home, and he and Dad get along incredibly well. Dad gave him a rifle for Christmas because he's part of the family now and they're really cute together. They have a lot of fun. So there's no question about who I am, but it's just not—my dad is twenty-one years older than my mom as well, so he's eighty-two, that's just not within his vocabulary. For him, a gay man has a particular image that his son who shoots and hunts and stuff doesn't fit. Even if I'm kinda fey in other ways, the fact that I know how to shoot, and you know, clean game and do all this stuff, doesn't quite fit the fag, you know? [*Laughter*]

SM: You've mentioned to me before about the different religious journeys in your mom's life… do you think she read your coming out in a causal way? Did she endorse your brother's interpretation that closeness with her had turned you gay?

DHJ: A little bit. One thing about my mom is she's not a homophobe. She had a lot people she was close to who were gay. But I'm her baby. I'm her only child. I was her only shot at grandkids, right? [*Laughter*] So I get it, I get why it was so hard for her. And I came out really casually over the phone, which didn't give her much of a chance to process things face to face, which was really our main way of dealing with difficult things. Part of it was, she was also the black sheep of her family. She was the second of seven kids, the oldest girl, and her mother was incredibly emotionally and physically violent to her. I was the first grandchild and when I was very young, my grandmother and mother had reconciled, and I would be visiting and my grandmother would say, "You're spoiling that child. The way you're treating him, he's going to be a serial killer by the time he's fifteen." She constantly judged me as deficient, in large part because I was my mom's child. I was good at school, so I kind of became the success story that helped my mom redeem herself with her own mother. She always saw herself as this failure because she didn't go to college, even though she was brilliant and courageous and had an amazing work ethic. But, to her, she felt like she was judged less negatively because she at least produced this son who was academically accomplished and was going to school and doing well and then became a professor and all this stuff. So I was seen as her greatest success and then, all of a sudden, to have the people who had judged her all her life say, "Aha!"

Later on, when things were a bit better, we had a pretty profound moment: she was talking with me and said, "You know, I've been in male-dominated jobs all my life, and I had to be twice as good as a man to be considered half as accomplished. And I always thought that yours was going to be an easier road. But now, no matter how good you are, no matter what you do, you're still going to be just another fucking faggot to a lot of people." And that really… that devastated her. And she wasn't saying that I was a "fucking faggot" to her, but she had been the victim of so much sexism in her life and she fought it; she didn't want me to have to fight like she did. And yet, that was what happened. So that was really hard for her.

It was her older brother Dan who kind of got her head around this because she just broke down into tears and she told him I was gay—and he's always been a good man to me—but he just let her cry for a while, and then he finally said, "Kath, 90 percent of the world is going to be against that boy all his life. Whose side do you want to be on?" And it was just kind of like, "Oh!" And that's all it took. It was like, "Oh yeah, my son's, damn it!" The one way to get her out of the dumps is to stoke her fighting spirit, and that's what it took to bring us close again.

SM: It was interesting for me to hear about the ways in which your family was able to adapt to different circumstances. For instance, you were talking about hunting with your dad but taking the time with your books; that was participatory and I guess reciprocal on your father's part to enable the space while maintaining the integrity of the relationship or what the event was seeking to accomplish. And it strikes me how that resonates with your critical work, particularly on expansive kinship and ethics of inclusivity, and I'm wondering if you might think aloud about how that model functions in terms of adaptability.

DHJ: I haven't really thought about it in that way, but just honouring who people are and making space for them to be who they are in different circumstances, without disrupting everyone else's experience—because part of it too was, yeah, I was reading but I was also hunting and I had responsibilities as a hunter. So when the elk were coming down, you stand up, you do your job. So there's space but you're also there as part of another thing, so it's a balance: you honour people's integrity, but you're also honouring what's bringing you together.

From the time I was very young, my mom decided I was going to be self-sufficient as much as possible. So she taught me how to cook; she taught me how to do laundry; she taught me how to clean. Even early on, when she had her restaurant, my first job at twelve was washing dishes, one hour a day, six days a week. That's a lot of work for a twelve-year-old kid. And then every year, it was one hour more until we lost the restaurant four years later, and then I was ready to work for other people. So yes, it was non-coercive, but I was trained to be accountable up until that point. It's not enough just to be non-coercive, you have to train people to be sufficient and independent and able to do their work and then you can be really hands-off because they know what's expected.

SM: Were there many Indigenous people at your school or in the community in Victor?

DHJ: No. As far as I know—there could have been some others—we're one of two Native families from the area. Um, maybe three. But it was primarily white. There were some folks of Mexican-American heritage, but it was primarily a poor rural white community. It's also a tourist area, so there's kind of a summer middle-class population. In Cripple Creek, the next town over, six miles over, that's where I went to school. Cripple Creek was the place with the name, with the touristy thing. That's where the moneyed people lived, and Victor was where all the poor folks—the supposed trashy folks— lived. I lived in Victor. So there was class distinction there. But even the pretty well-off folks would have only been solidly middle class in other places. No, I'm pretty sure we were pretty much the only Indians.

SM: And was there stigma attached to being one of the only Indian families?

DHJ: No. No. It was a kind of interesting situation. Class was more of an issue up there, at least for us. Dad was just a good old boy, and still is. He's just a much older good old boy. So yeah, he was the Indian. But people never really—my dad's a short man and a very slender man, but people wouldn't have said much to him about it. I mean, he dealt with some of that stuff when we'd go outside of town, a little bit, but nothing, nothing in town. There might have been more of it when Mom and Dad first got together. She was eighteen and he was thirty-nine—three times divorced, alcoholic, Cherokee truck driver. But a lot of that just had to do with "He's thirty-nine. She's eighteen." Well, she was seventeen when they first actually met. He thought she was in her twenties. And she pursued him. Once he found out how old she was, he tried to get away from her. And she said, "I'm gonna be your last wife, one way or another."

But what's interesting is that I had internalized a lot of anti-Indian stigma that wasn't even from the community around me, but just from popular culture. When I was about three, my dad—there was a friend of his that was Lakota, a truck driver who came to visit. And I guess—I don't remember any of this, this is the story my parents tell—we were at a restaurant, it wasn't even in that town, it was in another city my parents were living in before they moved back to my mom's hometown. But we were at breakfast with this Lakota guy and the whole time I was glaring at him—'cause he was very phenotypically Native. My dad's dark-skinned but has a buzzcut and "not the Indian you have in mind" kind of thing. But I was glaring at this Lakota guy through the whole meal, just with absolute hate, and Mom knew I was going to say something—I was always a very verbal child. But she couldn't very well spank me *before* I said anything! So she was going to take me to the bathroom to go pee, and I went over and I poked him. And I said, "Hey! My daddy doesn't like Indians." And, of course, they all started laughing and laughing and thought it was the funniest thing, and Mom said, "Your daddy *is* an Indian." And I guess I started throwing a walleyed fit in this crowded restaurant, "My daddy is not an Indian! My daddy is not an Indian!" Just screaming and crying and just horrified that my daddy was an Indian, and Mom kinda shook me and said, "Yes, he's an Indian, and that makes you an Indian, too." And I guess the story is, I kind of looked at her, snot running down my face, and I said, "I'm a little Indian boy?" Mom said, "Yes." And I said, "Oh." And I was fine. I was fine.

What interests me about that story is why at three would I have been so horrified that my father was an Indian? Three years old: I had already internalized so much anti-Indian imagery, so much anti-Indian rhetoric. You know, I knew what Indians did to little boys and their mamas. My dad loved watching Westerns, so I knew Indians killed people. They killed nice people. My daddy wasn't one of those. My daddy was a nice guy. You know, by the time I was old enough to really think about it, I had become a complete Anglophile. I wanted to be as far away from being a mixed-race Cherokee hillbilly with kinda ambiguous sexuality and gender norms. I wanted to live in the England I read about and saw on TV. I wanted to go to Oxford and wear tweed with patches and smoke a pipe and sit in oak-panelled drawing rooms and talk about big ideas with other sophisticated, cultured, civilized people. I'd watch Merchant Ivory films and just salivate, because I didn't want to be from where I was... I didn't see anything of value where I was from until I was in university. In high school, when we would have pep rallies, there would be contests, and I was always very artistic and so I was the one designated in my class to draw posters and stuff. And there were a few times our team, the CC-V Pioneers, was competing against Indian-themed teams, like the Lamar Savages or something. And I distinctly remember drawing really nasty stereotypical pictures of Indians scalping people and stuff and, in retrospect, it's just the most mortifying thing to think that I participated in that, and I did it without a second thought until I was about sixteen or seventeen and started being a little more attentive. And it really wasn't until I was about twenty that I had a bit of a turnaround, and then I sort of became an über-Indian and then I kinda pulled away from that.

SM: Born-again Indian.

DHJ: Oh God, awful! I was just awful. I hope I've become a little less obnoxious. But yeah, it wasn't really the community that was an issue that I grew up in. Yeah, there weren't any other Indians or very few Native folks, but it was popular culture that affected me.

SM: Do you think, from the images that you and I were privy to as kids, that the semiotics have really shifted in relation to Indigenous peoples? Or are children today beholden to the same regime of images?

DHJ: I think it's a bit less, well, it's less overt in terms of the cartoons. The one I always remember is just the old Bugs Bunny cartoon, which had this Indian with a huge red nose and these big black glasses. You don't see those anymore, just like you don't see those old Tom and Jerry cartoons anymore with the Mammy character. Those things have gone by the wayside, which in most ways is probably good, but I think it's a little unfortunate we don't have those more readily available to talk about and analyze; those stereotypes haven't gone away—they've just gone underground.

SM: And sometimes the invisibility of them makes them more dangerous.

DHJ: Yeah, yeah. So I think there's a better mix, but it's still the one-size-fits-all Indian. But we're back in the age of noble savages rather than ignoble savages that I grew up with. Either way, you're still seen as a dying people. But one gets to have really cool monologues and the others just howl and scream a lot. [*Laughter*]

I WANTED TO BE AS FAR AWAY FROM BEING A MIXED-RACE CHEROKEE HILLBILLY WITH KINDA AMBIGUOUS SEXUALITY AND GENDER NORMS. I WANTED TO LIVE IN THE ENGLAND I READ ABOUT AND SAW ON TV.

SM: Thinking of Chingachgook looking out over the vista.

DHJ: [*Sigh*] Yeah. Visually beautiful, philosophically bereft.

SM: Can even romanticized images be mobilized in positive ways?

DHJ: Oh, hell yeah. Yeah. I would much rather, *much* rather, have Chingachgook than the nasty, scalping, slaving Indians. It's not great; it's still a stereotype, but at least it's something with some dignity to it. And considering that Native people are so often represented as having no dignity and being so bedraggled and so debased, God, the alternative… If you only have two choices, take nobility, right?

SM: Do you view your creative work as both building from and reacting to the representational history that we're talking about?

DHJ: I think a lot of it is unconscious, that you just tell the story you want to hear. And I've always been influenced by strong women and by mountain folks and down-to-earth figures and people who kind of stand between the spaces and inhabit multiple worlds. So those are the kind of characters that I write about. The ones who are the standard heroes—I think of *The Lord of the Rings* and *The Lord of the Rings* movies, the character who interests me the least is Aragorn. I just don't care. [*Laughter*] I don't care about the King trying to get back to his throne. I don't care. I'm much more interested in the weird homosociality of the hobbits, the fey beauty and elegance of the elves. I mean, I'm more interested in these other figures who are more compelling in their complexity. So part of it is intent: wanting to be very complex in the kinds of characters I write about and the kind of narrative I deal with, but part of it… this would be the story I would write because those are the stories I want to read more of.

SM: The relationship between Tarsa, as female protagonist, and Shakar, as a complex female villain in *The Way of Thorn and Thunder*… I think of it as being quite significant given the history of non-Native depictions of indigeneity focussing on the hypermasculine through almost the erasure of womanhood from Indigenous communities. Why do you focus on those sources of power in the community?

DHJ: I think they were just interesting characters, right? But I don't think I can get away without mentioning that Tarsa was my first gaming character playing *Dungeons and Dragons*. Tarsa and Tobhi both were my gaming characters. So was Denarra from the book. So these were characters I inhabited. When I was a kid, I pretended to be a woman all the time. I'd play *Super Friends* and I was Wonder Woman or Batgirl. I'd play *Masters of the Universe* and I wasn't He-Man; I was either the flamboyant and unique villains like Skeletor or, more often, I was Teela or the Sorceress or Evil-Lyn. There was just something about womanliness that really fascinated me. And also, just beauty. I loved pretty things, still love pretty things, and I wanted to be very pretty. So I think when I was going to be playing *Dungeons and Dragons*, I could pretend to be a woman and I could kind of inhabit that space.

Well, of course, in retrospect, it's a little problematic; there are all kinds of ways that can go wrong. But Tarsa was my first character and so she was a character I explored a lot of gender play through. And then Shakar was a villain from early on when this was all a game. When I was writing the novel, it had to be about Tarsa. But Tarsa had become a very different kind of figure. She'd become much more powerful, she'd become much less demure than she'd originally been. She was very demure to begin with, and now she's just a kick-butt warrior who'd kick my ass all over the room. But not in a kind of Angelina Jolie-Lara Croft-*Tomb Raider* style but a warrior-ness that is rooted in accountability in a really significant way. That was just going to be the story I was gonna write.

SM: I want to ask you about reimagining what "warrior" means, what an idea of an ethical warrior stance might be, whether that's the physical warrior in battle on behalf of community or other ways of conceptualizing the warrior. And I think of Tarsa who, as a Redthorn warrior, moves between the "Blood of War" and the "Blood of the Moon" and recognizes those as integral to one another as opposed to polar opposites (with "Blood of War" as the domain of the male and the other as the domain of the female). Can you speak a little bit about the type of warrior figure that Tarsa needs to be in that story, I guess?

DHJ: A warrior to me is somebody who fights the good fight with everything they can with love at the centre of their concern. And there are a lot of ways of doing that. Tarsa doesn't always fight out of love. Sometimes it's out of hate. But every time she fights out of hate, it's disastrous—something awful happens. When she fights with love, she's looking for a future. Anybody can fight with hate, but that sometimes presupposes a despair about what's coming. You fight with love, you're looking toward a future free of fighting, right? You fight with hate, all you see is the fight and then it becomes self-defeating. And Tarsa is not self-defeating. Tarsa's driving force at her best is love. And that's the kind of warrior she had to be. So she goes from being a blood warrior, where she has to shed blood, to becoming an advocate for peace. But even as an advocate for peace, she's a warrior. The difference is, she's looking for other alternatives and is paying attention to the particular kind of balance that peace requires. As a Redthorn, it's an immediate experience, an immediate threat that you're dealing with. The Greenthorn Guardian that she becomes the head of, these are long-term warriors, these are long-term visioners. They're about building, they're about growing things. And that's the kind of warrior that she becomes and embodies by the end.

SM: I also want to think about Tobhi as a warrior figure because in many of the battle scenes it's quite palpable what a fighter he is, what a fighter spirit he has. But he's a dif-

ANYBODY CAN FIGHT WITH HATE, BUT THAT SOMETIMES PRESUPPOSES A DESPAIR ABOUT WHAT'S COMING. YOU FIGHT WITH LOVE, YOU'RE LOOKING TOWARD A FUTURE FREE OF FIGHTING.

ferent kind of warrior figure, as well. And he doesn't fall into stereotypical masculine warrior mode in a lot of ways. And my other reading of him has always been that he is, in a way, a literary theorist. He is the one who takes the stories of the leaves and seeks to put them to use. He doesn't try to just translate their stories but rather to see their relevance by mobilizing knowledge and experience and understanding—theory. Do you see any connection between Tobhi's warrior capacity and warrior *writers*, warrior *critics*? What the intellect can do on behalf of community?

DHJ: I love that idea of Tobhi as a literary theorist! I hadn't really thought of that. I really like him as a warrior—so I'll talk about the leaves—but when gets out there and fights, he's having fun, right? And he's doing what's needed, but he also kinda just gets a kick out of it. He enjoys that kind of physical tussle. But he is not motivated by hate when he's doing this. The reason he goes on this journey to Eromar is because he's been asked by Garyn and his aunties; his clan mothers have given permission for that. He is in service to those purposes and he takes it very seriously. And that's when he learns the leaves. It's not just a love of the people, it's a love of the gift. It's a love of the stories. And he has fun with it. And he interprets, he translates, and he's playing with it to understand the story in as many ways as he can. And eventually by the end of the book the leaves are etched on his flesh, they become part of him. So he becomes the embodied story of the people.

And I think that's something that theorists can do and that writers can do: we can give back stories to people that lift them up and lift ourselves up at the same time and show possibilities that are different than the ones we are given by mainstream culture and hopefully more enriching, more exciting, more loving possibilities. It doesn't mean that we don't deal with hard things or difficult things, but we're still telling stories about people who are loveable in many cases. Or stories about people who are worth listening to. Even if they're miserable, cantankerous, unpleasant people, they're worth listening to. So giving a space for voices that are so often silenced: I think writers can be really important in that. And that's war. That's war against pop culture. That's being a warrior against this overwhelming hegemony of dysfunction and deficit; it's a long battle, but you gotta start somewhere.

SM: When you talked about Tobhi ultimately being able to embody the story, it made me think of the importance of validating embodiment and sensual experience in *The Way of Thorn and Thunder*. Can creative work—like that which celebrates the sensual—reawaken in readers their own abilities to inhabit their bodies in healthy ways?

DHJ: I think absolutely it can. Absolutely. I know that I have seen that. I've experienced that with other books I've read. One thing I wanted to make sure of—and I didn't think about it consciously at the time—but when I was going through revisions, all of the main characters who are in love relationships are people with agency. There are certainly very few references to rape and other forms of coerced, exploitative, or non-consensual sex in the book. In the Darkening Road, there's kind of a hint that the Folk, the she-Folk, are threatened by he-Folk, as well as humans, kind of human marauders. But I wanted to make sure that the majority of characters, when they are in loving relationships, they have agency, that they're not victims of somebody else. And I think that's where some of these books can be useful. When you see people who are in love and have agency and exist in different kinds of bodies... just to have those represented—diverse characters, with diverse body types, diverse abilities, in diverse kinds of relational configurations, who can find pleasure in their bodies and in the bodies of others that is not about exploitation, but about actual pleasure—that alone, I think, is helpful and beautiful.

So yeah, I think just that focus on empowering passion is enough—for some readers, it won't be for all—but for some readers who are hungry to see some alternative to the really explicit stuff you can find on the Internet or in other books. I mean, so many fantasy novels are just about explicit violence and explicit sex that has nothing to do with love, nothing to do with respect or understanding. Those things get tiresome. And I wanted stories that are about *people* gettin' it on, not just bodies.

SM: In an Indigenous context in Canada, for instance, a lot of writing has demonstrated how Eurocentric patriarchal notions of impurity and the grotesque have been coercively attached to the female body as a "potential vessel of evil." I wonder also how the male body has been stigmatized and how even the silence around the male body potentially can constitute an act of dangerous erasure. Someone like [Métis poet] Gregory Scofield's work actually celebrates the male body in various ways, but that doesn't happen very often. And often when the male body is celebrated, it's as a physical instrument of power through, you know, the speed of the runner or the warrior in action. But the sensual male body is very seldom spoken about in literature.

DHJ: And it's usually the queer male body when it is celebrated.

SM: Can literature and story and even critical theory unpack and reverse some of that stigmatization or—I don't even know if I want to use the word stigmatization because I don't know if it adequately speaks to what I've been trying to get at—but rather this elision of the sensual male body?

DHJ: What strikes me is the male body is seen as capable of and a source only of violence and harm. When that's the only model you have, what a desolation, right? When your body, the only way your maleness is or should be rendered is through violence, through harm, through corrupted power. Oh, it's just tragic. We need to see the body— the male body—as being a giver of pleasure, not just a recipient of somebody else's acts, but a source of pleasure for the self and others. Whether it's sensual pleasure or just kind of gentleness, kindness, a nice handshake rather than a crushing one. Or a pat on

WHAT STRIKES ME IS THE MALE BODY IS SEEN AS CAPABLE OF AND A SOURCE ONLY OF VIOLENCE AND HARM. WHEN THAT'S THE ONLY MODEL YOU HAVE, WHAT A DESOLATION, RIGHT?

the back or tousling someone's hair or just a touch that is not a taking touch but a giving touch. But the models of hypermasculine maleness that we get: if the male body isn't giving harm, it's taking pleasure. It's always extractive. It's either penetrative or extractive—either assaultive or extractive. One or the other, there's nothing else. And that is such a catastrophic failure of imagination, as well as a huge ethical breach. To imagine that the male body is only capable of wounding. It's crippling to the soul to imagine that your only function in life is to hurt people. So literature ought to give us alternatives.

One of the scenes I'm proudest of in the trilogy—the omnibus[1]—is the scene with Tobhi and Quill, their love scene. I love that. Tobhi's a scrapper but he's nervous when he's with his beloved. And he's made it clear: he's had sex before, this isn't his first time. We don't necessarily assume it's Quill's first time; it might be, we don't know. But he's nervous, he's scared, like guys get, you know? Even in the age of Internet porn that's just all about exploitation and really degrading treatment, guys get spooked, guys get scared and nervous and excited and want to bring pleasure. So Tobhi, he's nervous and it's Quill who guides him and she's gentle and he responds in kind. And it's a very loving moment. That's one of my favourite scenes in the whole story because it's such a tender scene, and it's a straight scene, right? I mean, I didn't write a hot queer scene with that one. It's just these two very sweet, loving people who just want... it's about giving to one another. There's nothing about taking. Or if it's taking, it's after it's been given, you know, this reciprocity. Those kinds of scenes, those kinds of stories, when we talk with other men, talk about the pleasures given rather than simply the pleasures received. Even now, I don't know if there are a lot of conversations about, "Yeah, well, the first time I made someone climax, what was that like?" No, that's not the story we often hear. We hear, "My first climax." Well, what about the first time you gave pleasure to somebody else? And that's sexual pleasure. What about the time when you hugged someone and it was exactly what they needed? That's a warrior's act, as well, to know what's needed to be done and to do it boldly and without need of response. To fight against shame through love.

1. Because this interview took place directly before the omnibus edition of *The Way of Thorn and Thunder* was slated for release, both of us were just getting used to referring to it as "the omnibus" rather than "the trilogy."

PART THREE

WISDOM

KNOWLEDGE

IMAGINATION

DEEPER THAN A BLOOD TIE

A CONVERSATION WITH ADRIAN STIMSON AND TERRANCE HOULE

*21 MARCH 2012
Conversation among
Adrian Stimson, Terrance
Houle, and Sam McKegney
at Atomica Restaurant
in downtown Kingston,
Ontario. This discussion
occurred after Stimson and
Houle delivered artists'
talks at Queen's University
and prior to their
performance at Stauffer
Library Union Gallery.*

JUST BEFORE I BECAME A FATHER, I ASKED MY DAD, "DO YOU HAVE ANY ADVICE?"
AND I HARDLY EVER GET ADVICE FROM HIM... AND HE GOES, "THREE THINGS: LISTEN
TO YOUR ELDERS. LISTEN TO YOUR KIDS. TAKE CARE OF YOUR FUCKING SHIT." AND I
LOOKED AT HIM AND I GO, "OH, THAT'S PRETTY SOLID ADVICE."—TERRANCE HOULE

SHIT WENT DOWN AND IT WAS PRETTY BAD SHIT AND YEAH, I HAVE CERTAIN
NEUROSES BECAUSE OF THAT TODAY, BUT YOU KNOW, I'M WORKING ON IT AND I'M
LIVING MY LIFE AND I'M ENJOYING IT. AND DAMN IT, TODAY WAS A GOOD DAY. THAT'S
NOT TO SAY I DON'T HAVE MY BAD MOMENTS, BUT I REFUSE TO GET CAUGHT IN THAT
WHOLE WESTERN IDEA THAT YOU HAVE TO BE A CERTAIN WAY, AND THEN AT SOME
POINT YOU WILL BE HEALED.—ADRIAN STIMSON

SAM MCKEGNEY: I'm more than happy to frame questions for you both, but obviously you two have quite the repartee with one another, so feel free to take the conversation where you think it ought to go.

TERRANCE HOULE: I like that he's gay, he likes that I'm straight.

ADRIAN STIMSON: And I hate trying to turn him because he's already there.

TH: I'm eminently turnable.

AS: Yeah, he wears his straightness on his sleeve.

TH: Exactly.

AS: I think about the way we play and how the colonial project skewed that. We were incredibly playful historically. I think about the stories my dad tells me, and I believe the lines of sexuality are always crossed—there's never anything bad about that. There never was anything bad about it because it just was what it was.

TH: You have to get back to the idea of brotherhood that was intrinsic within almost any culture. But with Native people it was always: "Everyone is your brother. Everyone is your sister. Everyone is your elder." The ideas around relationships are very different. It's deeper than a blood tie.

AS: Oh yeah, very intimate.

TH: It's emotional. Even like the idea of counting coup—there's that relationship between warrior brothers, fighting alongside each other; the idea of adoptive family, you look at Crowfoot who adopted Poundmaker. When the Indian wars were happening, there was always this mythology around the Cree and the Blackfoot being enemies. That's just not the full story. We were people that all lived together in the Prairies, and there was that unison between tribes, adoptive connections. Adrian's got like, what, three names?

AS: Yep, yep.

TH: And they're not all from Blackfoot. So your identity is known in other tribes. And even as you grow, you keep your young boy's name.

AS: One of my elders came up to me a year ago and said he really thinks I should have my grandfather's name, and it's a really powerful name and so I may get another name soon. Because he did say, "You still have a kid's name," and I need to move through that.

TH: Yeah, grow up, eh? How old are you anyways?

For me identity is always the key thing. We all got Blackfoot names in my family. If you're not recognized in your community, then how are you recognized out in the

TERRANCE HOULE is an interdisciplinary media artist and a member of the Blood (Kainai) Tribe of the Blackfoot nation. Involved with Indigenous communities all his life, Houle has travelled to reserves and reservations throughout North America participating in powwow dancing and ceremonial elements of his culture. He utilizes performance, photography, video/film, music, and painting at his discretion in his artistic work. His practice also includes tools of mass dissemination such as billboards and vinyl bus signage. His recent solo exhibitions include "The National Indian Leg Wrestling League of North America," "GIVN'R," and "Iinniiwahkiimah," the last of which involves an artistic exploration of his Blackfoot name, which translates in English to "buffalo herder."

ADRIAN STIMSON is an interdisciplinary artist from the Siksika (Blackfoot) Nation in southern Alberta whose work ranges from painting to installation to performance. He received a BFA with distinction from the Alberta College of Art and Design and an MFA from the University of Saskatchewan. His paintings include "Bison Heart" and "Tarred & Feathered Bison," which speak to ideas of punishment and identity; his installation work utilizes fragments from historical residential schools as tools of decolonization; and his performance art often incorporates his character parody of Buffalo Bill—"Buffalo Boy"—to trouble colonial notions of gender in performances like "Buffalo Boy's Wild West Peep Show," "Buffalo Boy's Getting It from the 4 Directions," and "Buffalo Boy's Battle of Little Big Horny."

1. Trooper is a Canadian rock band that gained fame in the late 1970s for songs like "Raise a Little Hell" and "We're Here for a Good Time," the latter of which contains the refrain, "We're here for a good time, not a long time."

world? My Blackfoot name, I feel like I'm slowly moving into it as a man. And I never had a childhood name. Well, I guess, my grandma always called me "a little pig," *ach-e-me*. And that still sticks. She still calls me that. That identity will always follow you through. And I was talking earlier about how Aboriginal men have lost their identity, and I know all these people that don't have Indian names. And I'm like, "Well, how does your community know you if you don't know who you are?"

AS: If you look at the transition from tribal society, rites of passage, growing up together, sharing everything, all of that was beaten out of us in the residential school era. Traditionally, as you grow and you start to become a man, you share all this stuff. You get together as groups of young men and there are things that occur within that milieu that are very natural and involve learning about and understanding your body and how it functions. I don't believe it was ever thought of as being dirty or bad. And the convoluted thing is that you enter into residential schools, where a particular morality is pushed upon you and sexuality becomes so taboo that the opposite happens and it becomes abusive. At one point it was innocent and just a natural process, all of a sudden those same things become abusive, violent, and convoluted. I hope that we're getting back to our original way of being, that we're starting to return. That's certainly what we're trying to do. To show that this play, this sexual play between a Two-Spirited man and a straight man, doesn't mean that either of us can be labelled. That it is just play with a brother, with a friend. It may look sexual but, you know, I don't really want to blow him.

ALL: [*Laughter*]

TH: He does. He does. Be honest, man.

AS: I think that those things are shifting a bit, in time. Look at the whole queer movement and gay movement and the activism there.

TH: That comes with having that strong identity within your people. Adrian and I, we have such strong identities, and we've kept such strong identities—male identities—that, like you said, it's not about gender. It's about brothers playing and this acceptance within our roles, because we're both men still.

AS: And it's interesting, I think, how sexuality evolves. At a really young age, I certainly knew that I was different, then all of a sudden I went to this age when I was very heterosexual and girl crazy, having sex with girls all the time and girlfriends.

TH: In a Trooper shirt.[1]

SM: You were here for a good time but not a long time.

AS: Absolutely! So, you know, I've tasted all the fruits in the world. No, that doesn't sound right.

TH: Very biblical.

AS: And I still have friendships with some of the women who I dated when I was a young man. And then I became bisexual and had relationships with both men and women, and now I'm exclusively homosexual. But that doesn't mean that my appreciation of women has waned or that I worry that when I find a woman attractive it goes against my queer identity. I say it's fluid. I see sexuality as fluid. Who knows? God forbid if my partner ever passed away, maybe I would end up with a woman.

TH: If that happens, we're going to the strippers.

AS: Within tribal societies sexuality was fluid and it was quite acceptable for a warrior, a man, to team up with another man for a while. And he was never looked at as being queer or gay. It was just at that particular time, he wanted to be with that person. A Cree friend told me about how there were actually societies of men who were Two-Spirited who would leave the tribe and go off together for a period of time and have one hell of a party.

TH: Guys weekend! I've never said it out loud but I've always been conscious of being contrary in my work—going against the grain, being opposite, doing opposite things—and I've always wondered if people would pick up on it. I know that Adrian picked up on it early on, and I think that's what really gelled with the work that we've done.

AS: It's interesting because we're put in the opposites of "traditional" or "contemporary." I disagree with all that. I believe that we're both traditional *and* contemporary, and that what we're doing is part of the continuum of our Blackfoot history. When people get caught up in saying, "Oh, that's not traditional," they're falling into this Western idea of labelling and dividing…

TH: …an anthro kind of thing.

AS: I see it as much more fluid in the sense that I am still doing what my ancestors did way back then. I'm still doing it here and now. And it's the continuation of that into the future that I think is exciting.

TH: The idea that traditionalism is a stop in time—like the Calgary Stampede, with the Indian Village—yeah, it's a great thing that the Stampede's kept this thing alive, but at the same time, it's caught in time.

AS: It creates a lie of a dead culture.

TH: And dealing with the male body, I always love these powwow dancers that would never wear anything but arm bands and muscle and a big belly hanging out with the chest plate up. I'm like, "Yeah, that's a real Native powwow dancer who doesn't give a shit!" My father was always like that. He'd wear his glasses whenever he danced, so that's why in my work I'm always wearing my glasses. This was back in the seventies and the eighties. Powwow's changed now. It's more glamorous. But if you go to a real traditional powwow, it's a lot more fun.

AS: Or even a sundance. You go to a sundance and the people are stripped of everything and all they have is their identity and their humility and their faith. I draw from that in my own work. It's traditional, it's contemporary. When my mother said we grew up nomadically, to me that's traditional, as opposed to just ceremonial. I mean, why can't those things change?

Having said that, I also think it's really important that there are certain practices within the culture that are still maintained and nurtured, but I look at that as being part of the continuum as well because we're taking those histories through the context of here and now. I know within my lifetime, I want to get involved in certain societies; it's a crazy fast-paced world, but you've got to make the time. That would be another continuum within my own evolving understanding of my culture through time.

TH: I've been criticized for a lot of stuff that I've done by other contemporary Aboriginal artists—people who are, like, "Oh, I'm a traditional drummer," whatever. But I go back to my own community and I always show my work to my folks and my elders. There's this one older guy, and he's a sundancer. I show him the work, and he always looks at me and he goes, "Good. You're out there in the world. We need more people out there in the world doing and saying those things." He always respects what I do and respects what I say, even though it's out there—like boners under loincloths. And he gets it. That's the critique I want, to have him as an elder, a medicine man, say, "Yeah, that's it."

AS: Also, you have to be cautious of elders who come out really negative about things like that because it's not their role. From my experience, if they're troubled by something, they won't actually tell you what it is. But they'll give you clues. And it allows you to think through it—"Oh, okay, maybe I should do this or do that." Gentle. In our time now, there are many new elders coming out that have convoluted ideas about traditional history, layered with Western Christianity. Sometimes I would receive a negative reaction from a particular elder, but then you start unpacking their history and you see, "Okay, there it is." I would never go back and tell them they're wrong because they have a point of view and I respect that. But I don't necessarily have to take it to heart.

SM: In *A Recognition of Being*, Kim Anderson and Bonita Lawrence discuss what's at stake when traditionalism becomes filtered through a Eurocentric, gendered lens. So instead of being a way to honour women's power, menstrual taboos around the sweat lodge become an exclusionary means of asserting male power, for example.

AS: Yes, because women are already cleansing, but men need the sweat because men don't menstruate. Women cleanse every year, every month, and the men need to cleanse, so that's part of it.

TH: But ceremonies were made for that. Where I come from, women have their medicine and men have their medicine. It's not a gender or a feminist thing. You know, historically in our culture, women were way up here, and supposed "equality" has dropped them down here to the level of men. That was the demise of these things. And my mother was part of the *Motokiiks*. And my daughter goes there and my sister, and they're powerful. They're powerful. My mom and grandma are the most powerful people I know.

AS: The *Motokiiks* are the Buffalo women society. It's exclusively a women's society. Back on Kainai, there's a man in the *Motokiiks*. He's a Two-Spirited man, and he's taken on the woman's role, and he's very well accepted into that role. So that just blows my mind when I start thinking about these relationships and how enlightened we are.

TH: Being a father, I see my daughter now, she's eight, and she's just a strong little woman, you know? It's partly because of me and her mom, but also my parents. She has such confidence in what she does and who she is, and she knows she's Blackfoot. She's got three names: Nicole Long Houle. I can't pronounce her name in Blackfoot, but it's Peacekeeping Woman. And then she's got a Chinese name, which is *Woo-wong-ying-nee*. That she was given by her great-grandfather on her mother's side, who was Chinese. Buddhist. She has those names. And she's grown up even better than I did, more like her grandparents—my parents—with Blackfoot names and with that identity that I never got as a young man because I didn't get my name until later.

AS: As a Two-Spirited male who doesn't have any progeny that I know of—I had a lot of unprotected sex when I was a young man—in the Blackfoot way, I have adopted all of Lori Blondeau's kids. Her kids are my kids and I take care of them just like my own. A few years back, her one son, Chuck, was getting into trouble. She asked my husband and I, "Can you help me out?" And I was like, "Of course we can." So we took him under our wing and took him to Burning Man.[1]

He was a fifteen-year-old and she says today, "he left home a boy and came home a man." His biological father basically abandoned him; although he has had male figures in his life, he never really had a father figure. And so we've become his fathers, he's our kid. He calls us and visits us all the time, we care, we're building trust. And that's the same with his brothers and sisters. They are our kids, too. Absent fathers can really mess with a kid's development.

TH: Who doesn't have daddy issues?

1. Burning Man is a week-long event held in the Black Rock Desert in northern Nevada. It is described by participants as an experiment in community, radical self-expression, and self-reliance.

AS: Yeah, ha, I know. And it's so wonderful to be in this position where I can call them my kids, and they both—Nigel and Dakota—they refer to Happy and I as their gay dads. And they're just very forthright about that with all their friends and they're not embarrassed or try to hide it. They say, "No, you're our dads." So that's amazing because I may not have biological kids of my own—though I tried, Happy and I tried to have a biological child…

TH: If you ever need advice.

AS: …I'm not lacking, as a Two-Spirited person. I have many children in my life who I nurture. I look at that and that's the traditional way back home. There's aunties and uncles to step in the place of parents. Or usually what would happen as parents is, you'd have your kids and then you'd give them to your grandparents to raise. The grandparents would usually raise the kids.

SM: Can I ask you both what you've learned about being a man through the process of parenting these children? What is it you've learned about yourselves?

TH: Just before I became a father, I asked my dad, "Do you have any advice?" And I hardly ever get advice from him. My two older brothers have kids. I'm the middle child. And I asked him, "Do you have any advice?" And he goes, "Three things: Listen to your elders. Listen to your kids. Take care of your fucking shit." And I looked at him and I go, "Oh, that's pretty solid advice," and he goes, "Damn straight." And I go, "Well, I hope I'm as good of a dad as you are," and he goes, "Highly unlikely." And I thought, that's it: How do you become better than your forefathers or your fathers before you? He said later on—I had some friends with me to go talk to him—and he said, "If my life was the extension and this was the beginning and this was the end," he said, "I'm only here in the middle as a Native man." And I thought to myself, "Holy shit, I'm only at the beginning." And it takes a lifetime to realize these things.

My daughter has taught me more things about humility, about caring and nurturing, about being—she calls me a Daddy Mom. I have that experience of being a nurturing sort of mother but also being stern like my father in a sense. And, you know, she informs my work, she informs what I do as an artist. I made the choice to be a full-time artist because of her. Because when I graduated, Steph got pregnant, and it was either I get a job that I'm going to hate in an office or some shit like that or I just fucking go for it. And I've decided I'm going to be an artist. So she's going to grow up and be a part of that and see it her whole life. She's going to experience it and, in the end, that's going to make her that much stronger. It's informed everything.

AS: As human beings, we all have that empathy, that need to nurture someone. And I've been really fortunate to nurture these kids and to gain trust with them. I look at my own childhood and how spoiled I was, and I guess if I look at my partner and I,

MY DAUGHTER HAS TAUGHT ME MORE THINGS ABOUT HUMILITY, ABOUT CARING AND NURTURING, ABOUT BEING— SHE CALLS ME A DADDY MOM.

Happy is able to say no and I'm the one who can't say no, I tend to spoil them. I'm terrible sometimes! Terrible in the sense that I find it really hard to discipline. But I think I have what my father has: these certain looks that you know if you've done something wrong. I'd just look at them and that's enough.

TH: That's like my folks. My dad could say anything to me and I'd just be like, "Whatever and go fuck yourself." But when my mom got mad, that's when shit hit the fan.

AS: My father never hit me as a child. Never hit me or disciplined me in a physical way. All he would have to do is just raise his voice or look at me and it was enough to put the fear in me forever. And I greatly respect him for that. I think I picked up on that a bit. You never really know, unless you ask your kids, what kind of effect that you've had on them.

TH: As soon as we turned fourteen, old enough to get a job, my dad was like, "You're out there working. Don't sit idle on my couch." But, fuck, I remember my dad used to smack me upside the head all the time. "Smarten up!" I'm pretty stern with my daughter, but it's hard. She's taught me patience. I can't even fathom what my dad had to go through with us. But he came from a pretty abusive family. My grandfather was really mean and an alcoholic.

AS: I've heard that my grandfather was tough and could be pretty mean, too.

TH: And it was from residential school and things.

AS: They learned how to be tough—they learned it.

TH: They never had parents. Ours is the first generation, all us cousins, to actually have parents.

SM: The residential school system enforced a lot of shame and stigma toward the body. In your work, you both grapple with that history while affirming the body—particularly the male body—in various ways. Why is that affirmation so important to you?

TH: There haven't been a lot of artists that have dealt with the male body in contemporary Native art. James Luna is one of them. The granddaddy of it. He's been an inspiration in my work.

AS: I remember going to residential school as a young kid, I was a day school student, I spent a lot of time in those dorms. I went to day school so I could go home at night, but my parents were both working in the system at the time, my father was part of the first wave of Native people working in these schools, so I lived in those situations. I stayed in the dorm many times. The separating of the genders, on top of the strict military ideas of order and discipline imposed on little kids, that screws with the mind. And then, of course, you have a bunch of young men who are coming of age and dealing with all those hormones, and so you get the abusive stuff happening to the younger boys. Many times older boys in the residential school would molest me; although this was abusive, today I can't help but feel their actions were done in a very loving way. We were all kids in a very fucked-up system.

TH: You learn.

AS: Yeah, exactly, it's a learned thing. In my trajectory, I want to come to understand more. Of course, the residential schools were terribly disruptive, especially in terms of segregating male and female. I'm only at the beginning of understanding it and how that's going to reflect in my work in years to come because I haven't really begun to start unpacking my own experience, because it is hard, when you start to really think about the shit that went down. In many ways, I have come to terms with things that occurred, but there are things that are so deep that you're trying to like understand how that affects you now as human being… There's still a long way to go to unpack that history.

TH: For me, it's like a fearlessness. I got tattoos on my arm. These are my coup marks. This is based on my regalia, based on my father's regalia, based on my own knowledge of things. When I got these tattoos, I felt liberated. I felt like I had a connection beyond just the last 200 years of being an Aboriginal man. I'm actually wearing my marks on me that everybody can see and identify. And for me, it's been a process over these last ten years to really shed everything and get down to this body that I'm comfortable with. I probably learned it earlier with my father doing sweats growing up, but now my body is a symbol of issues that permeate Aboriginal men with our diet, with our health, with diabetes, all of these things that are plaguing our culture. We're not werewolves, hunky studs, you know? But that's the image.

Even with powwow, the flashy image is built around competition. I grew up dancing but I stopped because it got too competitive; that's just not my own ethics as a Blackfoot Ojibway man. I don't want to be a part of that. I want to be a part of these things that I've always grown up with and part of that is stripping myself of all these other things and being comfortable with who I am. One of the biggest compliments I get with my work is, "You're a real Indian. That's real Indian shit. You're not afraid. You're baring it. There's an honesty there." That's one thing that's lacking with us now. Even in contemporary Aboriginal art, I don't see a lot of honesty.

AS: And also I'm highly skeptical of the whole healing paradigm because, quite frankly, I think it can become another crutch.

TH: It becomes addictive.

AS: It's this Pan-Indian idea that we, Indigenous males, have to be a certain way and act a certain way and heal a certain way. I've done many "healing" paths, including the "Red Road." After a few years, I said, "What the fuck is going on here?" I really felt like my mind was being messed with. It was another dependency thing. I'm the kind of per-

> FOR ME, IT'S LIKE A FEARLESSNESS. I GOT TATTOOS ON MY ARM. THESE ARE MY COUP MARKS. THIS IS BASED ON MY REGALIA, BASED ON MY FATHER'S REGALIA, BASED ON MY OWN KNOWLEDGE OF THINGS.

son who's maybe a little skeptical, my practical side said, "It just is what it is." And yeah, shit went down and it was pretty bad shit and, yeah, I have certain neuroses because of that today, but you know, I'm working on it and I'm living my life and I'm enjoying it. And damn it, today was a good day. That's not to say I don't have my bad moments, but I refuse to get caught in that whole Western idea that you have to be a certain way, and that at some point you will be healed. I don't think we're ever healed. I think that life just happens and you just have to be practical about it, find the tools that work for you and enjoy it as much as you can.

TH: For me, at an early age, it was always just dealing with your body. I'd always hang out with these big chubby Native dudes at sweats, but then the body was still taboo.

AS: In *Putting the Wild Back Into the West*, I use my eagle feather headdress that my grandmother did all the beadwork on. And people say things like, "Oh, that's wrong. You shouldn't be doing that. Those things are really sacred." And I asked my dad about it, and he said, "No, you have been given the rights to that headdress. It's up to you to take care of it and renew it in your way." So by allowing other people to put on my regalia, I am sharing that power, renewing the energy that will be a part of that headdress's history and being.

TH: Sometimes Aboriginal people have adopted these Western ideologies and imported them onto their belief of traditionalism. What I see plaguing a lot of people are these weird ideologies—their attitudes just sound so Christian. It's like, "No, no, no, no, no, no," like when I was getting in trouble with the boner pieces.

SM: In the *Pitchin' Teepees* piece, your models actually perform the type of discomfort that's plaguing men in a lot of ways, around their own sexuality, around their own senses of self. Is the discomfort that's created for the male Indigenous viewer meant to spur that self-awareness that will hopefully allow that person to inhabit the comfort each of you have with your bodies—a comfort that others may not have?

TH: Native people are majorly sexual beings. We're one of the fastest growing populations. There's a society of kids having kids and the male role within that family unit has been broken. None of these men are looking after their kids. So my grandmother is looking after three or four generations of kids because my uncles can't fucking be men about their shit.

AS: It takes time for Indigenous males to unpack their own colonial programming and then really ask themselves those tough questions because you take a look at some of the shit that happened, a lot of sexual abuse, a lot of convoluted ideas of what sex is and isn't, I think our work pushes their button. Then they really have to turn around and ask themselves, what's wrong with this picture? Why am I reacting so negatively to this?

IT TAKES TIME FOR INDIGENOUS MALES TO UNPACK THEIR OWN COLONIAL PROGRAMMING AND THEN REALLY ASK THEMSELVES THOSE TOUGH QUESTIONS.

TH: My father was actually the one that gave me the idea for "Buckskin Mounting." *Brokeback Mountain* was actually filmed near my reserve, and I kinda wanted to steal it back in some way. And my dad was like, "Oh why don't you do a *Brokeback* parody thing, or whatever?" And I was like, "You want me to be gay?" And he was like, "It'd be funny." But we were scared, doing this homoerotic thing in a room of 200 mostly Native men. I guess our stereotypes took over of the straight Native male. Yet they loved it. I don't know how many people came up to me after and were like, "That was so funny." So my own reaction and my own stereotypes of Native male identity, they were just blown away by the acceptance. But then another time I showed it to a younger audience for a summer media program and this guy literally wanted to punch me out. [*speaking to Adrian*] You had to deal with some stuff in Edmonton last year.

AS: Oh yeah, I was doing *The Life and Times of Buffalo Boy*. It was really on the edge for a public show, and I had thousands of people come through over the days that I performed. The vast majority of Indigenous people that came in got it right away, but apparently this one Native guy was going to come and give me shit. I wasn't there at the time, but the volunteers were there. He never showed up. I was ready for him though— I was like, "Bring it on. I'll talk to you about what I do and why I do it, and if you have a real problem with that, well, then … talk to my cousins!" [*Laughter*] (My cousins are known for being big and tough.)

I think it's important, when you're challenged, to face that challenge right away and nip it in the bud. We can have a good discussion, and we don't have to agree, but you have to respect what I do. I respect what you say, but we can be different.

TH: That's the deconstruction of it, especially a male identity that is so machismo.

AS: You never know what's going to happen in these public realms. If somebody crazy comes in, I'll sometimes need someone to back me up and help me out. My older brother passed away this last year. When I was a kid, he was my protector. He'd take care of me. In grade five, I was getting beat up every day after school, this was in Gleichen, the town beside my reserve. Finally I broke down and told him what was going on. And so he went right to town, found the guy and beat him up. He never bothered me again. My brother was a macho guy, best hockey player, best ball player on my reserve, and has three daughters, his oldest daughter is Two-Spirited. She was a hockey player when she was young, and she just got married to her partner this past summer. And my dad, her grandfather, went to the ceremony and supported her. It's pretty amazing.

TH: The male body. It's raging hormones. My brother is like 6' 3", like 280, body builder, probably doing some 'roids or some shit, and he would always tell me his scrap stories. I had to grow up that way because everywhere we moved, we were always the Native family and I always got picked on. I had long hair and I just learned not to take shit from anyone.

AS: I was the other way. I was sort of a smaller kid, so others protected me. I always got protected. My dad actually wanted me to be a boxer. And so I was at Gordon Residential School Boxing Club, stuff like that.

TH: Your dad was a boxer, eh?

AS: Golden gloves. Yeah. And I was sort of learning how to box and my big bout was coming up, my very first bout, so I get into the ring and I get up to the guy and the guy just whacks me right in the face. "Waaaaaah!" And I just started crying. And my dad was like, "Don't cry, Adrian, come on!" I couldn't stop crying. I was hysterical. So that ended my whole fighting career. And he never put me in the ring again. He knew right away that it wasn't what I should be doing and I think my mom got mad at him, too. Again, being protected.

SM: Your grandfathers were both in the rodeo—is that right?

AS: We're horse people. The Blackfoots were horse people.

TH: My grandfather wasn't in the rodeo but he was a rancher, a cowboy. Actually, if you watch a movie called *Circle of the Sun*, which is an NFB film on my uncle Pete Standing Alone, my grandpa's in the film. My uncle goes and hangs out with him and they're punching cows and stuff like that. And I remember my grandpa, he was just a dude. He was a fucking dude. But horse culture and rodeo and riding and everything, it's always been a part of our people.

AS: My grandpa, too. He was like six-foot-five, really big man, really tough guy. I have this great photo of him in the Calgary Stampede where he's riding a bucking horse called Shorty. That's my grandfather. But he was also the very first person who taught me how to draw. He drew a farmyard for me, stickmen stuff. He was incredibly gentle with me. Very gentle, very nurturing. He had scarlet fever when he was a kid, which affected his heart; he died in the early '70s. And I remember he was always going back and forth to the Indian hospital on the rez, and coming through the field, this big man with this white cowboy hat. And I'd go running out to see him.

TH: Yeah, the white cowboy hat, eh? My grandpa always had a white cowboy hat. He was a smaller man but he was the biggest dude I'd ever seen in my life. What I always loved about the real cowboy culture is that it's fucking hard honest work. I've got mad respect for people who do that. Even just farming in general, it's fuckin' hard work. We're pretty fuckin' pampered.

AS: Waaay pampered. With fusilli pasta and sundried tomatoes. That's the new idea of macho.

TH: I want cheese on this. Even though I'm lactose intolerant, I'll fucking do it!

MANHOOD THROUGH VULNERABILITY

A CONVERSATION WITH JOSEPH BOYDEN

〰〰〰〰〰〰〰〰〰〰〰〰〰〰〰〰〰〰〰〰〰〰〰〰〰〰〰〰〰〰〰〰〰〰〰〰〰〰

OLD MEN SPEAK IN RIDDLES, NIECES, BUT IF YOU LISTEN CAREFULLY, THEY MIGHT HAVE SOMETHING IMPORTANT TO TELL YOU. —JOSEPH BOYDEN, THROUGH BLACK SPRUCE

14 SEPTEMBER 2011
Conversation between Joseph Boyden and Sam McKegney at the Arc Lounge in Ottawa, Ontario.

SAM MCKEGNEY: In *Through Black Spruce* the children playing on Sesame Street are described as having "blackfly halos," an image that reflects innocence but is simultaneously ominous. Could you discuss how you were using that image and then also reflect perhaps on your experience with youth in Moosonee and Attawapiskat and these other small Indigenous communities in northern Ontario?

JOSEPH BOYDEN: I think as writers we're always looking for the image. You can't overwhelm a story with these images because they lose their intensity. But I remember, from my own reality, walking down Sesame Street in Moosonee and seeing this kind of thing, and the kids are just completely unaware of something they've gotten used to, which for an outsider is something that's just a pain in the ass! But I wanted an image that captured that they are saintly in their own way. And I didn't want it to be a dark image. I was looking for that one image that would capture something I'd seen in my own real life in just a very precise way, without really wanting to believe at the time that people would down the road say, "Oh, this is a wonderful kind of metaphor for something."

There's certainly a dark connotation but then there's the whole reality of children being innocent and not ready to enter into this world of experience, which they're certainly going to do in Moosonee and everywhere else in the world… and it's Will, you have to remember, Will Bird, who is seeing them this way. They're going to enter into a world of his experience eventually. And he fears for that, I think. Will's a softie at heart, so that's why I think it'll be fun to talk about him and masculinity because he's a Two-Spirit person, in some ways. Not in the sense of sexuality but of understanding the feminine very very well.

Some of the communities—Attawapiskat, Kash [Kashechewan], Albany [Fort Albany]—are very remote, fly-in communities, of less than a thousand people, typically. It's interesting, I think, that young men anywhere, but especially in these communities, look to the older ones to see where they belong and how they should act. And oftentimes, when I come in as an outsider, as a stranger, it's with silence, it's with a lack of eye contact, it's with sometimes open, very passive aggression. They put up a vibe of, "Fuck you," you know what I mean? "I'm not even gonna look at you but if I deign to, I'd mess with you," kind of thing. And that's all bravado, right? I think any young man goes through this, so it's not just an Indigenous thing, but I think growing up when it's pretty hard-scrabble like it can be on the reserves, that bravado is—and I don't want to tie it to gangs—but it's certainly something necessary to survive, which is often unfortunate. They're not given the chance to experience that softer side of themselves in public or with friends. And again, that's a very overarching statement, 'cause I have so many friends whose children are these wonderful young boys and going into manhood who are absolutely gentle and sensitive. But when you grow up in a tough environment, which a lot of these kids do, you're going to reflect that very quickly and you're not going to allow your childhood or your innocence to blossom like I wish it could.

But then, once you break through, once I broke through, I'd go up to these communities and spend a few weeks at a time and come back a number of times a year. So at first this was the perception. And then when I'd break through and get to know the families and show them that I was here not to boss you around or anything, but to absorb what you want to share with me, and once people open up, it becomes a very different thing, right? It becomes a situation where the young men begin to warm to you because you can joke with them and immediately, as soon as I could see a kid crack a smile, I knew, it's a different relationship suddenly. And humour is always the way that I approach it. Situations either in small Indigenous communities or in Sydney, Australia, where I don't know anyone—humour is universal in terms of breaking through that shell, that icy shell.

JOSEPH BOYDEN, a Canadian of Irish, Scottish, Métis roots, divides his time between northern Ontario and Louisiana, where he teaches writing at the University of New Orleans. He is the author of the short story collection *Born with a Tooth* (Cormorant Books, 2001) and the non-fiction works *From Mushkegowuk to New Orleans: A Mixed Blood Highway* (NeWest, 2008) and *Extraordinary Canadians: Louis Riel and Gabriel Dumont* (Penguin Publishers, 2010). His novels include *Three Day Road* (Penguin, 2005), the Giller Award-winning *Through Black Spruce* (Penguin, 2008), and *The Orenda* (Hamish Hamilton, 2013).

But a lot of these kids, these young men, I could very generally say that many of them have lost what their grandfathers had, which was hunting skills and fishing skills and the ability to feed your family and to play a very active and important and strong role of quiet leadership in your family. And I think a lot of the troubles that we see now on reserves with a large male population that doesn't know what to do with itself—and that ends up turning to alcoholism, that ends up turning to violence, it ends up turning to marital distress—is because they've lost that important role with their families and with themselves. And that's gotta be devastating for a people who for 15,000 years have lived in an area and in the last fifty, the power dynamics and the sexual dynamics have all switched and just flipped on their head.

SM: That points in the direction of the contemporary attractiveness of things like gangs, which are such an important part of your second novel.

JB: Absolutely. It's what brings back the ego, what brings back the purpose in life. "I'm gonna be a tough guy. I'm gonna be a provider, but I'm gonna do it in a dangerous way." Yeah. Absolutely. And that I think that plays out even more in urban Aboriginal communities, in Winnipeg, et cetera, et cetera, than it does in the smaller isolated communities.

SM: That makes me think of the dynamic between Marius and Will in *Through Black Spruce*. Will self-represents as a person who had the role of the person you were just describing, the one who was able to support and feed the family, feed the community, and Marius emerges as a threat not simply because he is bringing forms of violence into the community through drugs and alcohol, but also because he offers this alternative model of male power.

JB: That's very interesting. I've never really thought of it that way until right now. But that's exactly what Marius would do, is he's offering an alternative. He's offering something to these young men that they've lost. I didn't think of that at all, but absolutely, that's what I'm sure goes on in reality.

SM: The role of Gordon Painted Tongue is also really intriguing, both as a reflection on male power and as an indicator of the struggles involved in coming into personhood as a man. On the one hand, he can be linked to a lot of stereotypes about Indigenous masculinity through his voicelessness…

JB: The strong, silent …

SM: … silent, stoic, stalking …

JB: Absolutely.

SM: And he's very physical, like, he's very much a body. And yet, he's the one who is non-traditional. He's the one who's learning the traditions from Annie. What sort of concerns were you working through in that characterization?

JB: I actually wrote a short story called "Painted Tongue" in *Born with a Tooth* that's about Gordon, but in another world before Annie and all of this. So I'd written that story years ago in the mid-1990s and it was considered really seriously for publication by a number of big U.S. magazines. And it made me realize that maybe I do have what it takes to become a writer. And I'm telling this story because what I did with this Painted Tongue character is I took this stereotypical drunk, urban, long-haired, dishevelled, monochromatic Indian that you'll find across any urban centre in Canada and I kinda flipped it on its head. And I went, "Who's the real person behind me?" Behind the long hair hiding his face, he's a sensitive little boy having to live tough on the streets. That's when I first realized that a powerful thing I can do in my fiction, especially with First Nations, is play with the stereotype and then explode it and make the audience go, "Oh, wait a second, an Indian girl can really be a fashion model?" Of course she can. Look at the young woman in the margarine commercial, "We call this maize." You know that one I'm talking about? So I'm taking the "beautiful Indian maiden" and showing her to be really tough inside.

So when I was writing *Through Black Spruce*, and I had forgotten about that story— you don't think about your old stories when you're writing new stuff, especially ten or fifteen years later—I was writing the scene where the protagonist Annie was on the streets of Toronto and comes across these old Indian street people and on the set—I'm writing like I'm a director—I see the scene, and I'm like, "Roll." What do we got here? Annie comes across these Indian people… And then Gordon, Painted Tongue, from years ago, without my consciously wanting him to, walks onto the set. And I'm like, "Cut. What are you doing here? You're from another world, get out of the story." And he wouldn't leave. He wouldn't leave. And it was like, "Okay, well, if you're going to stay, you gotta do something." And so he ends up becoming Annie's protector, you know, the tough Indian, silent, strong Indian type, who is just a child inside. He was the Painted Tongue from the old story, in some ways. And I was able to flesh him out and allow him to become more three-dimensional because I had more time to spend with him on the page.

SM: Was there ever a worry or a concern with the relationship between Gordon and Annie because she's such a strong character and yet he plays this role of protector? Was there ever a fear that people could impose upon the story a "damsel in distress" model where she requires the male hero to swoop in and save her?

JB: I think I could worry about all kinds of things when I write something and that would just end up shackling me, so I wouldn't write anymore. But what I realized quickly is I'm again flipping stereotypes by having Annie in the city as a lost soul, but in the bush, she knows what she's doing; she's been taught well by her uncle Will. Gordon, on the other hand, has never even caught a fish before. He's an urban Indian, so I'm kinda playing with the urban Indian/rural Indian thing. So Annie is on her feet in her own territory. As soon as she leaves her territory and goes into the city, she's not. Gordon: same thing, he's on his feet, he understands his world, his urban world of the streets, but you bring him out into the bush and he's done for. And so I really had fun doing that. You don't expect the young beautiful First Nations woman to be also able to hunt and fish and trap, and you don't necessarily expect an urban street Indian to be in the bush and not know how to catch fish or protect himself. And so I wasn't too worried with that. I'm constantly looking at, "Why does this stereotype exist of the Indian as the drunk or the Indian as the strong silent type? Where does that come from?" And it comes from certain very specific situations that have become Hollywood-ized. And so really exploring them and breaking them apart—fracking them, I guess—is what I do, where I inject the water and the heat into these stereotypes to explode them to see what's on the inside.

SM: Will is an interesting character because he's rich with traditions, he understands a role that is fast-leaving his community, and he feels responsibility toward that role. And yet, he has his weaknesses, too. You allow him his flaws. What is your relationship to him as a character?

JB: I have never used real-life people and just basically made them into my fictional characters, except maybe you could argue once, and that's Will Bird. I've got a dear, dear friend, probably my best friend in the world, named William Tozer, who's a Cree hunter and trapper and bushman, who lives in Moosonee, who's a few years older than me, not much older than me, but, he's going to be fifty, I guess, so yeah, he's six years older than me. And he and I have been friends for a long, long time and I'm fascinated by him. And when I first was thinking of the idea of writing *Through Black Spruce*, I thought, my friend William has the most fascinating life. And as a fiction writer, I didn't want to write non-fiction, I wanted to write fiction, so I said, what if my friend William really did lose his first family in a fire while he was flying home. (He did not have an affair. He wasn't flying home from an affair or anything. He was flying in from a pop-and-chip run up in Attawapiskat, and saw his house was burning down. He lost his wife and two kids.) I imagined, what if William did not meet his beautiful, wonderful wife, Pamela—they now have three amazing boys and an amazing daughter, Rain. So that's where the fiction took off, from the reality. I hope he comes off as funny on the page because my friend William in real life is hilarious, he's a trickster, he's a wonderful guy. So Will Bird is a "what if" scenario of what William Tozer might have been if he had not connected with his very powerful, wonderful wife, Pamela.

Will Bird, he's the bushman, he's a tough guy, but of course, he's got flaws. He can't stand up to Marius; he tries to and he shakes. But haven't we all been in that situation where we're faced with somebody's who's an asshole or a very dominant, physically overbearing person who wants to mess with us, and we wish our reaction was, "Yeah, I'll stand up and beat you up," but that usually isn't the case, you know?

SM: One of the things that I find really intriguing about the portrayal of Will and his circle of friends—because it's a very tight-knit male community of three, right?—is that although the story is simultaneously recognizing the negative way drugs and alcohol are affecting the broader community, there's a very sympathetic portrayal of how, actually, alcohol brings these guys together.

JB: When they sit down on a back porch together…

SM: Yeah.

JB: … and drink a case of beer together. Of course. What's more masculine than sitting on the back deck and opening a square of beer and drinking it with each other, right? It's the way males learn to bond. You need that in order to talk with men in a way that doesn't make you feel like a sissy or a woman or make you feel weird; you have to oil things up with alcohol. It's hilarious, it's funny. And it's true. But that relationship goes farther than that. Will and Chief Joe Wabano grew up together, I imagine them having grown up together. And then this weirdo outsider, Gregor—like, they're all misfits, you know? They're all total misfits. I look back at writing *Through Black Spruce*—my scenes with Chief Joe and Gregor and Will, short as they were, were really fun to write because they're all such misfit losers in so many ways, wanting to be tough guys, but they're like three stooges. And there's no way they're going to be tough guys as much as they want to put that across. And that's such a male thing, too, isn't it? The idea that you try to put off your vibe, your aura, that you're a tough guy and then other people look at you and go, "Oh. That's a strange little guy."

SM: Did you feel any compulsion to move to the present, because you had done historical fiction?

JB: Oh, absolutely, absolutely. When I finished *Three Day Road*—I've often told this story in talks and stuff—but when I finished *Three Day Road* and it began selling suddenly around the world, I got depressed and I shouldn't have been depressed. I was like, "I should be really happy: I'm travelling around the world, my book's in fifty countries and fifteen languages, like why am I …?" It's because I missed Xavier and I missed Niska and I missed Elijah and hanging out with them every day and having them talk to me and me talk to them, kind of in your own weird writer way. And suddenly they were gone. And that's when I realized, you know what, the Bird family has so much more to say. And that contemporary First Nations existence in Canada needs some light shone on it by somebody who at least knows a little bit, you know what I mean? And so that's when I decided, there's going to be at least a second book, probably a trilogy.

WHAT'S MORE MASCULINE THAN SITTING ON THE BACK DECK AND OPENING A SQUARE OF BEER AND DRINKING IT WITH EACH OTHER?

SM: And I understand the original title was *Suzanne Takes You Down*. Have you always been a reader of [Leonard] Cohen or …?

JB: Who's he?

SM: [*Laughter*]

JB: I thought I made that up. I'm teasing you. No, I loved it. That was my very early title just because, you know, a publisher always wants something rather than an untitled novel. Give us a title. They're buggin' me for one right now and I'm like, I don't know. But yeah, that was the early version. Yeah, certainly, like Leonard Cohen, you want to talk about masculinity? You want to talk about the Two-Spirit person. So often in First Nations, a Two-Spirit person is somebody who is bi-sexual or gay. Absolutely a Two-Spirit person can be, but I think it's bigger than that. I think a Two-Spirit person is somebody who can live within a female and male form—internally, obviously, I'm not talking about physically changing yourself—but internally can inhabit the skin of both male and female. And as a writer I've called myself once a Two-Spirit person. I think people were probably like, "I didn't know Joseph was gay." But that's not what I meant. I have seven older sisters. I grew up with eight women, my mother and my seven sisters, very strong women raising me, and so, of course, how could I not understand the female? That's where the woman's voice often comes from in my work.

SM: *Three Day Road* is a novel that addresses two crucial institutions of social engineering: the military and residential school. Were you thinking through parallels between those institutions as you wrote the story or did they simply speak to each other because of the characters and what they had gone through?

JB: There was a quiet war going on in Canada in the early 1900s. We weren't loud, like the Americans. The worst we had in some ways was the 1885 rebellion with Riel. In comparison—not to belittle it in any way—but in comparison with other battles, especially American battles against Indigenous forces, it was very minor, in terms of the death toll. Canada was very good at not being loud and brassy like the Americans, but acting in that British way of—I don't want to say deceptive because I'm not a hater of the British by any means—but a very insidious battle going on, a war against First Nations. The British Canadian way of controlling geography and of getting what we wanted from the First Nations was not to do the Custer kind of thing or the Ulysses S. Grant kind of, "let's wipe 'em all out," you know? "Let's kill the Red Devil." It was very insidious. It was, "We'll offer them things, we'll bring them Christianity, we'll create residential schools." So there's this quiet insidious war going on in Canada in the first half of the twentieth century.

But there's also this very loud war going on over in Europe. Very loud. In every way you can imagine. It's the first mechanized war. It's the first war to introduce weapons of mass destruction, in terms of gas and artillery shells and the tank. It was a modern mechanized approach and so was the British approach to Canadian Indians. It was a very scientifically social approach. And so there's this quiet little insidious war going on at home and there's a very loud war going on overseas.

SM: With relation to Xavier and Elijah's experience of being removed and placed in this entirely foreign environment of the war—certainly it's a greater struggle for Xavier, more than a little bit because of the experience that Elijah has from an institutionalized environment in residential school. So there's a way in which Elijah is prepared for the structure that he'll find himself in.

JB: Absolutely. The military structure and the residential school, of course. But what doesn't he have? He doesn't have the soul. Everyone loves him in his military unit. He's talkative, he's funny, he's everything that everyone would wish an Indian would be. He's heroic, he's brave, he protects you, he does all these things. But what he doesn't have is that connection to where he comes from. And that's what ultimately unhinges him, that he doesn't have the growth of Xavier. If you read the prologue of *Three Day Road*, on the first page: Xavier teaching Elijah how to trap and Elijah quickly realizing the power in killing but not the power in the actual pursuit or where that comes from or why you kill. He's so unhinged because he doesn't have that connection to where he comes from and who he is. He's ungrounded.

Whereas Xavier barely survives this war because his Auntie raised him to know where he came from, who he is, and what to do, what's right and what's wrong. It's not just a Christian value system, right and wrong, at all, it's very much an Anishinaabe and a Cree idea of morality. Christianity is very black and white, very Manicheistic. With Cree and Ojibway people, the understanding is that they aren't poles, right and wrong, that all of us contain both extremes and it's how we balance and fight and struggle with them and then ultimately treat others that determines who we are. Here's an example, Martin Luther King, who's revered as the great icon of the twentieth century for so many people, and in her diaries Jackie is talking about, "I'm sure he was drunk when he came into Jack's wedding and he was not the nicest of …" You know what I mean? Of course he wasn't! You put someone on a pedestal, they're going to get knocked down. But I think Indians ultimately understand that really deeply, at a core level, that no one is perfect, that we shouldn't necessarily strive for perfection, we should strive to reach out to others. That's a big tangent. But it's all about masculinity. Accepting your role as a masculine man is not just, "I'm gonna serve you the food that you need to eat, I'm gonna keep you alive"—it ain't that simple. This is a very different world that we live in.

SM: One of the things I'm fascinated about with the development of Xavier and Elijah is how Elijah is able to create a myth of himself throughout the novel that validates his own sense of self. So he has this sense of masculine self-worth that is refracted back

> BUT I THINK INDIANS ULTIMATELY UNDERSTAND THAT REALLY DEEPLY, AT A CORE LEVEL, THAT NO ONE IS PERFECT, THAT WE SHOULDN'T NECESSARILY STRIVE FOR PERFECTION, WE SHOULD STRIVE TO REACH OUT TO OTHERS.

to him by those around him, the military personnel that he's stationed with. But at the same time, it makes Xavier less and less sure of himself. So as the myth of Elijah creates the hero, that's when we hear Xavier say, "I'm becoming more of a ghost," right? Do you see a connection between these processes and the struggles of, say, young Indigenous men in urban scenarios seeking validation by those around them, and how that may encourage them towards models of masculinity that are unhealthy? Or is that the critic in me projecting onto your story?

JB: No, I love that reading. Who doesn't love or is not attracted to the idea of completely reinventing who are you and where you come from? And not in a giant way, but making yourself more attractive or approachable or even heroic to others? But Elijah doesn't have his—again, it goes back to identity, right?—he didn't grow up in the bush, he grew up in a residential school. He grew up with no mother, no father, and again, it goes back to the whole. And by the way, another aside: If you look at any group that has come from impoverished places, oftentimes you'll see fatherless families. You're going to see families without the male figure and the creation of gangs from that. From tougher socio-economic places, you're going to find young men wanting to band together because they've never had the father figure. Fathers are often either dead, in jail, or just not around. And so this is not just an Indian thing.

SM: That cycle that you're discussing seems to create its own perpetuation in the sense that from the absence comes an urge to seek out a meaningful male role, while none is actually modelled for you.

JB: And then you end up with a weak male role again. You end up with somebody who talks about honour and respect and protecting each other's backs, but gangs fall about immediately as soon as money or authority come into the mix. There's so often a lack of a male authority figure or a male figure who is benevolent or who is kind or gentle or in any way effeminate. There's just no room for it. And that's the failure of gangs. Gangs will always pop up and then be defeated, pop up and then be defeated, and then pop up in another way. They're like spores.

SM: Xavier is entirely broken at the beginning and then chronologically the end of *Three Day Road*. He's symbolically emasculated by virtue of his amputated limb and he requires the stories of his Auntie in order to usher him home. Niska has a lot of power as a character.

JB: People don't typically call Ojibway culture matriarchal, but the woman is everything. I don't think there's any traditionalist who would disagree with that. And the female is the powerful one. You don't invite a woman on her moon into a ceremony because the power of life that she brings and holds in her is too much for a human to deal with.

Niska's father allows her to watch when he takes care of a windigo when she's a young girl, because he knows, "You're the next, you're the next in line." And it's not so much that he's chosen her to be, it's just she has what he has. She has the natural, I don't want to use the word "power"—that crosses over male and female—but the family's raison d'être, which is they are healers. But in healing you sometimes have to excise the cancer. And that's what dealing with the windigo is: cutting out that bad part of us when it gets too overwhelming.

SM: That's certainly at the core of *Three Day Road*, and it emerges again in *Through Black Spruce* in the way that Will frames his duty to get rid of Marius. He calls Marius the "root" of the problem, saying he "needed killing."

JB: Yeah, he needed killing. That's an old Southern expression that I stole...

SM: In a novel that's so aware of the historical conditions that have created needs, or desires, in communities for forms of narcosis like drugs and alcohol, is there a way that Will is missing something regarding how Marius is himself a product of these conditions?

JB: Oh, absolutely. You know how Niska's father passed down to her the power? Well Niska didn't pass it down to Xavier. That power jumps over to Annie. And so Annie is the one who, without anyone being able to teach it to her, realizes, "Holy mackerel, I'm having these visions." In her contemporary world, she's had no one to teach her much except her Uncle Will, who can only teach her the bush. Uncle Will doesn't really have much of a connection to the shaking tent at all or the sweat lodges. That's not really his thing, you know? He's missing that. But Annie is desperate for something. And this is how I see so many contemporary Native people. They're not desperate but they're hungry for what has been lost over a few generations or five or six or seven generations of people going to residential school and losing their religion. I sound like REM, but they've lost their religion over the course of a hundred years.

Will gets Marius on a very intuitive level. He understands that Marius is not a good dude. Marius is a very frightening person and is a cancer in their little community. And Marius is directly linked, he's a blood relation to Elijah, right? Bad things will continue to reinvent themselves or gestate again in each generation unless they're dealt with, unless they're excised. I see it in my own family, for example. I come from a very large and complicated family and, as amazing as some of it is, there's a lot of darkness there, too. You have to deal with your past and where you come from to understand who you are and where you're going. I grew up without a father since I was eight years old, so I'm a fatherless guy, and my younger brothers, who were six and four, are even more fatherless. We grew up without a dad for the majority of our lives. If you don't know your history, you have to try to learn it in order to see what you're doing wrong now, if that makes any sense.

AND THAT'S WHAT DEALING WITH THE WINDIGO IS: CUTTING OUT THAT BAD PART OF US WHEN IT GETS TOO OVERWHELMING.

SM: Well, if you don't mind me asking questions about you personally—

JB: No, not at all.

SM: The final line at the end of your bio on the Penguin website reads: "I'm the father of a son, Jacob, and a writer." What do you see as the relationship between those roles—father and writer?

JB: Well, this is a question probably you and I will have to—well, actually it plays right into masculinity—but would take another half hour to deal with in terms of my relationship with my son, because he grew up and I grew up often apart physically because I've lived in New Orleans and he's lived in Toronto for pretty much all of his life. And he's twenty-one now, so he's at that age where he is his own man but I still see the boy in him. I especially see how I've not done my duties as a father and need to be reminded once in a while by my wife, Amanda (not Jacob's mom, obviously), that I did the best I could. That's all anyone can do, you know what I mean? My son's a good kid and a strong kid, and he's much his father in terms of searching for who he is and what he is at a very difficult age for a young man. You remember what it was like to be nineteen, twenty, and twenty-one and twenty-two? So that's where he is now and I'm almost reliving it when I think of him. When we talk, I almost relive those years, which were very tough for me. But it has absolutely everything to do with masculinities.

How do you deal with and raise your own children, facing that and saying, "No, I wasn't a perfect dad. I was far from it. At least I was there though." And that's what's important is that you're there when your child needs you. I think my son was lucky that I was there. I was lucky that my father was there at least for as long as he could be before he died. But I think so much of the issues of masculinity is needing a strong male role model, who is not just a tough guy or whatever, but somebody who can really show that effeminate side, ultimately is what it boils down to. That side that you're not afraid to be gentle and kind and overly fawning or doting. Brings up a lot talking about this. About my son's and my relationship.

SM: As a parent, it's difficult to show vulnerability because we're taught in various ways that to be masculine is to be strong, right? And so, to create scenarios in which vulnerability is actually a sign of strength is a really difficult thing to do. Which connects, I believe, to the role of the writer because literature allows people to experience vulnerability in a safe way.

JB: You can turn the TV off when you're watching a movie, you can close the book, absolutely, yeah.

SM: And also, for people—because it's a personal, one-on-one relationship with the book you're holding in your hand—someone who is very scared of their vulnerable side or who doesn't want to present it to others can still share that with a text, right?

So, to tie it back to the novels, *Three Day Road* got a lot of people reading books about Indigenous issues who would never otherwise pick up Indigenous lit. What do you see as the power or role of story in seeking other possibilities for masculinity?

JB: I can only give a personal example. Recently, CBC Radio had an idea for a program called *Bad Behaviour* and they asked me—and probably seven or eight other people—to write something and expose some little dark side, a small glimpse. So the original thing that I wrote was about being a punk rock kid and getting into a lot of trouble and watching friends die and a few go to jail and me somehow surviving. But they kinda pushed me and said, "Can you be more specific because it's only a four-or five-minute little story that you give to leave the listener thinking." I suffer from depression but hadn't for many, many years. And two years ago I was in a very bad place again I hadn't seen in decades, to the point that I was very fearful for my own life. And my wife Amanda, who's incredible, was trying to work me through it. It's very difficult being married to a person who suffers this kinda thing. But she was like, "Well, do something." I said, "You know what I wanna do? I wanna write about my own attempt at suicide when I was sixteen, a very serious attempt, and I'm gonna give this to them and blow them away and say, 'Fuck you,' to the demons."

So that's what I did, I wrote a piece called "Walk to Morning," and it's about attempting suicide when I was sixteen by jumping in front of a car and miraculously surviving. But then I realized as I was writing it that, number one, I am dealing with my issues really directly but, number two, now that I'm a figure that people might listen to, I can't in any way glorify the idea of suicide, so I brought in the bigger issue of Moosonee and Moose Factory and First Nations small communities across Canada. In Moosonee, there were eleven attempts—no, eleven successes—and probably 100 attempts in a community of 2,500 last year. And I finally realized that I feel like I'm a man since I've done this because I'm very vulnerable now. I've opened my most personal and dark times to Canada, and I've done it not just for me. I've done it because I'm feeling the pain of my friends who are losing their children. One of my friends lost two of their kids in six months, killed themselves. It's that kind of thing. I end the piece for CBC begging, if at all you feel the way I did, walk through till morning because I tried it at night and if I'd just kept walking, I might have…

And so that's part of being a man is admitting that you're absolutely vulnerable, that you fucked up, that you messed up. I've taken it up as a cause, this idea of not allowing certain issues that are deadly to be hidden: "We shouldn't talk about them for fear of them being like a contagion." That's not the way suicide works, I realize. That's not the way depression works. That's not the way drug addiction works. It's talking about and bringing it open on the table and saying, "Let's look at it." And that's ultimately for me at this point in my life what masculinity is.

AND SO THAT'S PART OF BEING A MAN IS ADMITTING THAT YOU'RE ABSOLUTELY VULNERABLE, THAT YOU FUCKED UP, THAT YOU MESSED UP.

AFFIRMING PROTECTORSHIP

A CONVERSATION WITH KATERI AKIWENZIE-DAMM

14 JULY 2013
Conversation between Kateri Akiwenzie-Damm and Sam McKegney on a bench in Wiarton, Ontario, while Kateri's sons Kegedonce and Gaadoohn played at Bluewater Park and were tended by Sam's daughter Caitlyn.

I AM EMERGING
HE TAKES ROOT IN MY DEEP DARK FLESH AND FORESTS SPRING FORTH
HE BREATHES ON THE SMALLEST PIECE OF ME
AND I AM AN ISLAND GROWING INTO CONTINENT, SPREADING MYSELF...
HIS SONG IS THUNDER ROLLING ACROSS THESE HILLS AND MARSHES
LAVA ERUPTS, FLOWING TO SEA
HE IS MY OTHER SELF REFLECTING
—KATERI AKIWENZIE-DAMM, FROM "EMERGING," IN A CONSTELLATION OF BONES
(COLLABORATION WITH TE KUPU)

SAM MCKEGNEY: Has your perspective on gender relations, and masculinity specifically, shifted as you've become in recent years a mother of boys?

KATERI AKIWENZIE-DAMM: Oh it's definitely shifted. In a way, I didn't really expect to be a mom of boys. I mean, I never really thought about it either way when I thought about becoming a parent. So now I have two boys. And I'm actually adopting another boy—

SM: Oh wow—Congratulations!

KAD: Thank you. Kegsy has a sibling, so he is going to be joining us. He's three years old so it's going to be a longer process, but maybe sometime in the fall or before Christmas he'll be living with us. Now I'm going to be completely surrounded by boys, which was not something that I expected, so I've been giving a lot more thought to "how do I raise them in a way that honours who they are, in terms of their identity in many respects, not just their gender?" But absolutely that's part of what I've been thinking about: being a woman raising boys as a single mom.

One of the things that's shifted significantly is my thinking, because I have a brother but I haven't lived day-to-day with all that male energy before. And my boys are so different, the two I have now. As I was telling you, Gaadoohn, the little one, I call him "The Ruffian," is so loud and he's got a big personality. He's really expressive. He can't talk yet so I think his speech delay has led to him being very expressive in many ways. Also, he's just a rough-and-tumble kind of kid. If you push him, he laughs, you know? He likes roughhousing. He's a lot rougher. Kegs likes roughhousing too, but he's a very gentle, happy-go-lucky, affectionate kind of kid. So just the fact that they're so different has made me have to think about how to help them to be who they want to be. Parenting is such a "learn as you go" type of thing. I can't parent them in the same way because they're two very different personalities. And I think that, being an adoptive mom, it's easy for me to see that they're so different from each other, and in many ways they're different from me and I accept that. When people have kids who aren't adopted, maybe there are some other issues that come into play that don't come into play for me. If my boys need help because they have speech delays, I don't take that personally or see it as a reflection of me. Some people get really defensive about those types of things and I don't. Because for me it's just a matter of, "what can I do to help them to achieve what they can achieve, and to be all that they dream of being?"

Gender is one piece of that. And you know, it *is* difficult as a mom of boys. How do I make sure that they get enough male influence? I have to recognize that I am who I am too and that I can't fulfill all of those needs for them. So I have to be mindful and try to present them with opportunities to hang out with boys and be around men who will mentor them and interact with them in positive and healthy ways.

SM: Is it difficult to negotiate or plan for those types of mentoring scenarios? I realize the boys are quite young now, but thinking to the future as they develop, do you

KATERI AKIWENZIE-DAMM is a poet, essayist, editor, publisher, activist, and spoken word artist from the Chippewas of Nawash First Nation. She is the founder and managing editor of Kegedonce Press, which publishes works by Indigenous artists and is situated on her home reserve of Neyaashiinigmiing, Cape Croker on the Saugeen Peninsula in southwestern Ontario. Akiwenzie-Damm's poetry includes the collection *My Heart is a Stray Bullet* (Kegedonce Press, 1993) and the spoken-word collaborative CDs *Standing Ground* (Nishin Productions, 2004) and *A Constellation of Bones* (Nishin Productions, 2008). Akiwenzie-Damm is editor of the groundbreaking collections *Without Reservation: Indigenous Erotica* (Kegedonce, 2003) and *Skins: Contemporary Indigenous Writing* (Kegedonce, 2000) and contributor to critical collections including *Looking at the Words of Our People* (Theytus, 1993) and *Me Sexy* (Douglas and McIntyre, 2008).

see lots of opportunities for those kinds of positive male-only spaces, and also forms of mentorship?

KAD: I think it's going to be an ongoing challenge for me because you can't really foresee how other people are going to interact with your children. You can't control other people and their interest in doing that, basically. Frankly, I thought my brother would be a lot more involved with them than he is. But he's not, and that was a bit of a shock for me. I thought that there would be much more influence there and there isn't. So, I guess that's also part of the reason why I've had to be more mindful of it.

Right now it's not as much of an issue—they go to daycare. My older son, Kegsy, is fortunate in that in his room at daycare there's a man and a woman instructor, so he gets both influences there. But that's not going to be the case when he starts going to school full time. From year to year he might have a male teacher, or he might not. It's definitely going to be a challenge. I'm very protective of them, I guess as most parents probably are. But I feel really protective that they are allowed to be who they need to be, and that people don't try to force them to conform to other ways of being. Like I'm really protective of Kegsy and his affectionate, nurturing ways because I think that boys can lose that very easily with outside pressure or pressure from the men in their lives. So I try to protect that for him and let him be who he is by nature. So it's going to be a challenge as a single mom, absolutely. And it's always going to be a factor in terms of having a new relationship too, because, I mean I thought I was picky before, but now…

SM: [*Laughter*]

KAD: [*Laughter*] I've been picky in the past, but I mean now my children are first and foremost in my thinking all the time. I could never be with a man who I thought couldn't have a positive, healthy relationship with them. So whether that means I'll be a single mom from here on or whether I'll be able to find somebody who can fulfill that and be a great partner all around, I don't know. I'll have to see how that evolves. But yeah, it definitely adds another challenge because there isn't a male figure in the house.

I have to say, because of all the work I've done around Indian residential school and children's aid scoops and so on, I know how risky it is to leave your children in the care of other people. I'm very aware of that, and I'd be lying if I said that it hasn't affected the way that I look at enrolling them in clubs and things like that. I have to really scope things out before I let somebody be with them in a non-supervised kind of way.

SM: Another layer of concern that arises with sports clubs and the like is that they often teach particular cultures of gender that can be extremely limiting. I think, for instance, about the forms of heteronormative masculine machismo that tend to be valued in hockey culture.

KAD: I've never pictured myself as a hockey mom… but whatever they need, I'm going to try to let them follow that and be there supporting them. So I guess if I end up being a hockey mom, I end up being a hockey mom. But circumstances are going to have to be what I think the boys need as well. And I can't totally control that.

Kegedonce has such nice long beautiful hair, and I'm sure at some point somebody at the daycare or going through the daycare said something to him, because all of the sudden he came home one day and said, "Boys don't have long hair; girls have long hair." I was trying to tell him, "well, you know, in our culture…" but he doesn't really understand the concepts yet of being Anishinaabek, or about our culture, or anything like that. But I did try to explain to him that it's not the same for everyone and everywhere, and that it's not true, that some girls have short hair, and some men have long hair, and so on. But, it was probably just an offhand comment from somebody or another kid, and it stuck with him. It made a big impact on him. It reinforced to me that you can't control everything. But it's not always going to be possible to put him only into situations where he can be who he is and he can express himself and he can follow his culture and so on without people pressuring him to be something else.

I think team sports are fantastic in a lot of ways. I played team sports the whole time I was a kid until university, and I got a lot out of it. I learned a lot about negotiating my way through life with other people that I wouldn't have if I had pursued individual sports and interests. I want my sons to be able to do that as well. Kegsy is already signed up for T-ball this summer and he's learning that he's supposed to listen to the coach, when really he's running off in every direction. It reminds me of when I took ballet as a kid, like all the little ballerinas were going one way and I was going the other way. Yeah, ballet was not my thing I guess. It was evident even then, at four or five years old. [*Laughter*] So I can relate to him, when he's supposed to be running the bases and he just keeps going. I think that type of group learning experience is valuable, and I don't want my fears to limit my children.

So it's really trying to walk this fine line, and I'm sure I won't always get it right, but I really try to communicate a lot with my boys. At night when I put them to bed (with Gaadoohn not so much because he can't talk yet, but with Kegs) we have a lot of conversations just lying in bed, before he falls asleep, just kind of going over the day and things like that. So I'm hoping that we can develop a relationship where if I make a wrong choice, or misstep, he can tell me about it and we can talk about it. That's the saving grace in all of this, because otherwise I'd just drive myself crazy trying to figure out what's the perfect thing to do every time. So I'm kind of giving myself a break and saying, "Okay, we'll try as much as possible to always do the best thing and on the other hand, we'll just try to keep communication open so that we can figure things out as we go, too." It's tough, I mean, they don't come with manuals. Is that a pun? [*Laughter*] No manuals… or woman-uals!

SM: [*Laughter*] Neither manuals nor woman-uals are available, as far as I know. What motivated you to confront the stigmatization of sensuality and the body, and to open up spaces for celebrations of the erotic in your work as a poet, editor, and publisher?

KAD: A bit of my background: I was raised Roman Catholic. For whatever reason in my immediate family—and, you know, I've asked my mom and she doesn't really remember why or how this ever happened—but I can remember as a kid having hugs and kisses at night, and then we got to a certain age and all of that stopped. And then there were a lot of taboos around talking about sexuality, relationships, and so on. My parents obviously weren't—I mean, it's obvious to me, looking back, that they weren't very comfortable with those kinds of conversations. So, I felt unprepared in some ways when I got older. I also felt that I learned a lot of fear and I guess shame, as if that aspect of myself had to be hidden. Like you didn't want to be too obvious about anything, didn't want to be too assertive or even let people know if you liked somebody, that sort of thing. I was very secretive about all that, crushes, desires, and everything as I was growing up, because I thought it would force me to have to answer questions that I had learned not to be comfortable answering. It also meant I felt I couldn't ask questions. So I just kind of put that in the background.

I thought that I had to live up to a certain image. Like I'm supposed to go to university and supposed to be a good girl, and all of this. And that came out of being raised Catholic, it came out of my family circumstances, and society in general. I also think that, being Anishinaabe, there were fears and things that got passed down. It wasn't until I was older that I started thinking that the source of some of that is it just isn't really a safe world for Indigenous women. But I didn't know that at the time. I just knew that there was a lot I shouldn't say, and that I shouldn't dress in certain ways, and I had to be really careful about all sorts of things.

I was a late bloomer, I was almost thirty before I fell in love with somebody—not that he necessarily fell in love with me—and I started looking for reflections of healthy relationships between Indigenous people in writing because I was a voracious reader and, doing the work that I do, it was a natural place for me to search for those images. I really started seeking them out. It was so strange to me because it got to be this big quest; it wasn't very easy to find those positive images and stories. I might have been in my late twenties, but probably a lot of kids go through that in their teens when they start reading love poetry and they're dating and falling in and out of love. I was looking for those reflections of what I was experiencing in my late twenties but I couldn't find anything. I was lucky because I knew a lot of Indigenous writers, and spent time with them, wonderful people like Jeannette Armstrong, Lee Maracle, Patricia Grace, and Haunani-Kay Trask—and all these people who were writing around love and relationships and so on. I also became aware of residential school and the impacts that it's had intergenerationally. Then right around this time, Phil Fontaine disclosed his abuse and all these horrible stories of abuse started coming out in the media, which was really great insofar as it could finally be talked about and addressed but, on the other hand, as a young woman, I felt surrounded by all these stories and images of our people being victimized, sexually victimized. There was no antidote to that. There wasn't much that I could look to and say, yes, there's all of that in our histories, but look at all these other positives. I could see the beauty in my own family because my grandparents had a fantastic relationship, but overall it felt like there just wasn't a lot to hold on to.

For somebody who was shy and who grew up the way that I did, I don't know why I decided to take that on, to collect and write and encourage others to write erotica, but I think it was partly for myself. I had this instinct that if that was something that I really needed, then surely there were other people, other Indigenous people, men and women, who needed to see depictions of themselves in positive, healthy ways, and interacting with each other in positive and healthy ways as much as I did. So, that's when I started collecting erotica for an anthology. It was quite the experience because I really was shy about it but I was compelled to do it. At first I thought that there were going to be a lot of people who would look at me like I was crazy, or like I was some kind of pervert, like I was just trying to amass this little collection for my personal needs or something. And a lot of Indigenous writers weren't writing erotica, but as soon as I'd mention it, they'd be like "yeah, *definitely.*" The light bulb would go on—you could literally see it. It's like they would brighten up and say, "Yes, I don't know why I haven't been writing that, but I'm going to." Sometimes, even a year or two years later, I'd go to my mailbox and there'd be a submission from them. Yeah. So that's how it started, and it became a seven-year-long project. Part of the reason for that was that a lot of people didn't have that kind of writing readily available. They just didn't.

SM: Do you think the fact that people weren't already writing those things or didn't have that type of writing available was evidence of having internalized that shame you're talking about or was it more of a tactical artistic choice to focus on other material?

KAD: It wasn't just one or two people who didn't have it or write it; it was more like one or two people who *did* have that sort of writing available. Like Richard Van Camp, when I contacted him he was like, "Woooo!" and he started sending me all of these stories. But it was generally the opposite, where there were only one or two people who did have something available, and other people were like, "yeah, I'm going to start writing something; I'm going to work on that." And they did. A lot of people did. There was so much support that it became obvious to me that people weren't even aware that they were limiting themselves, or that they hadn't felt safe expressing that side of themselves, even though in their other work they were quite fearless.

SM: Do you find the situation is quite different now than when you began the project?

AS A YOUNG WOMAN, I FELT SURROUNDED BY ALL THESE STORIES AND IMAGES OF OUR PEOPLE BEING VICTIMIZED, SEXUALLY VICTIMIZED. THERE WAS NO ANTIDOTE TO THAT.

KAD: I think so. I think there are a lot more depictions of love scenes, and there have been special erotica issues of Indigenous magazines, exhibitions of Indigenous erotic art and so on. I had really hoped that the day would come when people would be writing erotic poetry and erotic scenes in their stories and novels, and that it wouldn't be a big deal. Because it was kind of a big deal when I first started collecting it. People felt quite brave, I think; they were stepping out of their comfort zones. I even got interviewed by a Sami radio station one time, calling from Norway, because it was such a big deal—it was something really different, pushing at people's preconceived ideas about us and our literature. When people thought of Indigenous literature, that's not what came to mind; it was like protest literature or something about the environment, you know, those kinds of really limiting, narrow definitions of our writing. I think it's finally getting to that point where someone can write a collection of poetry and erotic poetry can be part of it. It doesn't necessarily have to be a big thing. It just takes what I would think of as its rightful place in our lives and our forms of creative expression.

SM: This positive movement in the Indigenous artistic scene—where the erotic is finding its place more comfortably within a range of expressive arts—is occurring at a time when other forms of media are commodifying sexuality in potentially dangerous ways. I'm thinking specifically of Internet pornography and the sexualization of young women in TV and film. Do you see art as, I don't know, a "corrective" is the wrong word, but how do you see artistic struggles toward positive sexual intimacy functioning within a broader cultural and media spectrum in which the erotic often functions according to power dynamics that are oppressive?

KAD: Unfortunately that might be the third step, you know? In some ways right now, people are just coming to a point where they're comfortable with that form of expression again, but I'm not naive about it. I think that at some point somebody's going to say, "there's this type of porn and that type of porn, so let's see what we can put together for people who have Native American fetishes." I can't control that though. I think that's a real possibility in this day and age, and all I can imagine is that if we keep creating our positive stories and images, that we help to counteract those kinds of exploitive images and stories. That's probably bound to happen at some point, but in my way of doing things, you just keep doing what you do and creating the beautiful and helping people to recognize the beauty and the positive, and to stay focused on that, so when that day comes there won't only be the images of exploitation dominating our thinking and the thinking of others in the society around us.

When I was growing up, there was such a dearth of anything erotic, about the only thing I can remember seeing was *Tales From the Smokehouse*. There was a copy of that book my grandparents had in their house and it was like, "Oh, what's this?" You know? I don't even know if I ever snuck it long enough to read the stories! The artwork by Daphne Odjig was so intriguing itself. Other than that book there were silly romance novels that used Indigenous people as cyphers to fill with their strange fantasies of who we are. Part of my motivation for doing the erotica work was that I didn't want other generations in my family—that's what I was thinking about first, but also anybody's kids—to grow up the way that I did, with no real and inspiring images of themselves to add to their sense of sexual identity and to help guide them in understanding who they are. You don't get everything from your family. You get a lot from your family, but you don't get everything, so those outside images are important and influential. I hope that my boys will benefit from that work that I did to help our people to start expressing that side of themselves, which sounds quite lofty, but I'm really proud of the fact that I was part of that reclamation and that I helped to move it forward in some way. If I do nothing else, I think that's not a bad legacy. I hope it helps them and other children in my family and community.

SM: People like Andrea Smith have firmly established that attacks on Indigenous understandings of gender and gender systems have been a fundamental element of the colonial process in North America. What is your sense of how your own community, for instance, is dealing with that legacy?

KAD: My sense is just from what I can see, and today people are more open than they were when I was a kid. I can remember hearing about a gay male being beaten up in the community when I was younger. I don't remember exactly how old I was but I think I might have been ten, or maybe a little bit older, possibly a little bit younger— somewhere around there though. And now there's a gay male couple living openly in the community—well, actually two that I can think of off the top of my head. I don't always hear everything that goes on in the community because I'm not working in the community, per se, but I haven't heard of them having any problems. I haven't heard comments from other people behind their backs or anything like that. So there's a kind of acceptance thirty years later that there wasn't when I was a kid… Did I say thirty? I shouldn't be dating myself. [*Laughter*]

That's not a huge amount of time, but I think that a shift has happened, and I'm glad to see it. I hope it continues and that people not only become more open-minded but that they really start to look at what the thinking was traditionally around gender identity, sexuality, and so on, because I think in some ways that knowledge hasn't been shared widely. There's been a concerted effort by the churches and the government to make sure that kind of knowledge wasn't passed down. So I hope there's a reclaiming. There has been to a certain extent, but I hope that it flourishes even more so that more people gain a better understanding. Because my community, probably like every other First Nations community in Canada, is still suffering the effects of residential school, children's aid scoops, ongoing underfunding for our children, and the impact that colonialism has had on parenting and the passing along of traditional knowledge, of sacred knowledge.

I DIDN'T WANT OTHER GENERATIONS IN MY FAMILY... TO GROW UP THE WAY THAT I DID, WITH NO REAL AND INSPIRING IMAGES OF THEMSELVES TO ADD TO THEIR SENSE OF SEXUAL IDENTITY

SM: Are there people in your community that you would feel comfortable going to to ask about certain stories and things—men's teachings, for instance—as the boys are growing up? Or is traditional knowledge accessible in that way?

KAD: That's a complicated question, maybe more so than it appears, or maybe I make it more so than it needs to be. Because I think that there are people who have that knowledge, or pieces of that knowledge, but it comes back to putting a lot of trust in somebody in a really important area of my sons' development. So I would be very careful about how that would happen or who would be involved in providing those kinds of teachings to them. Because unfortunately people have been so affected by colonization that those who appear to be traditional do not always act in traditional ways, in the best ways, and there are sometimes power dynamics that I really have to be aware of. Again, it's such a huge sacred trust to allow someone to provide that to my sons.

But I also believe that it doesn't have to be somebody from my specific community. If there are people who can help them with those kinds of questions, and they are from other Anishinaabe communities, I don't have a problem with that. Even men who would have knowledge from other Indigenous cultures and so on, I think that can be really helpful too, as long as I'm aware and able to mediate that to some extent. Because I learned a lot about who I am from travelling internationally and being able to talk to people from other Indigenous cultures like Patricia Grace, who's been a big mentor of mine, and Haunani-Kay Trask, who has changed my thinking in so many critical ways. They're a long ways from Anishinaabe territory! But it really helped me understand myself by learning from them about their cultures and teachings.

SM: Who are the artists today that are exciting you in terms of how they're challenging understandings of Indigenous men and masculinity through their representations?

KAD: An emerging poet whose work I find really interesting and I'm excited about is Giles Benaway. We've just published his collection of poetry *Ceremonies for the Dead*, and I find what he's doing really intriguing. I don't know if I could specifically say in terms of depictions of men, but I think that, as a poet, he has a kind of brave openness about him that I find really compelling. So he's one person. I really like the work that Daniel Heath Justice is doing, and Niigaanwewidam Sinclair, just in terms of the way they present themselves and the way that they talk about gender roles and ways of being. I think it's much more inclusive and thoughtful, and, in a quiet sort of way, really kicking the shit out of the stereotypes and the norms, the norms which were forced upon us, inherited via the dysfunction of genocide. Those norms, which should never have been norms, it's like they're taking a sledgehammer to them. But they do it in such a kind of quiet way, and I love that, because I think Anishinaabe people do that a lot.

At a Sunday church gathering or women's institute meeting on a Sunday afternoon, my grandmother could say the most outrageous thing that really confronted people's beliefs. And I'm sure that half an hour later, people would be sitting there having tea and go, "Did she say…?" You know? Because she would say it in such a way that it was very non-confrontational and sounded so logical and matter of fact. Some of the work that I see and that I admire a lot, it comes from people who are doing that kind of thing. I like the shit disturbers too. I always have. But I think that we need a bit of both, and so I like that work that's happening.

I think that what you're doing is important because just the fact that I'm having trouble thinking specifically of the way that masculinity is being represented in Indigenous arts in Canada, or even more broadly, tells me that it's an area where we need to be more thoughtful and more aware, and to not accept the depictions that are out there, which are pretty narrow when you think about it. There's the monosyllabic warrior stud type guy and there's the dysfunctional, abused or abuser inmate, ex-con—those kinds of stereotypes. But I think your work is really timely, and I hope that what you're doing and others are doing in this area is going to have the same ripple effect that the erotica work had, where my sons are going be able to find a wider range of depictions of Indigenous men that will maybe inspire them, influence them to some extent, and teach them both in that Nanabozho way of what to do and what not to do—because Nanabozho taught through both his good deeds and his misdeeds. They'll have more to draw on than I think Indigenous men have had in the past few generations.

SM: You and I have spoken before about the causal relationship between particular ideological conceptions of masculinity and eruptions of violence—particularly violence against women. Can you reflect on these connections?

KAD: There is an underlying acceptance of violence against Indigenous women in the mainstream. Absolutely. That's why so many women are missing and continue to go missing and that's why their disappearances don't get investigated in ways that lead to them being found or even their bodies being found. That's why funding for Sisters in Spirit can be axed with no public outcry. This acceptance also persists within our own communities. A lot of Indigenous men have learned what it means to be an Indigenous man from the worst possible sources, like residential school or CAS [Children's Aid Society] or jail, or parents who went through one or more of those systems and lacked the parenting skills that they needed in order to guide their sons. I don't think it's a surprise to anybody that perpetrators so often are the men in our own communities, because they've been taught that violence against Indigenous women is a legitimate option and Indigenous women also have been taught that it's an option for how they ought to be treated. It is an intergenerational thing where that way of thinking just gets passed down and passed down, and it leads to real outcomes in the real world. These ways of thinking don't just remain in people's fantasies without having any impact in the real world. They do impact our reality, they absolutely do. And the real outcome is that it's not safe for Indigenous women. I think that hasn't changed a whole lot. I mean there

> A LOT OF INDIGENOUS MEN HAVE LEARNED WHAT IT MEANS TO BE AN INDIGENOUS MAN FROM THE WORST POSSIBLE SOURCES, LIKE RESIDENTIAL SCHOOL OR CAS OR JAIL, OR PARENTS WHO WENT THROUGH ONE OR MORE OF THOSE SYSTEMS AND LACKED THE PARENTING SKILLS THAT THEY NEEDED IN ORDER TO GUIDE THEIR SONS.

are still constant reports of Indigenous women who are missing. That's still going on. And when things like Idle No More happen, violence is directed towards Indigenous women in response.

I think changing things within our communities means that we have to get back to some basics around who we are and how we interrelate. And it gets to that erotica discussion too, but it's beyond how we relate to ourselves in terms of our sexuality, but in terms of intimacy of all kinds. It's how my sons are relating to the girls at daycare, and how they are being taught to do that, and how they're being taught to talk to the women who are around them, how they're being taught to talk to the girls who are around them, and what's acceptable and what's not acceptable. It's about how they are being taught to see themselves and what it means to be a man and have power. Because power's not necessarily a negative thing. We all need to be and feel empowered. We all need to assert our own power in different ways, but there have been so many negative examples of power being expressed that as soon as you say "power," I think for a lot of people that means power *over* something. Power to bend something to your will. And that's what concerns me.

In terms of the healing of our communities and of ourselves, I don't know if it sounds old-fashioned, but I really think that one of the roles of men is to protect the women in their families and communities. And, in a lot of ways, that's not happening. That's why it's far too easy for other people to come in and create havoc, abuse our women, leave marks on our children's minds and spirits, and then walk away. I don't know if it comes out of guilt from the men, because maybe they've done things themselves that they're not proud of, or because that violence has been normalized in some ways, but if the men in our own families and communities aren't protecting us, there's no way that women can protect ourselves and our children against men. That's just the reality. Individually, maybe we can, but on a broad scale, old-fashioned as that might sound, I really think it's necessary for men to assume this role. When men don't protect the women and children around them, women and children are more vulnerable to being harmed. So I think we have to reclaim what's good about men having a protective role, being the protectors in the community. I believe that's a legitimate male role and a positive role that helps our families and our communities to stay safe and be healthy.

Some people might think I'm some kind of throwback or it's a really sexist thing to say, but to me it's just common sense. It's just the reality of accepting that I'm a woman and I have certain strengths and abilities, but if a guy is coming at me, what are my chances of protecting myself? If my brothers, cousins, father, grandfathers, uncles, whatever, are not there to intervene, I can't control that situation. I don't see women as weak in any way, but there are just some genetic imperatives that we can't escape. Like, men are not going to have babies. So, I don't care how much I work out, I'm not going to get the biceps that a guy would have. It's just how it is. So we have to be able to get past that self-censorship where we think, "I can't say that because that might sound

WE HAVE TO RECLAIM WHAT'S GOOD ABOUT MEN HAVING A PROTECTIVE ROLE, BEING THE PROTECTORS IN THE COMMUNITY. I BELIEVE THAT'S A LEGITIMATE MALE ROLE AND A POSITIVE ROLE THAT HELPS OUR FAMILIES AND OUR COMMUNITIES TO STAY SAFE AND BE HEALTHY.

bad to some feminists or some other women or some men," and just say, "This is what we need from the men around us. We need protection. Our families need protecting."

SM: And that sense of protectorship is generative in multiple ways because it not only provides a sense of safety and stability, but it also offers an important sense of purpose and meaning for the protectors.

KAD: There are so many men who don't know what their role as a man is anymore. It can be just something as basic as being watchful and protecting their families and communities. It could change our world as Indigenous people if that were happening. I think it would create a profound difference if men could simply—I mean, nothing's simple—but if they could take that on as a basic part of their responsibility as men.

And there are other things, like being a present and healthy parent. And part of that is protecting, but for men it goes beyond just being a protective parent; it has to extend outward. In our communities there's a role for everyone as far as the children go. And not everybody lives up to that. Some people have gotten into that nuclear family thing where they only really care about their own little family. But when kids are around at community functions, if somebody's doing something that's dangerous, people will speak up and speak to them, and as long as it's done in a good way, it's not a problem. There aren't arguments about, "you're not allowed to talk to my kid because he was running and screaming around the hall." There's still an acceptance that everybody has a certain responsibility for caring for the children in those kinds of gatherings. So if you expand that out, it should be all the time that we're vigilant about protecting our children and our community, about protecting each other. There are many things working against that kind of change, but it's something that we can strive to get back to that would really change our lives and change the future for our children.

INTO THE TRIBE OF MAN

A CONVERSATION WITH RICHARD VAN CAMP

5 JUNE 2011
Conversation
between Richard
Van Camp and Sam
McKegney at the
home of Richard's
mother, Rosa Wah-
shee, in Yellowknife,
Northwest Territories.

"ARE YOU A BAD MAN, TORCHY?"
"NO, BUT SOMETIMES I LEAVE AND LET THE BAD MAN IN."
—RICHARD VAN CAMP, "MERMAIDS"

RICHARD VAN CAMP: Writing is the greatest therapy; it is the greatest healing. You can fix things in fiction, and you can find things again and you can find yourself again in writing. You can find forgiveness in writing, and I think that for everybody out there who is hurting or grieving or is wounded, I think that there is great medicine in writing. And so I know that I like to write about men a lot. I think I've only been ever able to write two stories in a woman's voice, and I've been very lucky, I believe, to have pulled that off, but I have three brothers, and I have two fathers, and I think that that's why—and my best friends are men and they're beautiful men, gentle men, hard men, and men who are fathers and brothers themselves—so I think of fellowship, that tribe of man medicine that I'm involved with all the time with the uncles I've adopted and me listening at their supper tables or over the phone or through e-mails. I'm really grateful that I have that in my life. Yes. I'm ready to answer any question you have, Sam.

SAM MCKEGNEY: Thank you. Well, first I'd like to start by thinking a bit about stages of life, especially with the new baby book. I'd like to start with writing literature meant to be read by those who aren't its ultimate target audience. The child is the ultimate audience and the reader is the caregiver conduit. Does that require a different process for you as author?

RVC: Yes, I think so. When my mom's really happy—you can hear her in the next room—she does this thing, she goes "Hey-ya-hey." And it's beautiful. I don't even think she knows she does it. And so, at that time, my friends Marney and Zoe were carrying and expecting their first baby together. And so I was so near and dear to them that that was really the impetus to writing *Welcome Song for Baby*, so I knew it would be a song. I knew that it would be an honouring. I knew that it would be a welcome. And I know that we have blended families. I know that we have same-sex parents. I know that we have children being raised in poverty. I know we have children being raised in wonderful situations, and I know we have children that are being raised and welcomed into unthinkable situations. So what happened was this great lullaby came to me in a flash. And it really took me less than two days to write. And it was with that "Hey-ya-hey." That song and that beat. And I knew that I wanted it to be a wish. I knew I wanted it to be a welcome. And I knew I wanted it to be an honouring. And that's really how I wrote *Welcome Song for Baby*.

And then years later, I was in this very room, Sam, and I was playing with my niece and nephew, Vyka and Shaeden. And Shaedon, who's four now—he's the little boy on page 4 in *Welcome Song for Baby*, the little yawning one—he has seven books that you have to read. And watch, tonight I'll be reading the seven books to him. You know, I was giving my brother a break because he was running the tub. And he said, "Uncle Richard, you get to read the seven books tonight to Shaedon," and I said, "Alright." And we were cuddled up right here. Shaedon was really close to me. Vyka was kinda doing her own thing. I don't think she was walking yet. And I read Shaedon his seven books. And two of them were texture books where you feel the little wool of the lamb and the grass—I'm sure you know all about this—and the first one was "Where's Elmo's Blanket?" And then the rest were more about shapes and colours and different little things, and it hit me that none of these were honouring my niece and my nephew. None of them were. And I understand we need to teach texture and I understand we need to teach shape and I understand we need to, "Can you open the door and find the little bird?" I understand all that. But it hit me, there was no grace, there was no welcome.

The protector in me, that uncle in me, went, "We can do better than what's here. We can do better than 'Where's Elmo's Blanket?'" I got this little beat, and this little

RICHARD VAN CAMP was raised in Fort Smith, Northwest Territories and is the first published author from the Tlicho Dene. He is a graduate of the En'owkin International School of Writing, the University of Victoria's BFA program and UBC's MFA program in Creative Writing. He is the author of a novel, *The Lesser Blessed* (Douglas and McIntyre, 1996), which is now a movie with First Generation Films. He is the author of multiple short story collections including *Angel Wing Splash Pattern* (Kegedonce Press, 2002), and *The Moon of Letting Go* and *Godless but Loyal to Heaven* (Enfield and Wizenty, 2009 and 2012). He has written books for children, including *A Man Called Raven* and *What's the Most Beautiful Thing You Know about Horses?* (Children's Book Press, 1997 and 1998), illustrated by Cree artist George Littlechild, and books for newborns, including *Welcome Song for Baby* (Orca Book Publishers, 2007), *Nighty Night* (McKellar and Martin, 2011) and *Little You* (2013). And for the Healthy Aboriginal Network, he has authored two comics: *Path of the Warrior* (on gang prevention) and *Kiss Me Deadly* (on sexual health).

song and I said, "Shaedon, can you just wait here for a little second," and so he ended up going through some of the books himself. I sat down at that table there and I used a paper napkin and I wrote *Nighty Night, A Bedtime Song For Babies*. And I literally typed it up and I just left it, and then I came back and I ended up spending the night as an uncle, making sure that the kids were a-okay. I finished reading to everybody. And then probably the next day, within the next week, I sent it to Tonya Martin of McKellar and Martin. And then she wrote an e-mail probably three days later, and it was three words: "I. Love. It." And that's when I knew, we've got something. Like, if Tonya Martin loves it, then we're good. We're gold, because she's tough.

So when we're crafting stories that are for an individual reading, that's a whole different kind of medicine. That's a different kind of carving technique. When I wrote *Welcome Song For Baby*, I sung it as I was writing it. And *Nighty Night, A Bedtime Song For Babies*, I sung that, too. They deserved to be sung. So I think what I've written are really songs, whereas "Dogrib Midnight Runners" or "Sky Burial," those are more like hymns, if that makes sense.

SM: It does. And with the other children's stories, for instance, *What's the Most Beautiful Thing You Know About Horses?* I was really interested in that story's awareness of stereotypes about Indigenous peoples, at the same time that it doesn't condemn stereotypes.

RVC: Everyone knows "Cowboys and Indians." We all played it. Some of the Indians didn't want to be Indians when we were growing up; we wanted to be ninjas, right? And vice versa. And it's amazing how many cowboys want to be Indians these days. Go to any cowboy bar, right? Or any Indian bar. Go to any rodeo or powwow. But that was really welcoming people with a stereotype. Cowboy or the Indian, even though Indian is not politically correct 'cause we're Dene, we're Tlicho, we're Dogrib, right? But we can get into the magic of what it is to be Dene and Dogrib by saying, "My grandfather used to sneak into wolf dens to get their wolf cubs so he could breed them with dogs. This way his wolfpack would be deadly." So being able to say, you know, "This is 'Cowboys and Indians,' but keep reading and I'll tell you stories about how an eagle has three shadows or how frogs are the keepers of rain. There's magic here if you're willing to look past the stereotypes."

SM: The comic books from the Aboriginal Healing Network seek out a really important audience, particularly with relation to questions that this project is working on—finding models for healthy masculinity, healthy self-image, all of those things. Is that a difficult audience to write for and to reach?

RVC: *Path of the Warrior* was inspired by a shooting. It was inspired by the shooting of a young baby named Asia Saddleback in Hobbema reserve. And the story goes that when Asia was little, she was sleeping in her crib and she was shot in the heart, or near her heart, by a stray bullet. It was inspired by a gang member and it was inspired by a stray bullet that found her. And what that did, that shooting, was it mobilized Hobbema to bring back their traditional banishment laws. And the community realized that if a sleeping baby in her crib isn't safe, nobody's safe, so what do we have left to lose? And they started bringing the heavy equipment in to mow down the crack houses and they started banishing gang members and drug dealers, so they started getting rid of a lot of dangerous people. And they came up with this awareness that if you don't know where your parents are and if you don't know where your kids are then you're contributing to the problem. And it's time for elders to be elders and for parents to be parents and for teachers to be teachers. And it was a time of incredible reclaiming. So I was horrified when I saw the documentary about the shooting of Asia Saddleback. At that time I was living in Vancouver, where, yes, there are gangs, but I wasn't aware of how high Indian-on-Indian violence was, especially on reserves. I had heard about it, but Asia Saddleback brought it to me and that's because I'm an uncle and I just couldn't imagine the horror of having my niece or nephew shot in their homes in their cribs.

The welcome into a gang is prestige and power and respect and "The Life." But what is the underside of all that? The worst thing with gang violence is there's something called "blood in, blood out." And so when you're welcomed into a gang, you are beaten half to death by your gang members and then you're welcomed. It's a brutal initiation. It's a blood offering. And then, Heaven forbid, you ever want to leave. Well, then you're basically left for dead when they're done with you. And they burn everything. They burn your ride and take all your jewellery and your money and they burn your house down and everything else under the sun. So you're basically just left naked on the side of a road. And then after that, you're at their mercy if they want to hunt you even more.

What I really love about *Path of the Warrior* is that it is a call to being a protector for your community and for all those little ones who can't defend themselves. And so they say the most precious things in this life are defenceless. So you think of childhood, you think of innocence, you think of trust, you know. You cheat on your wife and then you go home and she doesn't know you cheated but you do. Her love, her faith in you is completely defenceless. Or when a child is molested, that child is completely defenceless. Or when a pet is harmed, you know, when an animal is harmed. Completely defenceless. Friendship is defenceless. There's no defence against what a friend can do to you. So *Path of the Warrior* is Cullen's path back to his destiny, and that's why I love that story so much and that's why I'm really happy when I get an e-mail from a mom who says, "I read my son's comic book and wept."

SM: There's a fine line in terms of maintaining the integrity of the story and passing on a message, like you were saying, because children are so adept at realizing when they're being spoken down to, so adept at realizing that, well, this is didactic, this is someone telling me what the moral is.

IT'S TIME FOR ELDERS TO BE ELDERS AND FOR PARENTS TO BE PARENTS AND FOR TEACHERS TO BE TEACHERS. AND IT WAS A TIME OF INCREDIBLE RECLAIMING.

RVC: With *Path of the Warrior*, I think it's a violent, horrible, bloody story, and that's why that image of blood on those babies' moccasins is really jarring and it's something that we haven't seen before. It's something that I don't think any of us ever want to see and that's on, I believe, the second page. And I think that's our hook. As someone who reads voraciously and watches tons of movies, I love that sensation of, "Are they gonna do this? Are you really gonna take me here and how on earth are you gonna absolve yourself of any responsibility from this in forty-eight pages with six frames on the page? Are you really gonna take me to this deep dark place?" and the answer is, "Yes, we are." I think that's the hook and I think that working with artists like Cree artist Steve Sanderson, who can convey emotion in face, emotion in gesture, I think that also was our trump card with *Path of the Warrior*.

SM: With relation to gang violence, what are the features of gang violence that become attractive to some male youth, in your analysis?

RVC: Well, I've never been in an Indian gang but I sure know about brotherhood and packing up with a team of friends. It's that sense of belonging and being heard and being welcomed into what I call the "Tribe of Man." And if you're not getting that welcome at home, you're going to be looking for it somewhere else, you know? So many of us, I believe, have lost our rites of passage and I think that's why so many people hunger to get tattooed, they hunger to be marked, so they're welcomed into manhood. One of the questions that I love to ask people is, "When did you know that you were a man? When did you feel that body wake up inside your blood? When were you welcomed into your inheritance as a man in a good way?"

SM: I've been talking with a lot of people about initiation rites and about ways in which ceremony can be brought back to celebrate the maturation process so people don't become shamed by their changing bodies but rather recognize their movement into different stages of their own life paths, which brings me to the issue of sexual health in *Kiss Me Deadly*: how did you conceive of the creative method to approach the topic of sexual health in comic book form?

RVC: When we were growing up, Fort Smith was the STI capital of Canada. My little hometown. And so the entire pitch just came to me in a flash, like: they fooled around, you know, typical small town, they fooled around—either with each other's best friends or cousins—and had unprotected sex because of drinking and lifestyle choices or "Baby baby, just the tip. Just the tip!" and then got back together. What interests me is, what does a couple need to do to make sure they don't give each other the dose? So many people don't go to get tested for STIs, because they just aren't aware of the test. They think someone's gonna get a big Q-tip and put a swab up my pee hole and a red-headed woman with huge cleavage is going to stick her finger up my bum, you know what I mean? Like you just get all these, I don't know if they're fantasies or what, but you get

SO MANY OF US, I BELIEVE, HAVE LOST OUR RITES OF PASSAGE AND I THINK THAT'S WHY SO MANY PEOPLE HUNGER TO GET TATTOOED, THEY HUNGER TO BE MARKED, SO THEY'RE WELCOMED INTO MANHOOD.

these misconceptions, and it's easier to say, "Deny 'til I die." Right? "I have an open wound, I have a chancre on the left side of my scrotum—it'll just, I'm just gonna go swimming for twelve days and hope the chlorine sterilizes this gaping wound." Do you know what I mean?

SM: Sure.

RVC: What I wanted to do was address every man's worst fear, which is you may have contracted something and you're giving it to somebody you love. *Or*, somebody you love has contracted something from your cousin and is about to give it you, right? And then at the same time I thought, so many of our youth—this happened to a friend of mine—his fourteen-year-old son would come and spend time with him because they were co-parenting, and his computer kept crashing. And so he kept taking it to the same rental place that would repair computers. And finally about the fourth time my friend snapped, "Look, I keep paying you guys eighty bucks, and my computer keeps getting these viruses over and over." And the computer technician bit his head off and said, "Look, I didn't want to say this, sir, but some of the sites that you've been trolling are probably illegal in about fifty states." So my friend realized that his stepson had not received the talk but had in fact been trolling the Internet, and that was how he was learning about sex. And so my friend realized that, after he saw some of the sites that his stepson was looking at, that these were really demeaning, humiliating, gruesome sites, and the truth is, I think, that is how many of our male youth are learning about sex now. That it has to be something that's punishing or it has to be power over someone or it has to be humiliating or women are meant to be objectified.

> THESE WERE REALLY DEMEANING, HUMILIATING, GRUESOME SITES, AND THE TRUTH IS, I THINK, THAT IS HOW MANY OF OUR MALE YOUTH ARE LEARNING ABOUT SEX NOW.

Another thing that I probably am going to receive a lot of flak over is that I have never been able to believe fully in the Medicine Wheel, because I believe it's a flawed system. And I know, I might as well slap a nun on the way home tonight because of what I've just said, but we talk about the physical and the emotional and the mental and the spiritual aspects of human beings, but where's the sexual? And people say, "Well, you know it's an amalgamation of all those," and I'm like, "You know what, if we're not talking about it, it's killing us and it's wounding us and it's harming us." You know, when we have eight times the national average of STIs here, lives are being demolished forever, you know? And yes, there are things out there that a prescription can take away, but there are a lot of things out there that they can't. And so, again, all the stories in the world aren't gonna make up for the perforating chancre on the tip of your knob. You know what I mean? And that's a direct quote from The Dene-Hawk-Richard-Van-Camp!

SM: Just thinking through the way you were discussing the shame and the stigma around sexuality, and beyond that, the way in which sex has been overtaken by objectification as opposed to being honoured as a relational reciprocal system—in a lot of your work, it seems to me that there's a movement toward awakening in men alternative ways of understanding sexual relationships. I think, for instance, of your story "Let's Beat the Shit Out of Herman Rosco" as asking men to question what they believe a normal and natural sexual relationship to be, right? And to think of themselves as givers and not just recipients of sexual/sensual pleasure.

RVC: And someone who cherishes, right? Somebody, again, who welcomes and honours, like a protector of that trust, yeah, protector of that gift of sexuality.

SM: And one thing I wanted to ask you about is that even as there are elements of the sacred in the sexual, you're an artist who is willing to talk about the fun of sex, that it's not simply transcendent, that it has its awkwardness, its humour, its sounds, and its smells…

RVC: I love planting those seeds. They say, once you've seen colour, you never go back to black and white. A long time ago, the Dene people traditionally would never put water on the floor in a cup. Ever. Ever. Because you're showing disrespect to that spirit that's in the cup. All water is life. All tea is life. There's a spirit in the coffee. So we always keep our water high. The traditionalists keep our water high. And if we're in a prayer and we're studying in a gym and we all have to stand, you'll see people, they'll look around, and they'll put like a little piece of paper underneath it to cradle that water for a little while 'cause you're showing respect, and when I pass that on, once you know it, how could you ever put that glass of water in your hands on the floor ever again knowing that, whether or not you believe in it, you are showing disrespect, in somebody's eyes, you're showing disrespect to that spirit of life that nourishes you. And that's what great stories do, is that once it's in your brain, once it's bouncing around in your cranium, how could you not respect, or at least wonder, or be curious about it, for the rest of your life?

SM: I've taught *The Lesser Blessed* three times in totally different curricular contexts, and in every case, students really relate with Larry as a protagonist. How much of Larry's relatability or his experiences speak to the anguish of going through the process of being a teenager and therefore are almost universal concerns? And how much of his story is a Dogrib-specific or Indigenous-specific story?

RVC: I don't know if I've ever told you this story, Sam, but after *The Lesser Blessed* came out, it was brand new, I was in Fort Smith at my dad's house and we had a few Dogrib elders over for breakfast one day and they were in town for a gathering. So my dad is a great cook and his breakfast Sunday brunches are not to be missed. He knows the ins and outs of harnessing the power of bacon grease to get everything going. I mean, your hair'll be shiny for a month, but trust me: it's worth it.

But what happened was, there was a little old lady, she was Dogrib, and she was showing us some of the purses she made, and she had some moccasins for sale and some earrings, and I didn't have a lot of money at the time, and I said, "Oh you know, I'd like to get these earrings for my mom. I'll trade you for my book," and she goes,

"Oh yeah, you're the author, the Dogrib author that grew up in Smith, eh?" And I say, "Oh yes, yes, I am," and I was still getting used to that title, you know? It felt good, but I wasn't sure if I could wear it. And she said, "I'm not much of a reader, but I'll trade you these earrings. I'll get it for my girl," she said. So I said, "Okay," so I went racing down to the room and grabbed the little box I had and fished one out and I came back. I dusted it off, I was so proud. And she said, "I'm probably not gonna read it, but if you could sign it for my girl, that'd be great, but can you tell me what it's about?" And I said, "Yeah," I said, "It's a coming-of-age story of a sixteen-year-old Dogrib Dene named Larry Sole," and she went, "Larry." And I said, "Yeah." And she goes, "Like your cousin?" And you know, I had a spiritual epiphany unlike any other. And I saw in a heartbeat the magnificent plan the Creator had for me while writing that book.

When I was in high school in Fort Smith, our cousin Larry came to stay with us for a while from Fort Rae, and he was gorgeous. He was a prince of light; he could speak Dogrib; he could sing in Dogrib; he could play guitar; he was so physically gorgeous. And the second he got off that plane, the phone started ringing off the hook. Married women, women who were engaged, women who were expecting: it didn't matter. They loved him. And I've seen that in a couple men, where they have that gift where women just fall in love with them, women become powerless. It's nobody's fault, but that's the medicine they have. And Larry had that. And what happened was, after a couple weeks of this, he was invited to a party, and I was just getting to know him and I really admired him and looked up to him. You know, I'll never forget his voice. He had the most calming voice. So he went to this party, getting ready to have a good time but there were no women there. It was all the men. And they beat him. They beat him horribly. And my parents had to go get him. And they wouldn't let us go downstairs to go and look at him because his face was so torn apart, you know? It was horrible. And we could hear him crying in the vents. And my mom prepared a yarrow compress for his face to help with the healing and swelling and everything. And it was really sad. And he moved back to Fort Rae shortly after. His heart was broken and then, within several months, he took his own life.

In the Dogrib tradition, we're not to speak of people who have taken their own lives. I think that is in the Catholic way, myself. I don't think that that is truly our way. And so, I realized when she said that, "Like your cousin," that I had written *The Lesser Blessed* out of a wish for how I hoped Larry's life could've been, but I didn't realize it at the time. And that's why "Dogrib Midnight Runners" is so important because we lost a friend to suicide who loved to streak in Fort Smith and he was a genius; he was the pride of our town for years. But he had a lot of problems and he chose to take his own life, and he left behind a little girl and a woman who loved him very much. I'm sure there are several women who loved him very much. He was a son, he was a brother, and he's gone. And Fort Smith is famous for many things and one of them is fighting. And there have been three times when our little town has stopped fighting long enough to

AND FORT SMITH IS FAMOUS FOR MANY THINGS AND ONE OF THEM IS FIGHTING. AND THERE HAVE BEEN THREE TIMES WHEN OUR LITTLE TOWN HAS STOPPED FIGHTING LONG ENOUGH TO WEEP TOGETHER. AND THAT WAS ONE OF THEM.

weep together. And that was one of them. And the reason I wrote "Dogrib Midnight Runners" was I was shocked when I returned to Fort Smith after Paul took his life and I saw people who never knew him but knew his mother weeping, weeping, weeping for his daughter and weeping for his mother. And I saw what a great thief suicide is and it always has been and it always will be because his name will forever be spoken in hushed tones, and think about what his daughter or son is going to have to grow up with in that shadow. And the reason I wrote "Dogrib Midnight Runners" was to reclaim that life and to honour that life rather than inherit and welcome that spirit of blackness and never being able to move on. And so the main character remembers in "Dogrib Midnight Runners" that the gentleman in the story, "Justin," who took his life, loved to streak, and so out of honour of his memory, the narrator, "Grant," decides to streak.

SM: That story says many things also about the communion of male friendship, about kinship among the men and their departed brother. And then, also, a sense of welcoming oneself back into the body. There's a lot of ways in which we are alienated from our bodies and taught to think of the body as something to be ashamed of. "Dogrib Midnight Runners" creates a space in which those men can imagine themselves differently through running naked, through being vulnerable in front of one another, right? Is that an important thing for young men?

RVC: I think so. Although, I mean, we were told by our grandfather to never go into a sweat because that's not our way. And I've been a doorman at a couple of sweats now, and I've been a helper, and I know that in some sweats people go in naked together and in some sweats people are clothed in bathing suits. Sometimes it's in towels. But I think that you're on to something there that it is important that in the natural world, you've nothing to be ashamed of with your body. You are who you are. This is your temple, right? Many of us are overfed and undernourished, you know? And if this who you are, this is who you are right now. It doesn't mean that that's who you are inside. This is who you are right now.

SM: In "The Night Charles Bukowski Died," there's a scenario of horrific bullying, of transgressions that require redress. But by the end of the story, as a reader you're unsure of whether violence can actually make things better, as the younger friend is cowering, weeping…

RVC: Mikey, yeah.

SM: And, then, the narrator gives the roar. Is that a roar declaring that this revenge had to happen or is that roar about the futility of what's available to us?

RVC: Again, it goes back to the most precious things are defenceless. That's the heartbreak that I like to play with: how far are you gonna twist the defenceless and how far are you gonna take somebody into those dark places when they're completely innocent, you know? Or sometimes, even when they're not so innocent but they've made their peace with what they're doing. And Torchy [from "Mermaids"] is a joy to work with because he has a code. Flinch [from "I Count Myself Among Them"] has made his way in the world on this really gentle red road, but deep down inside, he says, "I'm an attack dog. Don't make me do what they want me to do to you." He's trying really hard to be a good person. And that's what I like. Torchy's line: "I'm not a bad man. I just leave for a while and let the bad man in." What a terrifying thing to put out there: do you really want to see what the bad man can do?

SM: What would you desire young male readers—or any readers—to glean from your work about what a positive idea of warriorhood might be?

RVC: I think a protector and a nurturer and a giver. In my new collection of short stories, *Godless but Loyal to Heaven*, we see Torchy become a protector not only for his dearly departed brother, Sfen, but we see him become a protector for the family of his heart, Snowbird and Stephanie; on top of this he becomes a protector for a young man who he bullied; he also becomes a protector for the town and "settlers" who could potentially be moving into a new subdivision that is infected with uranium. In "Love Song" we see Grant from "Let's Beat the Shit out of Herman Rosko" try and become a protector for a Chinese mail-order bride; my new gladiator, "Bear," is a protector in "The Fleshing" and in "The Contract."

You know, my friend Gary Gottfriedson said, "Richard, you don't know what love is until you become a grandfather. You don't know what love is until you hold your first grandchild. You think you know what love is, you think you know what love is with your own children and the love of your life, but when you hold your first grandchild, it all makes sense. Every tear you've ever cried, every friend you've ever lost along the way, every horror you've ever faced, it all had to happen for that moment. And anything after grandchildren is gold." Gary's just become a grandfather again and I just see this joy in his life. And that's my wish for everybody is that peace and that joy, to have a safe home, to have a safe bed. To be able to realize the power of now. Not to wait to say you're sorry, not to wait to ask for forgiveness, not to wait to help.

They say you know you're rich when you're rich. And this has nothing to do with money. It has to do with family; it has to do with health; it has to do with the opportunities we wake to every day. My wish is that we celebrate everything that we have right now and to help others on their way. That is my wish. *Mahsi cho!*

INTIMATE LIKE MUSCLE AND BONE

A CONVERSATION WITH JOANNE ARNOTT

15 SEPTEMBER 2011
Conversation between
Joanne Arnott and Sam
McKegney at Sam's home
in Kingston, Ontario.

ALTHOUGH IT SEEMS TO ME
WHEN YOUNG MEN ARRIVE
GROWN MEN TURN AWAY

AND THERE IS NO HAND
INTO WHICH I CAN PASS YOU
NOW YOU ARE COME A MAN
EXCEPT YOUR OWN

—JOANNE ARNOTT, "INTO MANHOOD," FROM MOTHER TIME

SAM MCKEGNEY: Your collection of poetry, *Mother Time*, not only tracks the relationship between parent and children but it also recognizes the difficulties of growing up. I wonder if you could reflect on how poetry, throughout your career, has allowed you to investigate growing up, what growing up means.

JOANNE ARNOTT: I'm very strongly opinionated and also extremely shy—or I have been. And so, poetry and other kinds of writing have been a really necessary outlet for me. And as a poor person and not much in the academy, I need an outlet to express my level of thinking and my need to process intellectually what I see around me. If I'm living in a rooming house and everybody else is alcoholic and in the hole, and pursuit of life is getting the next cigarette, then writing becomes a lifeline, a way for me to be fully myself no matter what my outer circumstances. So I associate my writing with my ability to maintain my freedom as a human being, whatever or however adverse the circumstances. I think it's a really stabilizing thread in my life.

I have this idea of poetic information, that there's a kind of a multidimensionality that humans have, we interact on many levels at once. Poetry is a way, like a vehicle, to capture many more dimensions of a person's experience, and share those in the absence of the other. So then when you pick up my poetry and you read it, then you're able to access me in a multidimensional way. So what I mean by that is, how I feel in my body, what my emotions are, what my thoughts are, what my perspective is. I think that all of that can be captured and delivered. And there's also a lot of spirit in that as well.

SM: And how has that vehicle allowed you to explore your own process of growth?

JA: Of course, my primary experience of violence and being not safe is my family. And throughout my parenting years this has been a challenge, and a path of discovery. I started off going, you know, "I'm not gonna do what they did. I'm gonna be way better and smarter and so on," but there's this idea of blueprinting. It's like you can only know what you know and so I didn't, of course, in my twenties, have great insight into how my parents' lovely ideal wish for a great family, how that faltered. And so, despite all my best intentions and my snobbery, I ended up in a very similar situation, because I didn't understand how they got there. All of us had been growing up and coping in a stripped community, or denuded way, and this is one result of the diasporic push. Then I came to a point when I looked around and saw, "Okay, well, my kids are afraid of me. Now what do I do?" 'Cause this was not how it was supposed to be, right? Then accessing community in a different way, learning how to do that, and what the benefits might be.

It's like this: in where I was and am living there's a lot of resources for First Nations families in crisis. So, I just threw myself upon those resources and learned a lot, and through those connections and through some of my writing friends and allies, I was able to, on the one hand, grieve the disaster, and on the other hand, continue to hold on to this insight: that my children have a right to be mothered by me, and I have a

JOANNE ARNOTT (Métis) is a poet, essayist, and arts/community organizer originally from Manitoba who has resided in Vancouver for over two decades. She is a founding member of the Aboriginal Writers' Collective West Coast and The Aunties' Collective, and she is mother to six children, all born at home. Her collections of poetry include *Wiles of Girlhood* (Press Gang Publishers, 1991), *My Grass Cradle* (Press Gang Publishers, 1992), *Steepy Mountain Love Poetry* (Kegedonce Press, 2004), *Mother Time: New and Selected* (Ronsdale Press, 2007), *A Night for the Lady* (Ronsdale Press, 2013) and *Halfling Spring* (Kegedonce Press, 2014). Her non-fiction works include *Breasting the Waves: On Writing and Healing* (Press Gang Publishers, 1995).

right and a responsibility to mother them, and not give in to this huge push to separate "inadequate" parents from their children. Because the reality is, the move is to take all the little babies from these "fucked-up" people and give them to, you know, white Christian middle-class families. And so that does not interrupt that sense of denuding and destroying community. It just feeds right into it.

I also think it's really depleting for people to hold on to some idealized version of reality and reject where we actually are. So, it's kind of a balancing act between acceptance of what is and maintaining aspirations and hope and optimism and enjoyment and all those things that make life worthwhile.

SM: Your work demonstrates a real attraction to fantasy and magic, but always alongside a pull back to realities. Are there ways of ensuring a balance between a vision for something better and simultaneously recognition of what's around us? Or can one become sort of unmoored?

JA: Speaking personally, it's easy to become unmoored. What I vision, no matter how outlandish or different from where I'm at right now, it's something that I can realize and what I have to honour is the distance... I have to build up earthwork underneath the dream until that dream is resting on the earth, and that's the reality that we've come to. If I'm not happy with where I'm at right now, I still have this goal, I have this vision. And when I've accomplished something, it's very good to look back and go, "Well, you know, a year ago or three years ago, this was an undreamed-of possibility. And then it became this wisp of a cool idea—and now, here I am!" And just to honour the journey that I and we are making in an ongoing way. There's a lot of fatigue and a lot of heartbreak and discouragement that people can feel, which is legitimized by the reality, but it's also not the whole story. The past, it has a strong influence on the future, but it doesn't own the future.

SM: Do you feel that shame and stigma shape ideas about gender?

JA: Some of the very strong impressions that I have of my father are from a period of time when he was single parenting me and my younger siblings, and just this person so deeply weighted down with shame because nothing had worked out the way he thought it would. And he had a lot of anger-management problems and—what would you call it—a kind of a male arrogance, which he ended up having to pay a high price for in terms of losing a relationship that he valued very much. So he didn't have the good teachings that he needed to be who he really is on a day-to-day level and be able to maintain and nourish the relationships that he really wanted to maintain and nourish. So that's really tragic. And that is a fundamentally different way of looking at a "Capital 'A' Abuser" than is current in a lot of mainstream or settler analysis.

I was at a gathering in the early '90s on Hecla Island in Manitoba, a woman's gathering, and I arrived with some big questions that I needed answers for. I had been participating

THE PAST, IT HAS A STRONG INFLUENCE ON THE FUTURE, BUT IT DOESN'T OWN THE FUTURE.

in a healing circle with this very lovely Cree man, very charismatic healer, and I had just found out that he was secretly sexually abusing some of the women who were coming to him for help within a ritual or spiritual healing context. He was using that context as a shelter for sexual abuse. Consult a white feminist about what I should do in this situation, and its like, "Speak back! Name him, shame him," you know, "Get the name out there, and publicize all around!" And then talking to Chrystos, who was also at that time at the gathering, she had a completely different approach. Her insight was, "we're all damaged." So there has to be a more subtle approach to setting and maintaining healthy boundaries in a way that doesn't increase the shame. If I feel ashamed of something I've done, that means that I've disappointed myself, I haven't used my power to my own best advantage and to the best advantage of the people around me. And so rather than trying to separate this world into this false reality of "those are the bad guys and these are the good guys," we need to find ways to cherish and nourish people and the relationships between people and, at the same time, to eliminate all the cruel ways that we've learned how to mistreat one another.

SM: That really relies on recognition of the complex interconnectedness among people—the inadequacy, I guess, of the radical discreteness of individualism.

JA: What am I but this landscape of different influences and echoes and opinions? And the strengths of the people around me, their influence on me is profound, so I have to work very hard to make shields between me and anybody who's in my space—including the cat! I'm very sensitized to and connected with my environment and that includes all the forms of life—it's indiscriminate. So, you and I are not related by blood and we've only known each other a couple of years, but if you're in a room with me and my sister or my mother, you're not less real to me, and I may understand where someone within my so-called nuclear family, where they're coming from in a more predictive way just from longer exposure, but they don't actually have an impact on me before you do. It's all simultaneous, it's all happening, it's all in flow.

My mom was this working-class, white Catholic woman. She's got this whole brood of kids and the Monsignor comes to town in Winnipeg and starts bad-mouthing all those poor Catholics, and it's like, well, we're not allowed to use birth control, we're not allowed to do this, we're not allowed to do that, and now you're saying it's our fault—so this kind of class shaming within that religious context. So she really changed her life under the influence of the different feminists, like Betty Friedan and these different voices in the late '60s and early '70s. So she really defined herself as an individual; she "reclaimed her power," and completely, or incompletely, abandoned her role as a life-bearer, giver of life, and leader of her family. Because it wasn't valued by those early feminist voices, it wasn't valued at all. So she divested from this very frustrating, very debilitating role as an unloved mother of an unloved family in an unloving society to build up a sense of herself as a worker.

When I was a young woman, I wrote a play and I showed it to my mom, and she was quite indignant because I was reflecting my experience of violence at home in a very

WHAT AM I BUT THIS LANDSCAPE OF DIFFERENT INFLUENCES AND ECHOES AND OPINIONS? AND THE STRENGTHS OF THE PEOPLE AROUND ME, THEIR INFLUENCE ON ME IS PROFOUND.

abstract piece that was basically, you know, "The Violent Man, The Violent Woman." But my mom looked at this and she was horrified. She said, "It's the man's fault, violence is always the man's fault." So I have seen a lot of men walking with the burden of shame for all of the violence in families or in the world. You know, the light falls on it one way and you go, "Yeah! Yeah, that's right." And then the light falls on it the other way and you go, "Well, women are not powerless, women are not just the row of knick-knacks on the mantelpiece. We're the ones that are raising the children or not, we're the ones that are reproducing…" We reproduce culture whether we want to or not. And so if the culture, as happened to me, involves a lot of non-gentle treatment and non-respectful treatment, then that is going to recur no matter how clever I think I am. When the push comes to shove then of course I'm going to mistreat because that's what I've learned, and if I don't have a strong centre and a strong sense of safe place within myself, then that is going to come out in my own behaviour. So it really doesn't work for me to be really judgmental about anybody for anything.

My father was the only adult in my life that I wasn't separated from, he did not take off, he did not abandon me. But he also did not always treat me with the love and respect that I actually kinda woulda liked, [*Laughter*] if I may put it that way. So there's that sense that's left strong confusion around "What is love?" for me. So his first marriage ended as a disaster. I was one of the eight children who were from that first marriage and about half of us stayed with him and the others kind of went to different families, parts of the family, or became street kids or whatever. Eventually, just as I was leaving his household, he started a new relationship with the woman who became my stepmother and who's the mother of my youngest brother. I wasn't living with him in all of those years and there were unkind moments, challenges, but I see in the arc of his story a kind of a redemption narrative. My father died a couple years ago, and most of us gathered to be with him and, for the first time in most of our lives, to gather as a family within a community. I was able to have really intimate conversations with most of my siblings. And talking to my youngest brother, his experience of our dad was just so completely different than mine that they might as well have been two separate men. He said that our dad gave him a spanking once and he deserved it. And it's like, this is the man who threw me up against the wall and threw my siblings up against the wall, kicking everybody, beating with straps, temper tantrums all over the place. When you see a small child having a temper tantrum—as an adult man, he was like that. But my brother saw none of that, right?

So my dad had this complete disaster, this nuclear family that went "Kaboom!" And then he regrouped and he had this second marriage. And I'm very very grateful for the second marriage because there was a lot of inappropriate, criminally inappropriate things going on, which stopped because of the arrival of my stepmother, because she saw him as a good man, she saw him as really sexy and handsome and a real catch and he wanted to live up to that. My stepmother spent the last ten years of her life in a nursing home—I think it was Alzheimer's—so he spent the last ten years of her life going every day and feeding her and just this kind of a beautiful expression of loyalty. So in all the phases of his life, I associate my dad with loyalty. This is kind of a profound family man in that way. But how it was expressed in different ways at different times, it shows a learning arc.

SM: The first two stanzas of "Into Manhood" read:

Although it seems to me
when young men arrive
grown men turn away

and there is no hand
into which I can pass you
now you are come a man
except your own

(*Mother Time* 128)

Could you reflect on that poem and also just the struggles of coming into a sense of what appropriate manhood might be?

JA: That poem kind of reads like a prayer, but it's also very literal. There was a period when my oldest son—I'm trying to think of the age, like fourteen, fifteen, in that age range—and time after time, both my son's father and my then-husband, the boys would come and then the men would get up and leave. The men just didn't have a way of being comfortable with men when they were young, and so they did not have a way of receiving the young men. And so they would literally get uncomfortable and they'd get up and they'd walk away. And through this period of I don't know how many years, I kept going back and back to this.

And with my eldest son, his major challenge to be the person he can be... well, again, it's a story of loyalty. It's like he got into drugs and theft because of his loyalty to this little set of teenage boys, who are variously unhappy for various reasons, and they're bonding. He described this wonderful place where he'd been staying, where it was just this kind of a co-operative dream and they all help each other out; if you need something, they'll get it for you. And then a year or two down the road, it was like, "well, this is not such a great place!" And so it just depends, you can describe things in very different ways depending on how you're looking at it and what's important to you and what sides of it stand out to you. He had a year or so between when he was caught trying to rob someone and when he had to face the judge. So he used that time to withdraw from drugs and start to regain his health and start to find a way to be himself in a way he felt good about, right? But he got into trouble because he's got a capacity to love. Because he's got empathy for others.

So now he takes a lot of pride in being a worker guy, much like my dad. He works in demolition, strategic deconstruction. [*Laughter*] So anyways, for him, his brand or his path of masculinity is very, very worker-guy oriented. He's happy using his body. He expresses his creativity through music and visual art and whatever, but he's a highly social person, you know? And, like my dad, the defining part is the work, that's the grounding meditation.

For my second son, he's a much more feminine kind of a man. He's Two-Spirited. And has struggles around that, for sure. Once my second son had moved out of the house, when I would go to the train station and if I thought I saw him—you know how your eye's attracted to someone that you're missing—the people that drew my eye as maybe him were all young Asian men. So there's a way that has developed in popular culture—and this is West Coast, right?—through social and aesthetic cues around beautiful manliness that is quite urban, that my second son has been strongly attracted to and patterns himself on, whether he knows that or not.

So my third son is eighteen. In the moment, if you saw a picture of him, you would think "Creedence Clearwater Revival." He looks like a southern rocker and tragically where he finds his joy is in performing as a poet. And I always say tragically because, to me, it's like this vow of poverty. There's some kind of mix-up in Catholicism where poverty equals goodness. It's like, this is virtue. As my teeth come out, one by one, I resent that training more and more. It's like, there's got to be another way!

All of my kids are these creative dynamos, and I think, *I think*, they're suffering much less than what I and my siblings experienced; you would have to ask them. Because even avoiding the obvious traps of alcoholism or battering relationships or those kinds of things, which I have for the most part avoided, there's still so much intense, intense life force coming out. It's like you need to be an open channel to this certain amount of energy that flows through you each day, and if you're damming yourself up or dammed—doors are closed by others on your behalf—or you just learn the wrong ways of expressing that energy. I mean, I know they have all been marked, they all have experienced both depression and anxiety. And I don't know how to magic-wand fix it for them. But I think that they all have, too, a real fundamental understanding of emotional literacy that their dad, my brothers, the men in my family never had. Or the women either.

In one of my later visits with my dad there was a moment there where the violence against women by men in our family, where I touched on that, and he seemed to be, like, "I don't know what that could be." Puzzled, like I was pointing out something unrecognizable. And so, there's a way we have to have respect for real human limits. The image that I use is that there was a flat part to his brain, where he was not effectively taking in information. It's not like you could condemn him for not dealing with reality when he just couldn't process that. And that's after a lifetime of both receiving and participating in and delivering traumatic anti-girl, anti-woman, and probably anti-him, anti-male, disrespect and violence—physically and psychically, abuse of different kinds and quantities. I think a lot of what we've been talking about is just the whole issue of trust. And for a person who has been many times traumatized and who has been raised by people many times traumatized, who were also raised by people many times traumatized, there is a feeling of, "How much can I bear? How much can I consciously know?" And you just have to have a feeling of generosity toward our human limits, that sometimes I just can't know everything that I know.

SM: It appears from your descriptions like each of your sons has sought out ways of being creative that he can feel good about.

JA: I don't want all my kids to end up on welfare because they're too sensitized to spend eight hours with strangers, which has been a lot of my struggle, that need to be away from people because it's just too psychically overwhelming to be out in the noise and the expectations. So I'm encouraging them to get out there and develop those psychic shields that will allow them to come and go, in public and in private spaces. And part of my challenge has been the fact that people have not always seen me and brought out their best behaviour, you know what I mean? So this whole caste thing, class and caste thing, shows the need for a strong counterbalancing community. As the boys are growing up, I've been able to have them have contact with men who are not abusive and who model Indigenous manhood. So I try not to reenact the extreme isolation that I grew up with. I wish it were easier.

SM: Thinking about *Steepy Mountain Love Poetry*, I want to ask about the importance of healthy forms of desire. Could you reflect on embodiment and sensuality?

JA: What you ask reminds me of something that I feel very good about, because we've talked a lot about what I'm not so happy about in terms of my… journey. One of the things that I'm quite unhappy about is that I was born in a hospital; my mom was drugged and I was bottle-fed. And that's true of my siblings as well. And that my mother was born in a hospital and bottle-fed. And my brothers were circumcised. And so one of the very positive things that we've done, myself and my two ex-husbands, my team, has been to have support for me, in my childbearing, so that I would most of the time feel quite nourished rather than ignored or under attack. And a midwife's nourishing support of childbearing at home. So there's not heavy drugs, bright lights, this "the doctor delivers the baby." Well, *no*, the doctor doesn't deliver the baby! The baby and I have this kind of a dance and *I* deliver the baby or *the baby* decides to leave or it's kind of a thunderstorm, right? An interpersonal thunderstorm. It's like you can't really say who decided what but we did this, right? And then none of the boys have been circumcised and neither has my daughter. Happily. I breastfed them for, I think, between twenty and thirty months each. So there was an attempt to vary how we live our life from what our immediate ancestors had done and what the prevailing culture really actively pressures you to conform to, and in a way that honours our bodies and honours our sons' and daughters' bodies so that, hopefully, ideally, they will be less fundamentally traumatized in those ways that you can't ever put words to. It's one thing to be held, to be a small body and be held by a benign large body, right?

PEOPLE HAVE NOT ALWAYS SEEN ME AND BROUGHT OUT THEIR BEST BEHAVIOUR, YOU KNOW WHAT I MEAN? SO THIS WHOLE CASTE THING, CLASS AND CASTE THING, SHOWS THE NEED FOR A STRONG COUNTERBALANCING COMMUNITY.

SM: That space for safe intimacy, embodiment, and sensual connection is so important. I worry a lot now, for instance, about the fact that my kids are growing up in a generation in which many will learn about sexuality, in part, through Internet pornography.

JA: Yeah, that's another of those ungovernables. It's very delicate territory because I don't think we've seen an end yet to the reality that young Aboriginal women walking down the street are seen as someone it's safe to attack. That is just so. It permeates. I haven't visited a region in Canada where that is not so. And that high level of permission to, like, "do your best," you know? However oppressed you are as a man, if you're not happy, just find one of these and "do your best." So, I don't know how any of us develop and maintain these good loving sensual, sexual relationships with men of our choosing without that being a factor—without the interference of having unwanted sex, without having extreme disrespect and extreme danger of a life-and-death scenario, having those things inflicted upon us. Whether we blame ourselves, you know—I shouldn't have walked down that way, I should've… Well, too bad, I was too poor to buy a ticket, or whatever. So setting aside the question of who is to blame for any individual woman's victimization, we could just sit back and say, "Holy fuck! That happens a lot, all across Canada, in every community." And it happens systemically. And it happens that the repercussions are still not very much. And I think, within our lifetimes, that's changed. But it still hasn't changed dramatically.

And because women and men are intimate—I remember a massage therapist telling me once that muscle and bone are intimate, and it's true—and same with men and women. You know, it's not like separate species. We grow in the same families. We're berries cross-fertilizing. How do you measure the impact on my five-year-old son, his sense of masculinity, when I come into the house upset because my neighbour has threatened to cut me up and throw the pieces in the garbage? As a "joke"—and this was one of the good guys! A woman was murdered in our building and it was an Aboriginal woman and we think the murderer was an Aboriginal man. This was my neighbour's way of handling the stress, through involving my son in some pretty menacing humour, targeting his mom. And so, all of us in this little community of people are profoundly affected by the death. We don't have all the answers. And so, this particular guy, his way of dealing with that—I believe he may have been the person who found the woman's body—so his way of kind of processing his visceral shock was to talk to my son about cutting me up and throwing the pieces in the garbage. To me it's mind-numbing. It's like, you could say, "Well, that was disrespectful." But you know what? It's a fuck of a lot more than disrespectful. The thing is every mother's son has some part of the experience of the mother. Whether he has a conscious handle on what he's witnessing or not, it's all arriving, it's a part of his life, too.

Anyway, back to your original question: happy sex is like a thunderstorm, and so is a temper tantrum. Two different ways to discharge all that life force, with different social consequences for everybody.

SETTING ASIDE THE QUESTION OF WHO IS TO BLAME FOR ANY INDIVIDUAL WOMAN'S VICTIMIZATION, WE COULD JUST SIT BACK AND SAY, "HOLY FUCK! THAT HAPPENS A LOT, ALL ACROSS CANADA, IN EVERY COMMUNITY." AND IT HAPPENS SYSTEMICALLY.

TENDING THE FIRE
A CONVERSATION WITH NEAL MCLEOD

THE OLD OKIHCITÂWAK MEASURED THEIR LIVES BY THE IDEAS OF BRAVERY, COURAGE, AND SELFLESSNESS. WE NEED THESE THINGS IF WE ARE TO FIND THE RIVER WITHIN OUR BODIES. I NEED TO FIND MY WAY BACK TO THE RIVER LIKE MY FATHER BEFORE ME.
—NEAL MCLEOD, "WORDS FOR MY SONS"

20 MARCH 2011
Conversation between Neal McLeod and Sam McKegney at Sam's home in Kingston, Ontario.

SAM MCKEGNEY: The first thing I'd like to ask you about is the phrase "sons of a lost river" that recurs in *Gabriel's Beach*. What does that image mean to you—to be the son of a lost river?

NEAL MCLEOD: It almost sounds like an emo band or something—*Sons of a Lost River*, or *Sons of Nanabush* or something. I would say that it all centres around, well probably a couple of things. One is the historical events of 1885, which in English have been rendered as the Riel Rebellion or the North-West Resistance, but in our language they say *ê-mâyahkamikahk*, which means "where it went wrong." After those events occurred, for many along the Saskatchewan River, the whole world of the Cree and Métis changed drastically, particularly for men. Of course women were affected, but, after that time period, a lot of the men who were involved in those events were imprisoned,

NEAL MCLEOD (Cree/
Swedish) is a poet, screenwriter,
visual artist, curator, scholar,
and comedian. He grew up
on the James Smith reserve in
Saskatchewan and is currently
a professor of Indigenous
literatures at Trent University in
Peterborough, Ontario. He is the
author of the critical book *Cree
Narrative Memory: From Treaties
to Contemporary Times* and two
collections of poetry, *Songs to
Kill a Wîhtikow* (Hagios Press,
2005) and *Gabriel's Beach* (Hagios
Press, 2008), and he is a co-editor,
with Natasha Beads, of *Sounding
Out: Indigenous Poetics* (Wilfrid
Laurier University Press, 2014).
Having studied at the Academy
of Fine Arts at Umeå University
in Sweden, McLeod has exhibited
his artwork throughout Canada,
including as part of the 2005
exhibition *Au fil de mes Jours (In
My Lifetime)* at Le Musée National
des Beaux-Arts du Québec. His
comic work includes recordings
and short films with the Bionic
Bannock Boys.

some of them were in exile, and unfortunately some of them passed. The freedom that Cree and Métis men had after that time period was greatly hampered, probably until the 1970s I would say, almost a hundred years.

I call it "The Lost River" because it's a poetic journey, a poetic remembrance of the experiences, particularly of Cree and Métis men, after this time period. What are the consequences of getting institutionalized in terms of connections to land and territory, but also in terms of not being able to become initiated into *okihcitâwak* societies, and instead having to go to residential school? What are the consequences of that? What are the consequences of not being able to go freely to sacred places of fasting and honouring powers, such as *mihkomin sâkahikan*, that means Redberry Lake, or all the other places close to the Saskatchewan River?

I wanted to look at: how did we get to the point that we are at today, as Cree and Métis men? What is the historicity of that? How do you make sense of that? How do you make sense of being men in a context in which a lot of our power has, until relatively recently, been taken? And then, consequently, the anger that emerges from that, and quite frankly the violence as well. Not only how we have experienced that violence, but how we ourselves have inflicted that violence, and how that violence has been transferred across generations. Why do so many young Indigenous males in my home territory gravitate towards gangs? What do they find in gangs that they don't find in other places?

So, I think that's what that book of poems is about. It's also trying to find your way back from that place of dislocation. It's not enough to talk about your loss—how do you find yourself back? How do you make your way home? How do you find your balance, collectively and individually?

SM: What was it about the stories of your grandfather Gabriel Vandall that offered such a powerful resource in terms of being able to speak to that feeling of loss, but also the power and possibility of return?

NM: Quite a few of his uncles fought in the Resistance of 1885. In fact, one of his uncles fought in 1885 at Batoche and also in World War I as infantry, ironically, for the Canadian Army. He was sixty years old when he was in the infantry—he lied about his age, but he was sixty—and in the infantry, not some desk job. And I always thought, "What were the stories that guided the old people to be so fierce in their place in world?" His mother, who was named *Cîhcam*, she was the daughter of *Masâskapaw* who was the older brother of *Atâhkakohp*, who was a major Cree leader at the time of treaty. So, his father was a Red River Métis, but his mother was a Cree woman, and also a keeper of the Older Grandmothers' Lodge of the Cree. She died in 1966, a little before my time, but I've heard a lot of stories about her. So, with this man, I grew up hearing about him my whole life, and hearing about his stories, and how my grandfathers, along with their friends, they were outnumbered, like 200 against 5,000. I suppose I was always interested in those odds. I was always interested in the things they told themselves. How did they find the courage when many people would have just run away?

My father always talked about his grandfather, he was close to his grandfather that passed away. He died the same year as his mother actually, 1966. He received about twenty medals in combat, both in World War I and World War II. So, he fought in the same army as some of his uncles. They say he wasn't scared to die, and that's probably one of the reasons why he was such a great solider. Some people have the Bible, some people have the Koran, I had these stories to think about and to try and find my way through. So I think that's why I always gravitated to these narratives.

SM: The sense of masculine lineage is present and forceful in your work—both in your poetry and in *Cree Narrative Memory*. I wonder if perhaps you could speak to your connection to the masculine environment in which you grew up.

NM: I think that the reason why the threads of masculinity are strong in the work that I've written up to this point is that I was raised by a single father, and those are the narratives that I would have encountered. Also, the stories that my father heard were primarily from his grandfather, who in turn was informed by other men. So that's kind of where the narrative genealogy comes from. My father was particularly close to his grandfather, who was raised by some of these men who had fought in these battles, and also who had fought against Blackfoot in earlier times. It was a source of understanding their place in the world, and also in terms of understanding a time when they had power and were not simply emasculated through residential schools or through the colonial process of the Indian Act, or anything like that. I think all of these stories of warfare actually celebrated a time of strength, not simply in an archival sense of the past, but as the living present. I think they drew strength from these stories. My great-grandfather was quite successful as a farmer, and they were able to adapt to new circumstances. They were quite strong in the language, I would say, and even to this day are quite strong, those that remain. Some families had the threads of these stories kind of unravelled, but that didn't happen in my family. The stories were still spoken of, and it wasn't in some distant past, it was something people would thread into their lives. So, I'm grateful for that. I think some people, they haven't spoken the Indigenous language sometimes for three, four generations, or even longer, and it's a lot harder for them to thread things together.

But also, I had to work really hard at developing an awareness of Cree knowledge. Some people are fortunate enough to have spoken it their whole lives. I've heard it since I was very, very young, and when I really worked at speaking it, I was able to retrieve old memories that pre-existed when I had a clear concept of the boundaries of language. So, I was able to get the rhythm and pronunciation pretty easily. But, I had to work hard at retrieving the language, and I found it to be a very interesting and layered process. I try my best to speak Cree to my son, the youngest one particularly, and he has a fairly solid working knowledge of the language.

SM: Mentioning that being around the language gave you a certain access that actually predated your conscious connection to the language, I'm wondering how this relates to the theorization of memory as you discuss it in *Cree Narrative Memory*, and the idea that memory is not limited to conscious retrieval of specific information but extends beyond individual experience. I guess I'm curious about the relationship between memory and language?

NM: I think I would even perhaps say it in a slightly different way. I would say that memory is related to sound. Some of the earliest memories that I have are of my great-grandfather, his name was Peter Vandall, or *Kôkôcîs*, as his nickname was in Cree. We'd go visit him when I was a kid, up until I was about fourteen and he passed away. But he had a very distinct rhythm when he spoke Cree. So I think that the layering and the retrieval of memory is all about sound. It's about the echoing of those voices. So, if you have a clear voice that can thread all those things together—I know we're mixing metaphors—but it's almost like a vessel, a container. If you can remember a very specific voice, you can thread all those things together, or gather the sound together, and then other things can be grafted to it. And, when you realize that that old person heard some of those stories from people that were born in the 1830s, I mean how far back does that go? It's kind of humbling in a way, but it also contextualizes things.

I think that's another aspect: these stories connect people. And when people don't do that the language and narrative loss is extreme. I don't want to be disrespectful to my generation, but if you ask people about stories that stretch back a bit further, some people my age, they don't know the answers because they never sat with the old people and visited with them. And, partly that is just because that is not their temperament—they might be good at some other things—but once people stop visiting with old people, I notice that the language loss and the loss of memory is quite profound and deep. It only takes one generation where people are not keen on something for it to just begin to unravel. That's one of the ironies of oral history; if it's unattended to, it can unravel quite quickly. However, if it is nurtured and maintained, there is nothing more powerful. Because when you have a living voice that takes you back and traces you back to Big Bear, or some of these other great leaders, and also the grandmothers of course like *Cîhcam*, it's quite a powerful experience. Because when they tell these old stories they are almost able to bring those people back through their sound. I think that where I come from, people—younger people—are very hungry for this sound; they are very hungry for reconnecting.

SM: In terms of the ability to sit with the old people, and to listen to the sound and to experience that history, what advice would you give to people who, through no decision making of their own, have found themselves very distant geographically, or otherwise, from their own territories, their own communities? What responsibility do those people have to try to connect to that history?

> THAT'S ONE OF THE IRONIES OF ORAL HISTORY; IF IT'S UNATTENDED TO, IT CAN UNRAVEL QUITE QUICKLY. HOWEVER, IF IT IS NURTURED AND MAINTAINED, THERE IS NOTHING MORE POWERFUL.

NM: It's up to them if they want to or not. It's pretty much that simple really. Sometimes that sense of responsibility is fostered in families. For other people it's not. So, I can't make a statement about what my advice would be if they don't feel that calling. However, for those that *are* interested in it, there is nothing wrong with being honest and saying, "I don't know something. I don't know how to say this." It's never too late to retrieve a language. If you have a desire to go back and rethread it and retrieve it, it's there. Use anything at your disposal. I actually, literally, write out words from the Cree dictionary. Pretty much every day I write out words, which is kind of nerdy.

I don't want to romanticize oral traditions. But what's going to help preserve the language today? Something like Facebook. I was against Facebook, but I joined it about two and a half months ago, and I post words every day, and there's discussion about the nuances and the meanings. Digital technology can be quite liberating. It can thread together people who otherwise wouldn't be able to communicate easily with one another. And it's cheap or free. I mean, you have the basic cost of your device, but the Internet is relatively cheap. There's an online Cree dictionary, with about 50,000 words, so, you can cheat. Sometimes when I talk to my dad, I go online, and he'll ask me how I pick up all these hard words, and I kind of cheat and type them in while I talk to him. He doesn't really know, but I guess if you publish this article, this book, he'll know!

You got to have fun with it too. Sometimes people make Indigenous languages all dour. It's like a Scandinavian movie and the sky is all dark, and people are drinking tea, and there's a cuckoo clock that ticks randomly and jumps out, and everyone is all melancholic. I mean, language won't survive unless it's fun, it's that simple. If people see language only in a ceremonial fashion, it's probably not going to survive. It has to be a living, daily language. You have to text in Cree. You have to be cool in Cree. If you're cool in a language then people want to speak it. I remember when we started the *Crow-Hop Cafés* in 2000, my friends John and Bill Cook, they sang songs in Cree. When you can actually charm ladies—or men—in a language, that's a good incentive to want to learn it. There's a certain romantic cachet in speaking it; it boosts the ratings a little bit.

I think you got to have a sense of humour too, and you got to be a little thick-skinned, because you will make mistakes and errors. I've said some ridiculous things. Cree people like to tease, it's our national sport. Italians have soccer, we have teasing. It's not some sacred way or walking the Red Path or anything. It's just because people are constantly practising their wits, and it's an admired skill. That's probably why we're good at stand-up comedy and stuff, and also poetry and live performances, because it's imbedded in our culture to be like that. Accounting? Now, that's another matter. Just kidding. I'll leave that up to the third-party managers.

SM: On top of being a recurring line in *Gabriel's Beach*, "Sons of a Lost River" was also the title of a series of your paintings. And there are prints of your paintings included in the poetry collection, *Songs to Kill a Wîhtikow*. How do those visual images speak to the poetry for you? Did they come at the same time? Does the process of writing poetry create the need to express in the painting and vice versa? Or do they happen at different times while thinking about similar issues?

NM: Well, there have been many fine works of writing, of Indigenous literature, which talk about someone's life story and so on, in great details sometimes. I wasn't really interested in doing that about some of the darker elements of my younger days, so instead I simply used the metaphor of a *wîhtikow*. So instead of having to mention those things directly, I could just bundle it all up as a *wîhtikow*. It was immediately a very visual thing. It was not just simply for artistic reasons or aesthetic reasons though. Probably if I wouldn't have painted twenty-foot paintings of *wîhtikows*, maybe I would have had a breakdown, or maybe I would have gotten cancer or something, or unfortunate events of the past would have manifested themselves in other ways. So, for me, art isn't simply about aesthetics and artistic decisions. Let's face it, Cree people sometimes couldn't afford a $140 therapy session. So, you paint and write instead. It does the same job, but sometimes it's a little harder.

SM: Is it difficult sometimes to look at that artwork if it has come from a traumatic place?

NM: No, not at all. In the Introduction to *Songs to Kill a Wîhtikow* I talk about naming the darkness. If you don't name the darkness then you can never move beyond it, individually or collectively. That darkness can be the darkness of things that have happened to us collectively and individually, but also, how we ourselves are part of it as well. Honestly, I'm against the settler-Indigenous dichotomy, because it simplifies the universe too much. We ourselves can do things that are not conducive for social balance. I think part of the process of writing is trying to document and articulate these things in a way that is socially responsible. It tries to find a space where we can re-imagine things.

SM: That last comment made me think about the image from the other book of poetry, of being able to "carry the fire of Gabriel's Beach," and how that—in my reading—relates to the ability to acknowledge experiences that are difficult or traumatic and yet to endure. What does carrying the fire of Gabriel's Beach mean for you?

NM: Here's the balancing position, if you will. On one hand, you need a certain amount of fire, or resolution, to survive horrific and traumatic events, collectively and individually. If you don't have that fire, you will actually be engulfed. The legendary storyteller Louis Bird talks about how some people turn *wîhitikow* when their trauma just overwhelms them. However, on the other hand, the idea of the fire also relates to what happens when you go too far. The very things that make you good at warfare can make you pretty horrible in relationships, if we're to be honest. Especially from a masculine point of view. All those things that cause you never to bow down to rednecks can also be disastrous in personal relationships. So you see, that's the situation. That very fire that allows people to survive, and particularly males, that can be the fire that burns them inside.

THE VERY THINGS THAT MAKE YOU GOOD AT WARFARE CAN MAKE YOU PRETTY HORRIBLE IN RELATIONSHIPS, IF WE'RE TO BE HONEST. ESPECIALLY FROM A MASCULINE POINT OF VIEW.

I'll be honest—I have no problems talking about this because I'd rather people talk about it than not talk about it—I've been a violent male in the past, both with males and with female partners. When I was in my mid-twenties, I signed up for a program to deal with these things. I noticed that that was a pattern with males in my family. Some people would not talk about it, right? But I think we should talk about it and think about how we got there. That was actually one of the reasons why I wanted to document the poems and to write them down, to think about how we got there. Where did we go? What are all of these events? We always have individual choices, but there's always a context to those choices, and if things are threaded across more than one generation, it frames your individual choices. It takes more to re-imagine yourself out of those things. So, the fire, you need it to live, you need it for life, but it can also burn you inside, and sometimes those around you, I would say. Particularly when social circumstances and individual circumstances become difficult.

Historically, the Cree men who lived in the 1800s before the reserve period, their world was a less fragmented world, I would say. There was a context for violence. People would go through warfare and so on, whereas now we don't really have the same context for violence. Once again, I'm trying not to essentialize, but without that context for male aggression—and females can manifest it too, so it's not necessarily men—I think it's not surprising that there are so many Indigenous males where I come from in prison. It's still relatively recent, the shifts in the West, and realistically where I come from, we're not going to be assimilated in the next hundred years. So we have to radically think about what has happened in the past. So to me, the book of poems isn't simply a book of poetry per se, it's a map. I would like, ideally, to reach young men from where I come from, and have them realize that they don't have to be violent in the way that they are sometimes indoctrinated to think that they have to be, to be men. They can be men and not be violent. I think we're still collectively trying to figure that out, I would say.

SM: The really moving poem to your sons at the end of *Gabriel's Beach* speaks to the ability to nurture that fire in good ways that don't have to spill over into violence. How do you perceive your role as a father in relation to these issues?

NM: Well, I failed my one son because of alcoholism, I'll be honest. I was able to reconnect with him when he was older. That was Justin. Cody is raised a lot differently. He is not subjected to the quasi-militaristic training that I received growing up. He's completely oblivious to some of those things, which is good. But, I think we can have the Healing Foundation, we can have all these organizations that help us, which are very good. The Truth and Reconciliation Commission, and so on. But, we have to start off with our own sons. And, I'm speaking from the perspective, being a father with sons, that we have to start off with them. What kind of path can we create for them that is different maybe than the one that was created for us? To be honest about the past, not to romanticize it—that is the danger, like "everything in the past is good." Boys were

HISTORICALLY, THE CREE MEN WHO LIVED IN THE 1800S BEFORE THE RESERVE PERIOD, THEIR WORLD WAS A LESS FRAGMENTED WORLD, I WOULD SAY. THERE WAS A CONTEXT FOR VIOLENCE.

trained for warfare at the age of seven, which just doesn't happen today, right? So, how do we move from that culture to where children leave home at eighteen? There's some major differences. Where people would go on revenge parties, now people come and talk about Jesus and turning the other cheek.

SM: Linking back to our discussion of Gabriel on Juno Beach, how do you define the term "warrior"? In the opening pages of *Gabriel's Beach*, you translate the Cree term *okihcitâw* as "worthy young man," which seems connected to "warrior," but it's not exactly the same. So what are the nuances?

NM: So, number one, I'm not a word warrior. [*Laughter*]

SM: You're not into [Gerald] Vizenor?

NM: I like Vizenor, and I kind of find that idea interesting, but if I were to go to my own ancestors in the next level and say, "Yeah, I'm a word warrior." And they'll be like, "OK, well, we fought at the Battle of Old Man River, and Juno Beach, and you took your pencil where?" It just kind of doesn't have the same… In the old days they would recite their war stories, but writers talking about their readings doesn't really have the same cachet, I don't think. No disrespect to my fellow writers, my sister writers. But, your question was… What was your question again?

SM: Well, the first part is basically about the term "warrior"…

NM: Oh! Okay. I remember. I personally don't like the word "warrior." I mean, I'm not going to talk about anyone else's traditions, because it's not my place—Mohawks, or other nations—it's not my place, and I wouldn't feel comfortable commenting on it. But, there are actually two words: one is *okihcitâw*, that means literally—there are societies that were called *okihcitâwak,* and the chicken dance in contemporary powwows is a remnant of that old society, which is why in the West, particularly, all the old veterans go first, because it's a remnant of all these societies—but that word is originally an Assiniboine word, it's *ahkacîta,* which meant those societies. But it also has an older root meaning "Thunderbird"—interestingly, it referred to thunderbird. But then as it was absorbed into Cree it changed from *ahkacîta* to *okihcitâw*; it means to give away freely to others, or to provide for them. The word "provider" is probably a better translation.

The other word is *môsâpêw*, that's what they called Gabriel, my Auntie mentions that. Now, interestingly there are three layers to that word. One is *môsâpêwak,* that means the buffalo bulls that are on the side of a herd, because they are kind of lingering. So then, they use that as a metaphor today: *môsâpêw* is like a bachelor. But then, there is another layer of men who put aside everything for the benefit of others. The idea of warrior, it doesn't work for me. If it works for other people, then that's great, but it doesn't work for me. I know Cree words that describe the stories that I know better. But, maybe someone who was bereft of language, an Indigenous language, the word "warrior" would work for them, but it doesn't personally make any sense to me. It's a very narrow idea; it only focuses on one narrow aspect. Just like Yoda, right? Remember when he's in Dagobah, and Luke says, "I'm here to see Yoda the great warrior." And Yoda says—I'm not going to say it in the voice because I don't want to freak out your grad students—but he says, "War does not make one great." Well, same thing. It wasn't war that made them great.

One time my friend, John Quinny, whose grandfather *Pahpahakwân-Piyêsiw* or Prairie Chicken Thunderbird—it's quite an interesting name—he was with Big Bear, and he was with Wandering Spirit in 1885. As kind of a nerdy college boy, I said like, "Oh you mean he was with Big Bear? Wow. And he was with Wandering Spirit? What did he tell you about Wandering Spirit?" And then he just said, "Actually, he told me more about how to be a good person." So that's why I don't like the word "warrior" for me because it's a very narrow sense of what those old guys were.

SM: What are the lessons that one might shed light upon, or turn to, to teach young men about what it means to "be a good person"?

NM: They have an expression in Cree—"they," as if I'm not a part of it. It just sounds more dramatic—*they* say *kaya pakacî*, which means "don't give up"; *âkakêyimomô*—"keep going." That's probably number one. Number two is, probably, to take responsibility for your life, and not to blame society for everything. Sometimes people are just assholes. You can't blame colonialism for being an asshole and you can't blame the fur trade. Like, really? So, I think that taking responsibility for your life is key. And to try and think of creating a world, or helping to create a world, that extends beyond yourself. So, instead of simply thinking about your own artistic career, how can your work actually help people, even in a small way? I admire people who are very active in social activism, but, okay, cleaning a house, cooking, I don't have time to go out and work in a soup kitchen or something. The best I can do—I'm not a warrior—but the best I can do is to write, and to paint, and put some ideas out there, and maybe document some things in our language for others to think about. Beatrice Lavallee said that the old Grandmother Lodge of the Crees, that old entity, told her the two key things are *tâpwêwin* and *nêtawêwin*—"speaking well" and "truth." So you have these two words and the only way to make sense of them is to thread them into your life. There's no dogma, per se, right? That's why our spiritual traditions are a bit different.

SM: Are there any other things you want to discuss with relation to masculinities?

NM: Some people want to radically deconstruct gender. It's contingent and so on, and maybe it is. But in my upbringing, there is a clear cluster of things that make up what we might call Cree men, or Cree masculinity. Now, I would say that there's a whole cluster of things like being brave, and thinking of others, and not being a coward—that's one of the biggest things, don't be a coward. But the key is that it has to be tempered by

SOME PEOPLE WANT TO RADICALLY DECONSTRUCT GENDER. IT'S CONTINGENT AND SO ON, AND MAYBE IT IS. BUT IN MY UPBRINGING, THERE IS A CLEAR CLUSTER OF THINGS THAT MAKE UP WHAT WE MIGHT CALL CREE MEN, OR CREE MASCULINITY.

and contextualized with all the grandmother stories as well. Because if you only have stories about warfare and stories about the men, you'll only have half of it. It wasn't until I was older that I got to hear about my grandmother *Cîhcam*, and I really got to know Louise Halfe and Beatrice Lavallee in kind of a deeply personal way, and I really got exposed to some of the grandmother stories. So I would say that to talk about Cree masculinity and Métis masculinity—Métis from the West—you have to also think about the grandmother stories, or it would be very incomplete, I would say. I think we have a responsibility to re-imagine these things and to make our traditions live in the present, to take the best from the classical ideas and then to weave them into a living present.

A LIBERATION THROUGH CLAIMING

A CONVERSATION WITH GREGORY SCOFIELD

HIS MOUTH BRUSHING MINE
IS A FLAT STONE
SKIPPING THE LAKE'S SURFACE
AND OH HIS TONGUE
A SPAWNING FISH JUMPS
OVER AND OVER THE WATERFALL
IS MASKWA PAWING
ALL HIS WINTER HUNGER
SO I YIELD UP ROOTS AND BERRIES
AND LIE BACK
MY WHOLE ABUNDANT SELF
—GREGORY SCOFIELD, "ÔCHÎM ♦ HIS KISS"

5 JUNE 2011
*Conversation between
Gregory Scofield and
Sam McKegney at
the Trader's Grill at
the Explorer Hotel in
Yellowknife, Northwest
Territories, during the
Northwords Writers'
Festival.*

GREGORY SCOFIELD (Cree/ Métis) is a poet, teacher, social worker, and youth worker whose maternal ancestry can be traced back five generations to the Red River Settlement and to Kinesota, Manitoba. He has published an autobiography, *Thunder Through My Veins: Memories of a Métis Childhood* (Harper Flamingo Press, 1999) and several books of poetry, including *Native Canadiana: Songs from the Urban Rez* (Polestar, 1996), *Love Medicine and One Song / Sâkihtowin-maskihkiy êkwa pêyak-nikamowin* (Kegedonce Press, 2008), *Singing Home the Bones* (Polestar, 2005), and *Louis: The Heretic Poems* (Nightwood Editions, 2011).

GREGORY SCOFIELD: Coming to my own masculinity began with me having to work to be in touch with my own body. Because at one point I was so disconnected with any of the male role models in my life that it was like being in a very asexual place, you know? So part of being able to get in touch with my masculinity was being able to specifically get in touch with my body. I started working out, I started building up parts of my body, I started feeling the places where I was physically strong. And there was a kind of liberation within that process—a liberation through claiming. It was like, okay, this is my body, and I'm starting to claim parts of my body, other than my male parts. I'm claiming other parts of my body because I don't have an issue with the emotionality; I don't have an issue with the spirituality. But it's really the physicality. And so once I was able to do that, I felt like I was physically strong and able to protect myself. It's very different when you go into a situation where you feel as though you are protected. You negotiate very differently with life and with people. And in my case, I began to negotiate very differently with other men and women in my life. And in being able to negotiate differently, I was able to start coming into my own power. And from there, of course, other pieces started to fall into place.

Finding my dad, finding who he was, finding what type of person he was, being able to forgive him and all of the other men—the terrible ones, if you will—enabled me to put them in a place of powerlessness. I was able to now protect myself physically, emotionally, mentally, spiritually. I was able to look after myself. And once I was in that space, of course, I was open to create and write.

SM: Colonization has been described as a process of alienation from the body. How does one reintegrate elements of selfhood? You illustrated this for yourself as a process of taking ownership over your body in a particular way, but how can one encourage embodied experience for others?

GS: When we're talking about masculinity, the male context, that kind of recognition would have required, for me, probably one of two things: First, a sense of love or of being loved in an unconditional way. So I'm not talking about being loved for sex, I'm not talking about being loved for what you can provide. I'm talking about just being loved for your whole, individual self. Second, it would require an offer of confidence and encouragement to find self-confidence. Because, really, it's within that confidence that a person is able to make good decisions. And really, the decision that you're making, in this context, is around trust. Do I trust this person? Do I not trust this person? So, without confidence, without love, people are oftentimes in situations where they make decisions based upon need, which can lead to unfortunate results.

SM: When I initially talked to one of the writers interviewed in this project, she said she was very uncomfortable as a woman talking about masculinities, saying something along the lines of, "It's not my place to discuss these things." And I suggested to her that ideas about being a good man don't just come from men. Your poetry often attests to the profound influence of the women in your life in providing foundations for you to become the man you've become. So my question is, are there roles for women in creating space for manhood and evaluating what proper masculinity ought to be?

GS: In my case, my women—in particular, my mom, my auntie, my grandmother, the three major women in my life—really had no choice but to provide for me and foster what they thought would be the healthiest things for me. You also have to keep in mind that I grew up primarily with a mother whose young adulthood was in the sixties. She was very well-read, she was very astute on matters of politics and Eastern philosophies and religions. You could talk to her about anything. So of course she really fostered reading and learning in me. Being a product of her generation, my mom was very open to me becoming whatever I wanted to be. She never led me in any one direction. You know, she never pushed me to become this, that, or the other thing. If anything, she really took a step back when it came to my own personal decision-making.

Because I lost her so early on—I mean, she was forty-eight and I was twenty-six when she passed away—I wasn't able to go through the process of figuring out my sexuality and saying, "Mom, this is who I am," and what have you. But honestly, in hindsight, I remember these conversations with her and she would drop these little bombs—not even bombs, but these little permissions—every now and then, saying things like, "You know, honey, I don't care who you love, as long as you're safe, healthy, and happy." And of course, I had no idea what she was talking about. I was just like, "Oh Mom, my love life isn't of any importance to you!" But in hindsight, basically what she was doing was saying, "My boy, be whoever you're going to be and be the best you simply can be."

And, you know, it was really the same thing with my auntie. My auntie was a wonderful storyteller and a wonderful entertainer and a wonderful nurturer, so she was able to foster those qualities in me. Growing up with her, I learned to cook, I learned to sew, I learned to do bead work, I learned to scrub the house from top to bottom, I learned how to fold clothes properly—all of these things, so of course they have played a huge role in my life. They certainly were the ones who lifted up the toilet seat and taught me to pee standing up. They weren't the ones that, at fifteen or sixteen, gave me condoms and taught me not to get anybody pregnant. That was missing. But in an odd way, I didn't seem to miss it. You don't miss what you don't know you don't have, right?

But the thing that became glaringly clear—and I'm going to go back to this—is that I didn't know how to sit and have a conversation with another man. I didn't know how to do that. And especially an older man. I didn't know how to be comfortable to do that. My first instinct is I wanted to get up and go away and have it finished, be done.

SM: Do you feel that was influenced both by the absence of your biological father and by the violence of some of the men that were...

GS: Absolutely. Oh yeah, absolutely. For me, it was a longing for what I didn't have and an absolute loathing for the things that I did. So that is a hard dichotomy to navigate. I think I'll spend the rest of my life reconciling that. I'll spend the rest of my life finding ways to come to terms with that and to heal that. And, of course, a lot of that—without sounding pie-in-the-sky about it—is forgiveness. Probably one of my biggest inspirations in looking at my own masculinity has been working to become the type of man that I would like to have had in my life. So to become the type of father to my nieces and nephews, to be the type of lover to my partner, to be the type of friend to my friends, to be the type of big brother that I could be, to be the type of little brother that I could be. That's what I've marked in my growing and evolving masculinity—to strive to be those things.

SM: In the last section of *Thunder Through My Veins*, you describe cradling yourself in your own "fatherly arms" as an image of coming into strength, of becoming the father needed by your own childhood self. Is that part of the same process?

GS: Absolutely. It reverts right back to what we were discussing about the physical strength in this part of my—I don't know if it's a poetic ideology, if it's a childhood ideology, if it's just an imagining—but part of being that small boy that I once was carries this idea of a fatherly type that is physically strong who is able to hold you and shelter you from the world, yet reassures you with this kind of quiet love. That's always been part of the process and it all started physically. It's like I had to take one of those senses and I really had to hone that one sense before I could go on to the other ones. It's almost like taking steps in a way in order to become the kind of man that I wanted to become.

What's really neat about finding my dad—and believe you me, my dad certainly had his faults—but physically, my dad was a big guy, you know? According to my stepmom, my dad and I share a lot of things in common. My dad was very mischievous. My dad could be very charming. My dad was very bright. He was very protective. He was very just. So it feels quite wonderful to know that those qualities that I've fostered within myself, had I had the opportunity, I would've had parts of that from him as well. And, you know, I've certainly come to terms in this particular life that that was not meant to be a part of my path. So I've been able to stop that whole ceremony of grieving, and I've been able to work towards this ceremony of celebration, of being able to say, "I also embody these things."

SM: Did your perception of any of this change when you found out that your father did seek to find you?

GS: It's a powerful thing to be able to ask those questions: "Why? Why didn't you do this? Why didn't you do that?" Each of us as children—whether it's with mothers, whether it's with fathers—each of us as children inevitably at some point has the burn-

PROBABLY ONE OF MY BIGGEST INSPIRATIONS IN LOOKING AT MY OWN MASCULINITY HAS BEEN WORKING TO BECOME THE TYPE OF MAN THAT I WOULD LIKE TO HAVE HAD IN MY LIFE.

ing question: "Why?" And the particular poem that you're referring to was basically me being able to ask my dad, in spirit, why he didn't do certain things.[1]

And so how did I feel, you're asking, when I found out that his vacancy from my life was not necessarily his whole idea, 100 percent? What's really important about that—and I think in the context of what you're working on with masculinity—is that there is absolutely no way that I can find only my dad's story, because in finding my dad's story, right beside it was my mom's story. There's an old saying that goes, "There's three sides to every story: his story, her story, and the truth." So, what happened in that situation was, yes, I certainly got to find out my dad's story, and I certainly got to find out a lot more of my mother's story, and things I wasn't supposed to find out, or that she didn't want me to find out—which, I will say, she had every right not to tell me. There were things I was not supposed to find out. And then underneath all that stuff was the truth about *why*. Why was he not a present figure in my life?

And so, in finding that truth, there was certainly a lot of reconciliation and a lot of emotion towards both my parents. There were times that I was equally angry at both of them. There were times that I took the side of one over the other. There were times that I would take the other side. There were times that I was incredibly proud of one. There were times that I was incredibly proud of the other. And there were times that I loved them both immensely. And, at some point, I was able to reconcile that besides being my mom and my dad, they were both individuals... individuals who were allowed to make mistakes.

But the bottom line is that despite everything that my childhood was punctuated with, I was extremely fortunate to grow up with a mother who loved me tremendously and who worked diligently to keep me from being lost in a system where so many other kids were lost. And somewhere in the world, which happened to be England, there was also a man there who thought about me a great deal and who continued to question his availability, or lack thereof, in my life. So, at some point, you stop asking "why?" and you sit with the knowledge of "because." You sit with that knowledge and try to apply it to being a better person.

There are wonderful things that I share with my male friends that are completely male-based. We deal with them because we are male and we are products of a system and an environment that has taught us we have to behave a certain way. And so that is how we approach things. And there is solidarity in that. There is solidarity in knowing that we can transcend those places, and that we can do them as strong, healthy, kind, brilliant men. That we can forge ahead, and not be our fathers, or not—I can't say not be our fathers, because it diminishes them somehow—but not be limited by what our fathers were limited by and not be limited by what our grandfathers were limited by. And the same thing can be said to be true with the women in our lives.

SM: One of the central difficulties of the project that I'm working on emerges from label-ling and biological determinism: the idea that the male-female binary is a form of limita-

1. The poem referenced here is "If" from the collection *Singing Home the Bones* (Polestar, 2005).

AT SOME POINT, YOU STOP ASKING "WHY?" AND YOU SIT WITH THE KNOWLEDGE OF "BECAUSE." YOU SIT WITH THAT KNOWLEDGE AND TRY TO APPLY IT TO BEING A BETTER PERSON.

tion. And in queer and Two-Spirit theory a lot of work deconstructs that binary opposition. But what I've noticed is that, in doing so, it often effaces maleness. Is there a danger or a cost when we try to avoid maleness because of its connection to patriarchal history?

GS: First of all, in relation to the ideology of Two-Spirited theory, I always back away from that three-hundred fold. I mean I don't consider myself Two-Spirited. I don't really work within that context, if you will. Not that I'm disparaging of it. It's just that I think it's very multi-layered insofar as the politicization of the word and how it's come about and its interpretation and its reinvention and the reinterpretation of things.

I see very much what you're talking about in regards to the lack of male representation within that context. I think basically you answered your own question because I think there is a paternalistic, misogynistic, kind of loathing, in a way. I won't say fear because I think people have worked really hard to get past that fear. But I think that there's such a loathing of historical oppressive maleness. And there's still a lot of work to do to stem the societal—and I'm not just talking cultural, I'm talking *societal*—representation of those binaries of maleness and femaleness that you're talking about because there's still this stigma. There's still an expectation about what denotes masculinity and strength. I mean, look to the sports that we see on TV. Look to how our sport figures conduct themselves, look to the simple debates about head shots in hockey. Until there's a gentleness woven into that expectation, then it's going to be one of those things that's constantly in tension, especially by a group of people who—and I'm not just talking Two-Spirited—in these discussions around masculinity, look more towards the maternal.

SM: Can I ask you about embodiment and sensuality in *Love Medicine and One Song*? In "Ôchîm ♦ His Kiss" the kiss of the beloved is described as "maskwa pawing / all his winter hunger," and the speaker in the poem continues: "so I yield up roots and berries / and lie back / my whole abundant self" (10).[2] It's a beautiful image that demonstrates agency because it's a decision: "*I yield up.*" And yet to yield oneself up is to be totally vulnerable. Can you speak to the tensions involved in that need for physical intimacy along with the danger such intimacy might bring?

2. *Maskwa* is the Cree word for bear.

GS: The best metaphor that I can give is that it's the scariest ride at a carnival. You wanna go on it, but you don't wanna go on it. You buy tickets for it, and you walk around the entire carnival, doing all the other rides, eating, doing everything but going on that ride. So finally, it's getting darker and it's getting darker, and the lights have come up and the food smells are all around and you've got one ticket left. And it's getting time to go home, but there's that niggling feeling—*I really really really wanna go on that ride*.

So you look at this person that you're with and you go, you know what? I think I'm ready, I think I wanna go on this ride. And so you're waiting in line, the anticipation is building. You're questioning yourself, "why am I doing this, should I be doing this," yet at the same time, you're really titillated. And you're really filled with this anticipation and this ball in your stomach and you just don't know what's going to happen. The line moves. You and your friend are being ushered into one of the cars and the door is being locked. The gears are being revved up and you start to move. At that moment, you've completely yielded up your entire self. At this point, there is no going back. You cannot withdraw into yourself. You cannot get out. And even if you scream, they're not going to stop anyway. In that split second, you're thinking, "Oh my god, why did I do this? Why did I do this? What am I going to do?" And then at some point, you just absolutely let go, and say, "Well, I'm doing it." And then the car starts to flip and you go upside down and the blood rushes to your head and you're screaming and you're laughing and you realize you do have a bar to hang on to and that at some point it's going to be over and it's okay and at some point very soon you will be upright again. At some point, it will stop and you'll be on the ground, the arm will lift up, the door will open, you'll stagger out of the cage, and you'll be dizzy and you'll be very grateful and so happy that you went on it. And then you'll be ready to go home.

So, to me, that's what that poem is like. In order to experience the absolute and utter jubilation of being turned upside down, you need to first of all say, "It'll be okay, I think I can be turned upside down. I will be grounded again at some point." But really what you've done is given yourself permission. You've allowed yourself to be vulnerable. And in allowing yourself that vulnerability, you've allowed yourself that experience. And allowing yourself that experience, you've allowed yourself all of the things that have come with that experience: the terror, the jubilation, the excitement, the panic. You've allowed yourself all of these amazing emotions, which once you've landed again permeate, they just radiate throughout your body and they become a part of your knowing.

SM: There are many poems in that same collection that linger over elements of the body in a way that remaps the body as a form of landscape. They claim the body in a way—they claim its beauty and they celebrate its beauty. At the same time, they bring in images that don't tend to exist in poetry. They show the erotic potential of muskeg, of frogs, of slugs, of rocks. Are those two processes intertwined? The recognition of the landscape as significant, sacred, and sensual, and at the same time recognition of the body?

GS: They're one and the same. One of the most amazing experiences I had while I was working on that particular book was working on a poem called "Ceremonies." And I was sitting and I was writing, and I can't tell you if it was late or if it was early or what the day was or what have you, but the image, the idea was—I was thinking about the sweat lodge, and I was thinking about the symbolism of sweating and its benefits and just how long it had been since I had actually gone to a sweat. And I was thinking about this, and the lines came to me, "My mouth, the lodge, you come to sweat." And I thought, I can't write that. I can't write that because that's taking a sacred ceremony

IN ALLOWING YOURSELF THAT VULNERABILITY, YOU'VE...ALLOWED YOURSELF ALL OF THESE AMAZING EMOTIONS, WHICH ONCE YOU'VE LANDED AGAIN PERMEATE, THEY JUST RADIATE THROUGHOUT YOUR BODY AND THEY BECOME A PART OF YOUR KNOWING.

and sexualizing it. And then I started to think... the sweat is a sacred purification. It's the womb. It's the womb of Mother Earth. You're being born and you come out. And what I'm describing is just as much a ceremony, is just as sacred. "I heat the stones between your legs. My mouth, the lodge, you come to sweat." That was the line. And that embodied, that one simple act, embodied an incredible ceremony. It embodied an incredible sacredness, and I took a stand on it and said, "This is sacred, and this is what *Love Medicine*, this is what these poems are about."

And so what you're saying about the land, about the ceremonies, about the things that come from that land, it's all interconnected. The muskeg, the reeds, the rocks, the smell of the earth, the bogs, all of these things are medicines from the earth, and those are the things that we possess within our own bodies. We don't have to look very far. Parts of our bodies are muskeg. Parts of our bodies, there are frogs there. And it was really just throwing those physical elements up and being able to give them to the spiritual energies where they exist. To me, people have oftentimes taken the spirit out of sex and sexuality. And if they haven't entirely taken out the spirit of sex and sexuality, they've long since stopped looking to the ceremonies that accompany those things. When you think of these sacred ceremonies—of give-aways, naming ceremonies, fasting—sex and sexuality is all a part of that. You name things on someone's body. You fast those things, you hunger them, you crave them, you sing those things, you dance those things, you taste those things, you feast them.

SM: Young people often don't have people telling them to treat the body as sacred, to find sensuality in ways that are celebratory. Do you seek to reach those audiences as well with your poetry? How can your songs be heard by those who most need them, I guess is what I'm asking.

GS: I sing different songs to that audience. Not because what we're talking about is not appropriate for them, but I sing different songs to them because what we're talking about takes a long time to come into, if you will. So I sing songs to them or read poetry that aims to inspire them to find their own experience and be able to articulate that. Because sex and sexuality is still so new to them, and rightfully so, that it remains a private thing. And they need to be able to hold that privately and do what they want to do with it and not necessarily have to share it or talk about it. But just because they're maybe not talking about one little area doesn't mean we're not talking about other areas—and they're all rivers that lead to the same lake.

SM: It's interesting to me how poetry is so private, so intimate, especially when read in solitude, and yet it can also be so social. When I attend a reading by a gifted reader of poetry, I feel like I inhabit my body differently. I feel like a more embodied person when I'm in that moment of engagement because there's the sound, there's rhythm, volume, and cadence, there's the visual element, and there's the audience of other bod-

PEOPLE HAVE OFTENTIMES TAKEN THE SPIRIT OUT OF SEX AND SEXUALITY. AND IF THEY HAVEN'T ENTIRELY TAKEN OUT THE SPIRIT OF SEX AND SEXUALITY, THEY'VE LONG SINCE STOPPED LOOKING TO THE CEREMONIES THAT ACCOMPANY THOSE THINGS.

ies being interconnected through a common experience. Do you feel that the poetry does different things when it's in its book form versus when you are reading it aloud?

GS: Poetry does different things when it's lifted off of the page. When I'm reading the poetry, I'm essentially presenting it the way that I wrote it. I'm very mobile when I write. I have a very hard time sitting still. I always say that poetry is like a rattle. Our bodies, as poets, are like a rattle that needs to be shaken to move the words off the page. Your body needs to vibrate and you need to shake it up and you need to get the sound going. There are so many different sounds that you can make with that rattle. So, I guess, the same could be said for those words actually being delivered onto the page. Maybe you're shaking your rattle and all of those little seeds are spilling over the page and you have to arrange them.

The primary difference between the written word and the spoken word of the same piece is that without having heard me, you're going to read the poem with your own filters. You're going to be reading the poem in the voice in which you would read or maybe the voice in which you've once heard someone else read. And what becomes different is not that there isn't a spirit in the words on the page, but rather that when you are reading, you are being charged with sorting through the words and stanzas to find the spirit. Whereas when somebody's reading aloud and they're shaking the rattle, the spirit is being flung, the spirit is being directed, it is being moved around the room, so you have no choice but to move. It's like a wave. You have no choice but to move with that spirit and to be taken by it. And the spirit will resonate with you, even after the poet stops speaking. That's what I actually take a great deal of responsibility with: I know that I'm rattling and I know that I'm spinning the spirit of the poem around the room like a lasso. I'm spinning it and I have to be careful with that lasso because I want it to envelop as many people as possible and I want the spirit to resonate with them long after we're done.

AFTER AND TOWARDS

A DIALOGUE ON THE FUTURE OF INDIGENOUS MASCULINITY STUDIES

///

NIIGAANWEWIDAM JAMES SINCLAIR: I've read this manuscript a few times now and it's been interesting to watch it change, develop, and culminate. Accompanying you from the original envisioning of this project to now, I've watched this research evolve and shift alongside your findings. While no doubt you had your take on these issues from the beginning, this book was really driven by the many people you interviewed and the many miles you logged. It's remarkable work. I can't get over how it's so readerly now— like an ongoing conversation. In earlier drafts, you could read the interviews in pretty much any order and get basically the same experience. The way you have constructed it now gives the reader both an idea and a pathway, like a call and response. For instance, when Lee Maracle raised the notion of a "warrior," there was Daniel David Moses and Taiaiake Alfred addressing what this might mean. When Janice Hill raised the issue of sex and sexual violence, here came Tomson Highway, Louise Halfe and Jessica Danforth to discuss it. When Warren Cariou and Alison Calder brought up the influence of place and geography in men's lives, I suddenly realized that Ty Tengan had already opened up

13 AUGUST 2013
A Conversation over Skype between Niigaanwewidam James Sinclair in Winnipeg, Manitoba, and Sam McKegney in Kingston, Ontario.

NIIGAANWEWIDAM JAMES SINCLAIR
is Anishinaabe (St. Peter's/ Little Peguis) and an assistant professor at the University of Manitoba. He is a regular commentator on Indigenous issues on CTV, CBC, and APTN, and his written work can be found in the pages of *The Exile Edition of Native Canadian Fiction and Drama*, newspapers like *The Guardian*, and online with *CBC Books: Canada Writes*. Niigaan is the co-editor of the award-winning *Manitowapow: Aboriginal Writings from the Land of Water* (Highwater Press, 2011) and *Centering Anishinaabeg Studies: Understanding the World Through Stories* (Michigan State University Press, 2013), and is the editorial director of the Debwe Series with Portage and Main Press.

my thinking on the subject. And so on and so on. It was almost like one voice would lead me to a question and another would answer it, personally and indirectly.

I found it very compelling how all of the pieces gestured to or framed what healthy Indigenous malehood—rather, *malehoods*—might look like. I'm thinking about Basil Johnston's point that young men are shaped by grandmothers, Tommy Thrasher's idea that the land teaches kindness, and Kim Anderson's centralization of courage and bravery. Some really foundational work is offered by Brendan Hokowhitu and his brilliant theoretical centralization of sport as a teaching conduit for health and collectivity through responsibility and honour. So many interviewees brought up the continuing role of ancestral languages, pop culture, and fatherhood. There is much involved in describing healthy Indigenous malehoods. Thinking about them now, there's too many to list. They're interwoven too, like a spiral.

I was also intrigued by how some speakers contradicted one another. As they say, the number one thing Native peoples do well is disagree. [*Laughter*] There was Taiaiake Alfred offering rather harsh critiques of Indigenous art and literature, for instance. Then, and almost in response, we had Daniel David Moses and Joseph Boyden talking about the empowerment of Indigenous identities and communities through writing. I also found interesting the ways in which raising children—and specifically young men—was represented differently from say Kateri Akiwenzie-Damm to Neal McLeod and how this contrasted an experience like the one Daniel Heath Justice bravely shared. Reading the back-and-forth between Adrian Stimson and Terrance Houle was both hilarious and jarring too.

I found listening to all of these remarkable voices very pleasurable and of course very educational. As someone who's researching and writing in this relatively new field of scholarship, *Masculindians* provided an opportunity to experience a real Indigenous spectrum across Kanata, Turtle Island, and the globe. There are certainly other areas that could have been included in the conversations, but with any book you have to make choices; you either work forever or you actually *finish* it.

SAM MCKEGNEY: A number of things stuck out for me as exciting and somewhat surprising as I went about conducting the interviews, a couple of which I'm wondering if we can reflect on together. The first was the number of times protectorship came up as a principle or an ethic. Kateri Akiwenzie-Damm speaks about reclaiming what's good about being a protector and about protectorship as a role that men can take on that not only gives them purpose but also serves the family, the community, and the nation. Richard Van Camp talks about protectorship frequently in his work—he talks about the protector in him as an uncle, about warriors as protectors, and even about protectorship and sex, noting that being a good lover means protecting and honouring the gift of sexuality (which is an interesting way of thinking about it). And Joseph Boyden grapples with what it means to protect and be protected in his novels. So I'm wondering about your thoughts on the idea of being a protector because popular

North American culture often valorizes the idea of the protector through hypermasculine tropes that ultimately disempower the protec*ted*—often women and children who become reconceptualized as the objects of the protec*tor*. But that of course isn't the only way of being a protector and that's not the type of protectorship these writers are seeking to reclaim. Do you see being a protector as a valuable subject position or ethic for Indigenous men to pursue, and what are the safeguards that prevent it from being conscripted into patriarchy?

NJS: Many interviews identified protection as an element of warriorism, fatherhood or some notion of virility, but I think the way men support, secure, and bring health to community is what most were really talking about. Understanding the multiple ways Indigenous men are and can be connected to community—in both good and bad ways—is perhaps the biggest challenge Indigenous men face today. Kateri Akiwenzie-Damm said it best when she said: "There are so many men who don't know what their role as a man is anymore." I think this point really emphasizes how important it is to define protectorship, for to do so is to assist Indigenous men to uncover some of the many gifts they can bring to the table.

One of the legacies of colonization has been the separation of men from their roles within families, communities, and nations. What's replaced these are hegemonic forms of corporate, neo-liberal individualist identities that ossify cultures and replace meaning with a one-size-fits-all Lockean chant of: "Pick up your bootstraps and get on with the business of making money, buying a house, and consume, consume, consume." Indigenous masculinity is so much more than this.

When I think about protectors I think about my grandfather. Raised on our traditional lands near St. Peter's, he was removed to residential school and, like many, brainwashed through a demeaning process that included replacing your name, language, and identity. He was also taught from a very early age that being Indigenous was backward, savage, and heathen and that everything associated with protecting that was wrong. Residential school therefore not only physically removed him from community but ideologically separated him from experiences of love, kindness, and beauty that would have grounded him and kept him connected.

He rarely spoke about this—I mean, who would—but the horrifically violent sexual, mental, and psychological abuse residential school students endured is well documented. His answer to this experience was to lie about his age to fight in World War II with his buddies. Can you imagine that? He'd rather face bullets than priests. Well, the army had this habit of sending Indian soldiers to the front lines. After many of his friends were killed and he himself was injured, he returned an enfranchised Indian with no support, no rights, and completely isolated. At the same time, he had no high school diploma. Trying to support a young family, he worked up north in the mines and performed labour in Winnipeg, returning to see his family sporadically on weekends. What he had been taught in school and was now put in the position to do was to work, compete for jobs, and "progress": live the good old-fashioned Western dream of being a "man all on your own." Soon, however, with war injuries and wear and tear on his body taking hold, this way of life was unsustainable. And, when he lost my grandmother—the only woman he would ever love—shortly after she gave birth to my uncle, Grandpa really had a hard time.

For a long time he had struggled with drinking but after this it consumed his life. I imagine what inspired much of this was a long history of loneliness, both imposed and self-imposed. He found isolation at residential school, at war, in the mines up north. This was no doubt very frustrating, and when Grandpa drank he wanted to fight, so he did. He fought my uncles, my dad, my aunt, and pretty much anyone else he could find. Soon he had pushed everyone away, he was literally all alone. For many years I judged him harshly, but now I think I understand him. I can only imagine the challenges he faced trying to make a living in a world that exploited, abused, and rejected him. Closer contact with his family, community, and nation would have facilitated a sense of protectorship in the institutions and relationships that he came from.

The cool ending to this story though is that my grandfather did learn to become a protector in his own way. Just after I was born—and in large part because my father told him that he could never come around his grandson while he was drunk—he quit drinking. He chose a relationship with me and his other grandchildren instead. I cannot imagine anything more brave, dignified, or warrior-like. I can honestly say that I never once saw him drink and only knew a loving, sensitive, generous man. He was also one of the funniest people I have ever known. It took him a very long time—and many unforgiveable acts—but he became a protector of me, my cousins, and our family, inheriting something that had been waiting for him his entire life.

Protectorship is something you earn. Indigenous men don't start off as protectors; they inherit it through work, mentorship, and being recognized. Being given the position of being a protector is a gift that begins via modelling and mentoring. There's a ceremony Anishinaabe do just about the time you hit puberty. It involves your uncle—and sometimes your father but not always—taking you out for a fast, a vision, or some time in the bush. The men share in camaraderie, stories, and teachings while learning about community, their bodies, and the hard work it takes to have healthy relationships with everyone and everything around them. When they return to community, they often come back changed, grown up a little, and interested in enacting the senses of connection they learned while out on the land: They are initiated into manhood.

Traditionally this happened on the land but, like most events today, even this has changed. I'm reminded of Joseph Boyden in this book talking about grabbing a case of beer and sitting on the back porch or Richard Van Camp describing youth camps. For me my first initiation happened when my uncle took me to the A&W in Selkirk. There was no fast here—only onion rings and root beer [*Laughter*]—but my uncle spent hours talking about sex, how to drive a car, school, fatherhood, love, and dreams. I've

> PROTECTORSHIP IS SOMETHING YOU EARN. INDIGENOUS MEN DON'T START OFF AS PROTECTORS; THEY INHERIT IT THROUGH WORK, MENTORSHIP, AND BEING RECOGNIZED.

been on some more traditional trips but this first initiation ceremony was really sacred and formative.

SM: Are there any parts to Indigenous manhood that you think are especially gained from being on the land today?

NJS: When I was much older, I received and experienced one of the most important teachings a man can ever be given: how to earn a fire. I've returned to this whenever I think about what we might call Indigenous masculinity. You can learn everything you need to know about being a man by building, making, and nurturing *ishkode*, a fire. Ishkode is our grandfather, a sacred gift-giver. From the preparation, welcoming, singing, striking, and care a fire requires, everything you need to know about Indigenous malehood is given through this relationship. You never earn a fire through a match. Lighting a match is the exact problem of Indigenous manhood.

Lighting a fire via a match and some wood at 7-Eleven might cut down on time, but it's truly the most meaningless possible way of beginning any fire. You haven't collected the flint or dry grass, you haven't created the spark, you haven't fanned it to make it light or sung the right welcoming song or placed the young flame into just the right place in the kindling. To really nurture a fire into being takes inviting and welcoming your grandfather in, making him comfortable and nurturing him so he feels welcome. A fire requires sensitivity, care, and concern, as well as patience and understanding. If you're not aware, gentle, and swift at the precise moment he arrives, he may leave and you have to start all over again. You're literally frozen until you learn how to make the healthiest and most complete space for that fire to thrive. You can't have warmth, you can't cook food, you can't continue—well, I guess you could, but that's what you would call the "hard road."

When we're talking about protectorship, what we're really talking about is earning the responsibility of belonging to a family, a community, a nation—because being recognized as part of all of those networks necessitates that you build, maintain, and care for relationships and keep ties strong. Being a man involves constantly building, nurturing, and protecting the fires that warm, feed, and help grow the world around you. If you let these fires go out or, worse, don't build them in the first place, a web of relationships might break, grow weak, or perhaps never even exist.

SM: One of the moments in the collection that I find significant but also challenging conceptually is when Lee Maracle points out that I'm misusing the idea of a role. When I ask what her role as Wolf Clan Stó: lo entails, she insists, as I understand it, that I am mistaking what is truly an identity for a discrete set of tasks. "It's not a role," she says. "We *are* that. It's not a role. I'm not a role. I'm a Wolf Clan, backward and forward visionary." It reminds me a bit of Sakéj Henderson's rejection of the idea of "culture" because it oversimplifies and carves existence into a discrete set of concepts; he uses

YOU NEVER EARN A FIRE THROUGH A MATCH. LIGHTING A MATCH IS THE EXACT PROBLEM OF INDIGENOUS MANHOOD.

the word "worldview" instead to honour the whole, the "unified vision." I'd like to ask you about the idea of "inheriting a role" because, especially at this stage in Indigenous masculinities studies, we're talking a lot about "male roles and responsibilities" and it becomes something of a mantra—maybe it's useful, but maybe we're not interrogating it enough or not thinking it through in sophisticated enough terms. Do you consider the framework of "male roles and responsibilities" to be limiting or utilitarian as a means of conceiving of and navigating personhood or identity?

NJS: I always find it odd that when I go to ceremonies there are certain activities that are classified as "man" jobs—fire is often one, cutting wood is usually another, carrying certain pipes, singing certain songs, and so on. When I hear the word "role," I often hear: "Here's the five things men have to do and here's the five things women have to do" in order for these roles to be maintained. These of course can be platforms for important kinds of work like facilitating uncles mentoring young men, for example, but they are often couched in physical essentialisms that fall apart under scrutiny. When roles are considered in terms of them being "jobs," it reduces them into acts minus purpose. As I see it, any act is a stage for the establishment, maintenance, and extension of relationships. The word "role" in English kinda misses this. So, returning to my last example, let's say that men carry the role to build and maintain fire for a community. Well, after this good work is done and ceremonies are over, we return to our jobs and well-built homes and the question arises: what is the firekeeping then? How is a garbageman a firekeeper? How is a lawyer a firekeeper? How is a father playing Snakes and Ladders with his daughter a firekeeper? How does firekeeping fit into a world that values matches and wood from 7-Eleven? And, one of the most important questions today: Who cares for fire when men are absent, have forgotten how, or refuse to do it? It is precisely when we think of traditional "roles" in these contexts that our cultures suddenly appear archaic and outdated.

What I think Lee was getting at was that Indigenous identities are irreducible to fixed jobs, tasks, or actions. Indigenous identities reside in times, places, and in relationships with the world around us. Like our animal relations in the clan systems she cites, we make do with what we have, using what we know and understand about the world and ourselves. Nothing in the world is arbitrary; everything is an opportunity, a gift, to understand how you as a man, woman, animal or clan member, and so on, relate to an infinite universe.

So, in certain situations—particularly when Indigenous men have abandoned their homes and children, and left fires smouldering—women have had to create and protect fire. At the same time, men have also at times had to care for the water. All of these moments have not collapsed Indigenous senses of gender but rather strengthened them to show that networks of relationships—communities—are ongoing and dynamic vessels of Indigenous continuance. It's our responsibility to grow, strengthen, and care for these communities in which manhood and womanhood are parts, not vice versa. Roles—if we are going to use that word—are not jobs at all, they can be anything that shows how we carry ongoing ties with multiple beings, human and non-human, throughout the universe. Caring for fire is not a role, it's a way of being.

There are so many different ways you could learn about being an Anishinaabe-inini, an Anishinaabe man: by looking at the sun, spending time with the earth, but I learn about it best by looking at our animal relations. Our animal relatives were the ones who offered to care for us when we arrived, nothing about this has changed. They still teach us. By examining the interrelationships among animals and Creation, we can learn all we need to know about how to live with dignity and respect and understanding. Their roles, of course, aren't fixed.

Animals are always resilient and flexible. *Nikaak*, geese, right now are travelling south and every morning I watch them travel and think about how they get to this moment every year. *Niigaak* are very territorial, especially when birthing and feeding, but when they need to be—when they need to migrate, for instance—they join together in groups to get that work done. In other words, there's a time to work together in community and there's a time to separate and raise a family. There are roles within family and community, and these reside in specific purposes and places and times and geographies—they're always shifting. I think that roles can be useful when they involve articulating and affirming the multitude of responsibilities Indigenous men carry within larger networks. Keeping those networks strong and healthy provides platforms for understanding the many gifts we carry.

SM: So for roles to be of value within those specific contexts, they need to be characterized by malleability and senses of reciprocity and—as many discuss in the interviews—accountability to the larger community?

NJS: I think "accountability" is a tricky word within our field of Indigenous masculinity studies because it brings with it negative connotations—that there is something to be accountable for. It reminds me of a crime. If we're talking about the responsibility of being a father, that for me is not about being accountable at all; it's about a life-long journey and trying to understand how at every moment you have someone else to think about. Being a father constitutes every part of my being, every word I write, every step I walk, and it illustrates to me how every action I take involves another life. That for me is not about accountability, it's about ethics.

SM: I guess accountability can carry with it an almost punitive connotation. It's also an economic metaphor because it implies a sense of indebtedness, which complicates things further. But I wonder if accountability can also speak to a sense of acknowledging integral connections beyond the self—an honouring of self*less*ness and responsibility as a way of understanding oneself. I mean, you can hold yourself accountable to your own values in a way that isn't only disciplinary. It can be a way of articulating your responsibility to the larger network so that, as you were saying earlier, the web doesn't break. But I see what you're saying about it perhaps implying that Indigenous men always already have something to atone for, which is problematic.

NJS: Yeah, that was my exact response when you said "accountable." The time I felt most uneasy in reading the collection was when interviews lapsed into a judgemental tone, sounding like: "Young men have to do such-and-such a job that I remember doing and they have to live up to this idea that I have for them." It's always problematic to take your circumstances and project them onto another. In fact, it's somewhat romantic too because our memories almost always cut and paste, replace and erase. I think this kind of rhetoric also obscures the very nature of Indigenous communities, which were based in seasonal, mobile, and dynamic principles. We have to be really careful about being prescriptive about what people ought to be and ought to do. Here I'm reminded of when Tomson Highway tells us about writers and artists being curative magicians in the way they can shift perspective. We in the field of Indigenous masculinity studies have to become like magicians; we have to think about where Indigenous men have come from, where we are going, and the way we continue to face ongoing assaults on our identities, our sexualities, our bodies, and try to figure this all out in a world that won't let up. We really have to gain perspective and context before we start creating ideals that Indigenous men have to live up to.

That might be where we will have to sit for a while, trying to figure out what's happened. So much research needs to begin with: How did we get to this point? Why is it that in the early nineteenth century Ojibway missionary Peter Jones goes on a hunting trip with other men—which is supposed to be a beautiful and empowering moment in his life—and witnesses the men around him get drunk and pass out? The entire experience is a formative nightmare. As he awakes he realizes he has no fire, he's hungry, and he's literally frozen; so he deduces: "Well there's a real problem with tradition here" and turns towards Christianity. I think this moment doesn't provide us with a forum to judge him—as so many scholars have—but to think about why he made that decision and what choices were available in his context. Our research needs to address Indigenous men without tossing them on the proverbial scrap heap; it needs to really seek to understand what they were facing and why they might have made the choices they did. This is not to forgive egregious acts, not at all. It's to figure out our relations and the gifts—good and bad—they have left for us.

SM: That kind of nuanced understanding of the complex conditions that inform decision-making and behaviour comes up in the work of many of the authors in this collection. I'm thinking of Louise Halfe's portrayals of the father in *Blue Marrow*, for instance, or the opening section of Lee Maracle's *Daughters Are Forever* or Richard Van Camp's work. As Joanne Arnott says, we need to have "a feeling of generosity toward our real human limits."

Looking to the work that needs to be done and the work that is ongoing, do you feel as though there's enough effort towards envisioning alternative horizons of possibility? Do you see the necessary creative energy and vision or is too much of the work on Indigenous masculinities confined to interrogating what has informed contemporary conditions? Is it maybe more about diagnosis, according to a Western model, than about creative engagement that offers alternative imaginings?

NJS: I'm a little biased because I spend most of my time reading and writing literature, so I personally find the most exciting critical moves going on in the work of some of our creative writers. I can't get enough of Richard Van Camp's work, which is constantly pushing the idea of what beautiful and healthy male relationships look like. In so many depictions of male interactions in fiction we get violence and, if it's anything else, critics quickly label other male relationships homoerotic. Richard resists these safe reading strategies and instead challenges the reader. I'm thinking of the short story "Dogrib Midnight Runners," which asks: Why can't we have naked men going for a jog and that being about health, safety, love, respect, and honour? How can we have discourses about male love that are not irreducible to just bodies and sex and instead are about embracing our inheritances and responsibilities as men, as fathers, and as brothers? These are some exciting interventions.

Thinking back to the interviews, Tomson Highway and Joseph Boyden and Kateri Akiwenzie-Damm all talked about how mentorship is crucial to the creation of healthy Indigenous men. There is never enough talk about how patience, honesty, kindness, and love set the stage of rich senses of Indigenous malehood. It's much easier to write about the despair Indigenous men have endured and the harsh reality that has come out of this—substance abuse, absent fathers, poverty—than it is to write about beauty. Violent relationships are much easier to write about than healthy, nurturing ones. I think that's where our field needs to go. I don't see enough writing about healthy relationships with the men in our lives. I include myself in this criticism too.

Writing about positive male-male interactions is risky. It's tough. Mainstream culture loves violence, rape, and shock value. At the same time it might involve more work; few really write about complex, beautiful Indigenous men without romanticizing or sexualizing or using them as a foil against other, awful images. There's also admittedly a lot of absent fathers, gang members, and men in prison from our communities who have done some awful things. We also have this cult of male individualism that so pervasively affects Indigenous men in the public eye—chiefs, political leaders, cultural ceremonialists—men who dance and sing songs about family and community but then do horrible things to women, use and abuse and exploit the people around them.

I think our field has an opportunity to really uncover, identify, and perhaps even define the complex gifts Indigenous men inherit and have to give. It's worth considering. And indeed our field could make contributions to healing some of the cycles Indigenous men find themselves in by theorizing what Indigenous men do and have done to make this world a respectful, honourable, and beautiful place. What are the precipitating factors and outcomes of communities where Indigenous malehood is recognized, talked about, and debated in healthy and positive ways? Do we have to dream about this or can we ascertain examples and disseminate this information so others can know about it? That for me is what our field could do while still working to uncover some of the ugly stuff. That could be a great contribution.

SM: In their recent book chapter on Indigenous masculinities, Rob Innes, Kim Anderson, and Jonathan Swift do an excellent job of mapping out three strands of work needing attention for Indigenous masculinity studies to develop into a field with purpose and positive impact at the community level. These involve interrogating the history of disenfranchisement, dispossession, and social engineering that informs contemporary conditions—that's the first strand; the second strand is looking to elders, knowledge keepers, and those with experience of other Indigenous ways of being in order to "dig up what we can about healthy Indigenous masculinities"; and the third strand involves using that knowledge and critical awareness in imaginative ways that might engender a variety of possibilities for non-dominative yet empowered Indigenous masculinities, which in turn might work in the service of balance, health, and empowerment within communities and nations. And your comments just now show how those strands need to be braided together in a visionary way, and perhaps how literature is already actively doing that.

NJS: I agree with all that, but for me it's all about where this work is grounded. All the gifts that we need to survive and endure and create and imagine are here—everything's around us. You don't need anything more. We have a tendency within Indigenous studies to be as human-centred and gender-centred as the institutions that surround us. We sometimes don't centralize the other gifts that are available around us.

I told that one story of watching the geese go overhead, and another story about fire as a being, fire as a grandfather. There are so many more stories I could tell but they all have to do with how the world teaches us, and it's our job to read, listen, and interact with Creation, not vice versa. It's not that any of those three categories you listed off lack this, but I'd like to hear more work from Indigenous researchers about how we can look to the cycles and seasons and animals and earth and water for solutions to problems we have created for ourselves. Ironically, it has precisely been when we have ignored or run against the natural gifts that the universe provides us with that we have gone so terribly wrong. I hear a lot of people say that Mother Earth is our teacher and so on, but not enough about how the world *actually teaches us* in our work. If we want to be truly healthy in our relationships with one another, then we have to interact with the world in a healthy way. This is exactly the problem with pollution, and in particular water contamination. Take oil fracking in Saskatchewan and Alberta, for example.

When we think in human-centred ways, the world will teach us that we are ignoring most of the rest of Creation. Sometimes we need a harsh lesson and the world might have to teach us by killing us. It's simple. When we think of ourselves as the primary gift-givers to Creation and not dependent receivers of its gifts, we do things like fracking. When we think of ourselves as a nephew to the sun, the moon, the water, and as part of a great cosmological family, we don't. This is exactly the problem with Indigenous men. We too often think of ourselves as independent, supreme seekers of the great capitalist dream and make choices without humility. When that changes, that is truly when we will begin to understand the possibilities of healthy Indigenous masculinities.

SM: You were pointing to some areas that are perhaps not fleshed out enough in the interviews in this collection. Are there other ideas, areas of discussion, or arguments that you were surprised didn't crop up or were underdeveloped?

NJS: I don't see the collection as lacking because that implies that there is a list of ten things that need to be talked about, and that's something that happens when you're at a more established point in the field. When you have a critical mass of scholarship, then you can say, "Well, you'd better have these three theories in there." The problem, as Lee Maracle puts it, isn't that there aren't theorists, it's that "they just haven't been published." There are men and women with this knowledge and experience, but they're not working in universities.

If there was something that I wish there was more of in the book, it's what Gregory Scofield talks about as "claiming." There is lots of reaction to experiences with fathers, oppression, and policies, and discussing these is definitely important. At the same time though, sometimes when we focus on problems—the social production of hypermasculinity, for instance—we fall into the position of presuming: "If we only get rid of this, we'd be fine." Meanwhile, what's left to fill the vacuum? I found Gregory Scofield's interview to be the culmination of a thread in the book around claiming the erotic, the body, and the complexity of sensory experience. He talks about liberating himself through validation: "Here's what I know" and "here's what I experience." I really appreciated that honesty and that bravery. And there's no question about the truthfulness. It's the essence of claiming a position, a territory, and a meaning.

A second area might be more discussion about what economic conditions are necessary for a healthy and responsible Indigenous manhood. What kinds of economic production are we imagining when we think about communities with ethical Indigenous men? For instance, we are often in conflict with forces around us that seek to reproduce us as individualized corporate beings. This might get us thinking about the role of educators, of artists, of writers, and how these allow a certain measure of freedom in producing healthy Indigenous masculinities while at the same time confronting rampant individualism. Publishers are constantly looking at what sells the most, for instance. How might a responsible Indigenous construction worker or lawyer or investor look in today's world? We need more talk about how Indigenous men can build a life based on cultural teachings within an increasingly globalized world. And

IT'S SIMPLE. WHEN WE THINK OF OURSELVES AS THE PRIMARY GIFT-GIVERS TO CREATION AND NOT DEPENDENT RECEIVERS OF ITS GIFTS, WE DO THINGS LIKE FRACKING. WHEN WE THINK OF OURSELVES AS A NEPHEW TO THE SUN, THE MOON, THE WATER, AND AS PART OF A GREAT COSMOLOGICAL FAMILY, WE DON'T.

I'm not just talking about urban environments; the biggest influences today on reserves are television and video games.

SM: A number of interviews broach questions of economics, but there's more work to be done to analyze the larger economic structures in which systems of gender are embedded. Joanne Arnott talks about how poverty is stigmatized alongside race and gender, and Taiaiake Alfred talks about the influence of the capitalist rewards system on forms of masculine aspiration. I was really struck by Alison Calder's argument that socio-economic conditions actually create the circumstances in which particular forms of activity coded as "masculine" become attainable, whereas other socio-economic conditions make other forms of masculine performance desirable or attainable. What serves as capital in specific gendered spaces is incredibly context specific. So in the context of any individual experience of manhood, different socio-economic matters will come into play. Here I'm referring to the level of immediate lived experience, but as you were suggesting earlier, the broader socio-economic structures actually affect our capacity to have these conversations about masculinity in the abstract at the level of discourse. Funding structures influence what is published and what is broadcast and what kinds of research projects have success at the institutional and national levels. And coming back full circle to the immediacy of quotidian realities, when you can't get food into your mouth or the mouths of your children, then the question "What does masculinity mean?" perhaps becomes irrelevant. It becomes a luxury. On the other hand, maybe, as Terrance Houle suggests, that moment has everything to do with what it means to be a man. Perhaps the actions taken in that moment are the creative and imaginative embodiment of those meanings and responsibilities that theory is endlessly seeking to understand and make legible. Maybe those actions *are* the theory.

NJS: I once witnessed an act in a Cree community that speaks to this issue. These two men bagged a moose and they brought it back to the community. In their backyard they were skinning the moose. They were cutting it up, and they got to the point where their freezer was full. It was the dead of winter, and there came a point where they started walking down the road and began delivering moose meat to the people on the road—I was staying a couple doors down. What they said was that there was no storage, no ability to store all the meat. And one of the elders where I was staying said, "Well, that's what we used to do in the old days." So everyone had moose meat that winter. Interestingly, what happened the next winter is that these same young men caught a bunch of muskrat, and they started doing the same thing, delivering it down the road. This started a chain reaction where young men became suppliers for all of the elders living on their road. Now, there's an entire network and body of relationships that has been forged on this one road in this one Cree community as a result of one single act.

Perhaps, it might have started through a lack of storage, but it turned into an act of kindness. It was a gesture of kindness and sharing, and if I were to say anything about what Indigenous men should be, it would be that. It's the gesture of kindness that is a choice. In that moment of choice, a community formed that lives on years later. We can talk about how that existed hundreds of years ago, and that's all fine and good, and we can talk about how it should be like that in the future, but all I can say is what I saw and what I felt, which was based in a specific time and moment: A choice. And, that the moose meat tasted amazing! If I saw these young men today I'd go up and shake their hands, see how they're doing, and ask if they've gone hunting lately. I don't know anything other than that—I don't know anything really beyond their names and their families and that that gesture of kindness is something that changed an entire community.

SM: Is that act something you would describe as a claiming in the way that Gregory articulates it?

NJS: Absolutely. It's the claiming of being a good neighbour, a good relation. Every part of Indigenous cultures—if we're talking about anything pan-Indian—every single ceremony that I've ever been a part of is about being a good relation. There's nothing more simple than that, or more essential. A good relative is not always an idealized romantic image either. It's sometimes where you have to stand in front of a bulldozer. It's sometimes where you have to stand up for the water or you have to remind others of the sacredness of the Earth. It's sometimes where you have to make food. It's sometimes where you have to open a door. Every single part of being an Indigenous person, in the most meaningful way that I know, is about being a good relative and about thinking of somebody or something other than yourself.

SM: That highlights for me the urgency of decolonizing settler masculinities as well, because that celebration and honouring of interconnectedness that you're talking about is not often discussed in the context of mainstream North American masculinities—especially beyond one's nuclear family, in a sense that incorporates the land, the water, and the other-than-human entities around us as agentive beings. The economic systems that support and are guarded by the Canadian and U.S. nation states—in terms of global capitalism and resource extraction—are intimately involved in the production of mainstream ideas about gender. And those economic and gender systems undoubtedly influence Indigenous masculinities—not in a programmatic way, of course, because Indigenous masculinities are not *created* by those systems, but those systems exert pressures that have consequences; there is dynamic interplay at work. So I think that settlers from various socio-economic, geographic, and cultural positions need to be interrogating how our ideas about gender continue to be conditioned by settlement and the dispossession of Indigenous nations. We need to be aware of how settler masculinities were forged historically in the arena of conquest, which, as Qwo-Li Driskill suggests, required a masculinity that rapes and murders.

SETTLERS FROM VARIOUS SOCIO-ECONOMIC, GEOGRAPHIC, AND CULTURAL POSITIONS NEED TO BE INTERROGATING HOW OUR IDEAS ABOUT GENDER CONTINUE TO BE CONDITIONED BY SETTLEMENT AND THE DISPOSSESSION OF INDIGENOUS NATIONS.

At the same time, we need to be aware of the variety of masculine models available to settler men today—and to women—and the variety of economic, popular cultural, and educational influences on contemporary settler masculinities. The disparate forms of social and economic capital available to different settlers in different settings indicate that we need to avoid simplistic assumptions here as well, and we need to be imaginative about how we leverage that capital in the service of decolonizing gender. For example, the forms of social capital to which I have access as a settler scholar are different in a university classroom than at a community gathering or in a hockey dressing room or at a bar or in my parents' backyard, and the onus is on me to interrogate the kinds of privilege those manifestations of social capital enable, to understand that they emerge from the history of settler colonialism, and to seek out ways of performing my own gendered identity that denaturalize settlement, destabilize privilege, and pursue justice. I guess what I mean is that we need to maintain contextual specificity and to avoid easy answers in order to do the work that needs to be done—both for Indigenous *and* settler masculinities. We need to take Brendan Hokowhitu's advice and always court complexity.

NJS: Oil fracking doesn't exist unless you internalize conquest, control, and domination over the land. It's the most violent, destructive, and abusive act one can do to the land and the water, but it goes beyond that. It's suicidal. How many days can anyone survive without water? With uninhabitable land? With no animals because you've murdered all your relatives in the soil? Fracking is the most inane and nonsensical way of living in the world this side of the atom bomb. You only invent fracking to destroy yourself, and an economic system built on this foundation is self-destruction. It's as simple as that. So much of fracking, resource exploitation, and conquest has always been tied up in what manhood means in settler culture. To control, to manipulate, and to settle is such a stereotypical male trope that lives throughout novels, movies, and sporting events. American football to me is the essence of this: The conquest of another's territory and the romanticization of settling another's land, all performed through hypermasculine posturing and the cult of individualism.

SM: What do we need to commit ourselves to so that such corrosive masculinities give way to more balanced and responsible ways of being? How can this conversation connect with and enliven other conversations about Indigenous masculinities? How do we nurture this fire in a good way that might serve to warm and sustain our networks of relations?

NJS: This work is being pursued very strongly within Canada—and also, I believe, in New Zealand and Australia—but this is an opportunity for us to reach out to our relatives south of that great forty-ninth parallel, to Native Americans who may have a lot to teach us about what they're doing. The second thing is to really investigate connections with the work researchers and writers in queer studies have been doing for decades now. Queer studies and Indigenous studies have long been engaged in similar work and masculinity is a potential intersection. I'm thinking about Craig Womack's work around the ways in which gendered positions often fall apart when engaged in poetry and song and dance but reassemble themselves in moments like Creek stomp dances. I think more cross-investigations in these paths would lead to exciting findings and pathways forward.

The last thing I'd suggest is to bring these discussions back to the grassroots. Right now we're talking on Skype as two professors, and most interviewed in this book are funded, trained, and supported by universities. We don't want to leave out our brothers and uncles who are not in these places when we have these discussions about what it means to be an Indigenous man. One thing we do have access to in universities is young people. This book will probably end up predominantly in the hands of university students but I'm thinking how this work could also reach out to other youth as well. I'm interested in how this work can reach into places like the Manitoba Youth Centre, a youth correctional facility I have worked at. The young men I worked with there are all former gang members and know intimately the processes that have constructed them as sons, uncles, and fathers. They know much about experiences with abuse and poverty, policy and law, and how they have overcome these forces—some good, some bad—through senses of loyalty, the formation of families, and resistance. They just don't use the same language we do to describe what this means. And many of them can't read and most can't write. I think these young men, however, have a hell of a lot to share that would dialogue in complex ways with voices in *Masculindians*. If we don't reach young men like these and include them in our conversations, if we don't engage them in some way about what it means to be a responsible and ethical man within a family, community, and nation, we're really not getting very far in our work.

If we can engage Indigenous men in discussions surrounding where they come from, help them define for themselves and for us what it might mean to be an Indigenous man today, and join together with them in a collective vision about where Indigenous masculinities might be headed, then we are doing this work in a good way. If we centre ourselves on gestures of relationship—both by producing healthy work and by assisting in the creation of healthy men—we will really be doing something long-lasting. But if we have conversations only amongst ourselves, we'll be doing neither the work nor our communities any service. We'll not really be creating a field, we'll be creating a fad. However, as the voices and the spirit in this book demonstrate, we are already beginning to eclipse these limitations, and I hope we retain and reaffirm our commitment to building in these crucial directions together.

IF WE CENTRE OURSELVES ON GESTURES OF RELATIONSHIP—BOTH BY PRODUCING HEALTHY WORK AND BY ASSISTING IN THE CREATION OF HEALTHY MEN— WE WILL REALLY BE DOING SOMETHING LONG-LASTING.

BIBLIOGRAPHY

1. INDIGENOUS MASCULINITY THEORY

Abram, Susan Marie. "'Souls in the Treetops': Cherokee War, Masculinity, and Community, 1760–1820." PhD diss., Auburn University, 2009.

Alfred, Taiaiake. *Peace, Power, Righteousness: An Indigenous Manifesto*. Toronto: Oxford University Press, 1999.

———. *Wasáse: Indigenous Pathways of Action and Freedom*. Toronto: Broadview Press, 2005.

Anderson, Kim, Robert Alexander Innes, and John Swift. "Indigenous Masculinities: Carrying the Bones of the Ancestors." In *Canadian Men and Masculinities: Historical and Contemporary Perspectives*, ed. Christopher J. Greig and Wayne J. Martino. Toronto: Canadian Scholars' Press Inc., 2012. 266–84.

Ball, Jessica. "Fathering in the Shadows: Indigenous Fathers and Canada's Colonial Legacies." *The Annals of the American Academy of Political and Social Science*. 624, 29 (2009): 29–48.

———. "Indigenous Fathers' Involvement in Reconstituting 'Circles of Care.'" *American Journal of Community Psychology* 45, 1 (2010): 124–38.

Bayers, Peter L. "Charles Alexander Eastman's *From the Deep Woods to Civilization* and the Shaping of Native Manhood." *Studies in American Indian Literatures* 20, 3 (2008): 52–73.

———. "William Apess's Manhood and Native Resistance in Jacksonian America." *MELUS* 31, 1 (Spring 2006): 123–46.

Bombay, Amy, Kimberly Matheson, and Hymie Anisman. "Decomposing Identity: Differential Relationships Between Several Aspects of Ethnic Identity and the Negative Effects of Perceived Discrimination Among First Nations Adults in Canada." *Cultural Diversity and Ethnic Minority Psychology* 16, 4 (2010): 507–16.

Brave Heart, Maria Yellow Horse. "Wicasa Was'aka: Restoring the Traditional Strength of American Indian Boys and Men." *American Journal of Public Health* 102, 2 (2012): 177–83.

Bulman, Jack, and Rick Hayes. "Mibbinbah and Spirit Healing: Fostering Safe, Friendly Spaces for Indigenous Males in Australia." *International Journal of Men's Health* 10, 1 (2011): 6–20.

Clark, David Anthony, Tyeeme Clark, and Joane Nagel. "White Men, Red Masks: Appropriations of 'Indian' Manhood in Imagined Wests." In *Across the Great Divide: Cultures of Manhood in the American West*, ed. Matthew Basso, Laura McCall, and Dee Garceau. New York: Routledge, 2001. 109–30.

Cromley, Elizabeth. "Masculine/Indian." *Winterthur Portfolio* 31, 4 (1996): 265–80.

Devries, Karen M., and Free, Caroline. "'I told him not to use condoms': masculinities, femininities and sexual health of Aboriginal

Canadian young people." *Sociology of Health and Illness* 32, 6 (2010): 827–42.

Goldie, Terry. *Fear and Temptation: The Image of the Indigene in Canadian, Australian, and New Zealand Literatures*. Montreal: McGill-Queen's University Press, 1989.

Hardin, Michael. "Altering Masculinities: The Spanish Conquest and the Evolution of the Latin American Machismo." *International Journal of Sexuality and Gender Studies* 7, 1 (2002): 1–22.

Hare, Jan, and Jo-ann Archibald, Karlee Fellner, and Dorothy Christian. "Editorial: Indigenous Youth as the New Warriors." *Canadian Journal of Native Education*. 34, 1 (2011): 1–6.

High, Casey. "Warriors, Hunters, and Bruce Lee: Gendered Agency and the Transformation of Amazonian Masculinity." *American Ethnologist* 37, 4 (2010): 753–70.

Hokowhitu, Brendan. "Authenticating Māori Physicality: Translations of 'Games' and 'Pastimes' by Early Travellers and Missionaries to New Zealand." *International Journal of the History of Sport* 25, 10 (2008): 1355–73.

——. "In Conversation: Brendan Hokowhitu and Kim Anderson." Bidwewidam Indigenous Masculinities website, Fall 2012. http://www.indigenousmasculinities.com/recent-stories/18-visiting-scholars-interview-with-brendan-hokowhitu.html.

——. "The Death of Koro Paka: 'Traditional' Māori Patriarchy." *The Contemporary Pacific* 20, 1 (2008): 115–41.

——. "Māori Rugby and Subversion: Creativity, Domestication, Oppression and Decolonization." *International Journal of the History of Sport* 26, 16 (2009): 2314–34.

——. "Producing Elite Indigenous Masculinities." *Settler Colonial Studies* 2, 2 (2012): 23–48.

——. "The Rediscovered Self: Indigenous Identity and Cultural Justice." *American Indian Quarterly* 35, 2 (2011): 265–8.

——. "Tackling Māori Masculinity: A Colonial Genealogy of Savagery and Sport." *The Contemporary Pacific* 16, 2 (2004): 259–84.

Hokowhitu, Brendan, and Jay Scherer, "The Māori All Blacks and the Decentering of the

White Subject: Hyperrace, Sport, and the Cultural Logic of Late Capitalism." *Sociology of Sport Journal* 25 (2008): 243–62.

Jackson, Steven J., and Brendan Hokowhitu. "Sport, Tribes, and Technology: The New Zealand All Blacks *Haka* and the Politics of Identity." *Journal of Sport and Social Issues* 25, 2 (May 2002): 125–39.

Jeancart, Danielle P. "Imposed Identities: The Colonial Construction of Indigenous Masculinity." PhD diss., Trent University, 2012.

King, Richard C. "On being a warrior: Race, gender and American Indian imagery in sport." *International Journal of the History of Sport* 23, 2 (2006): 315–30.

Klopotek, Brian. "'I Guess Your Warrior Look Doesn't Work Every Time': Challenging Indian Masculinity in the Cinema." In *Across the Great Divide: Cultures of Manhood in the American West*, ed. Matthew Basso, Laura McCall, and Dee Garceau. New York: Routledge, 2001. 251–73.

Laine, Thom. *Becoming Brave: The Path to Native American Manhood*. San Francisco: Chronicle Books, 1992.

Laker, Jason A. *Canadian Perspectives on Men and Masculinities: An Interdisciplinary Reader*. Don Mills: Oxford University Press, 2012.

Lazur, Richard F., and Richard Majors. "Men of Colour: Ethnocultural Variations of Male Gender Role Strain." In *A New Psychology of Men*, ed. Ronald F. Levant and William S. Pollack. New York: Basic Books, 1995. 337–58.

Maynard, Margaret. "Staging Masculinity: Late Nineteenth Century Photographs of Indigenous Men." *Australian Historical Studies* 24, 66 (2009): 129–37.

McKegney, Sam. "'beautiful hunters with strong medicine': Indigenous Masculinity and Kinship in Richard Van Camp's *The Lesser Blessed*." *Canadian Journal of Native Studies* 29, 1/2 (2009): 203–27.

——. "Masculindians: The Violence and Voyeurism of Male Sibling Relationships in Recent First Nations Fiction." In *Literature for Our Times: Postcolonial Studies in the Twenty First Century*, ed. Bill Ashcroft, Julie McGonegal, Ranjini Mendis, and Arun

Mukherjee. New York: Rodopi Press, 2012. 375–85.

———. "'pain, pleasure, shame. Shame'—Masculine Embodiment, Kinship, and Indigenous Reterritorialization." *Canadian Literature* 216 (Spring 2013): 12–33.

———. "Warriors, Healers, Lovers, and Leaders: Colonial Impositions on Indigenous Male Roles and Responsibilities." In *Canadian Perspectives on Men and Masculinities: An Interdisciplinary Reader*, ed. Jason A. Laker. Toronto: Oxford University Press, 2011. 241–68.

Moreton-Robinson, Aileen. "Bodies That Matter: Performing White Possession on the Beach." *American Indian Culture and Research Journal* 35, 4 (2011): 57–72.

Ottosson, Ase. "Where are the Men? Indigeneity and Masculinity Realigned." *Asia Pacific Journal of Anthropology* 11, 1 (2010): 75–83.

Parker, Robert Dale. "Who Shot the Sheriff: Storytelling, Indian Identity, and the Marketplace of Masculinity in D'Arcy McNickle's *The Surrounded*." *Modern Fiction Studies* 43, 4 (1997). 898–932.

Rogers, Richard A. "Deciphering Kokopelli: Masculinity in Commodified Appropriations of Native American Imagery." *Communication and Critical/Cultural Studies* 4, 3 (2007): 233–55.

Rymhs, Deena. "'It's a Double-Beat Dance:' The 'Indian Cowboy' in Indigenous Literature, Art, and Film." *Intertexts* 14, 2 (2010): 75–92.

Selmeski, Brian R. "Multicultural Citizens, Monocultural Men: Indigeneity, Masculinity, and Conscription in Ecuador." PhD diss., Syracuse University, 2007.

Sheidley, Nathaniel. "Hunting and the politics of masculinity in Cherokee treaty-making, 1763–75." In *Empire and Others: British Encounters with Indigenous Peoples, 1600–1850*, ed. Martin Daunton and Rick Halpern. Philadelphia: University of Pennsylvania Press, 1999. 167–85.

Sweet, Timothy. "Masculinity and Self-Performance in the Life of Black Hawk." *American Literature* 65, 3 (1993): 475–99.

Tengan, Ty P. Kāwika. *Native Men Remade: Gender and Nation in Contemporary Hawai'i*. Durham: Duke University Press, 2008.

Valaskakis, Gail Guthrie. *Indian Country: Essays on Contemporary Native Culture*. Waterloo: Wilfrid Laurier University Press, 2005.

Wilson, Michael T. "'Saturnalia of Blood': Masculine Self-Control and American Indians in the Frontier Novel." *Studies in American Fiction* 33, 2 (2005): 131–47.

2. INDIGENOUS FEMINISMS

Allen, Chadwick. *Blood Narrative: Indigenous Identity in American Indian and Maori Literary and Activist Texts*. Durham: Duke University Press, 2002.

Allen, Paula Gunn. *The Sacred Hoop: Recovering the Feminine in American Indian Traditions*. Boston: Beacon Press, 1986.

Anderson, Kim. *A Recognition of Being: Reconstructing Native Womanhood*. Toronto: Second Story Press, 2000.

Barkdull, Carenlee. "Exploring Intersections of Identity With Native American Women Leaders." *Affilia: Journal of Women and Social Work* 24, 2 (2009): 120–36.

Barker, Joanne. "Gender, Sovereignty, and the Discourse of Rights in Native Women's Activism." *Meridians: Feminism, Race, and Transnationalism* 7, 1 (2009): 127–61.

Barrios, Patricia G., and Marcia Egan. "Living in a Bicultural World and Finding the Way Home: Native Women's Stories." *Affilia* 17, 2 (2002): 206–28.

Blaire, Heather, Janine Tine, and Violet Okemaw. "Ititwewiniwak: Language Warriors—The Young Women's Circle of Leadership." *Canadian Journal of Native Education* 34, 1 (2011): 89–104.

Chenault, Venida S. *Weaving Strength, Weaving Power: Violence and Abuse Against Indigenous Women*. Durham: Carolina Academic Press, 2011.

Culhane, Dara. "Their Spirits Live Within Us: Aboriginal Women in Downtown Eastside Vancouver Emerging into Visibility." *American Indian Quarterly* 27, 3 (2003): 593–606.

Green, Joyce. *Making Space for Indigenous Feminism*. London: Zed Books, 2007.

Hall, Lisa Kahaleole. "Navigating Our Own 'Sea of Islands': Remapping a Theoretical Space for Hawaiian Women and Indigenous Feminism." *Wicazo Sa Review* 24, 2 (2009): 15–38.

Hamby, Sherry L. "The Importance of Community in a Feminist Analysis of Domestic Violence Among American Indians." *American Journal of Community Psychology* 28, 5 (2000): 649–69.

Herndon, Ruth Wallis. "Racialization and feminization of poverty in early America: Indian women as 'the poor of the town' in eighteenth-century Rhode Island." In *Empire and Others: British Encounters with Indigenous Peoples, 1600–1850*, ed. Martin Daunton and Rick Halpern. Philadelphia: University of Pennsylvania Press, 1999. 186–203.

Hladki, Janice. "Decolonizing Colonial Violence: The Subversive Practices of Aboriginal Film and Video." *Canadian Women Studies* 25, 1 (2006): 83–7.

Jaimes, M. Annette, and Theresa Halsey. "Chapter 16: American Indian Women: At the Centre of Indigenous Resistance in Contemporary North America." In *Dangerous Liaisons: Gender, Nations, and Postcolonial Perspectives.* Anne MacClintock, Aamir R. Mufti, Ella Shohat. Minneapolis: University of Minnesota Press, 1997.

Johnston, Kerensa. "Maori Women Confront Discrimination: Using International Human Rights Law to Challenge Discriminatory Practices." *Indigenous Law Journal* 4 (2005): 19–69.

Kenny, Carolyn, and Tina Ngaroimata Fraser. *Living Indigenous Leadership: Native Narratives on Building Strong Communities.* Vancouver: UBC Press, 2012.

Lajimodiere, Denise K. "Ogimah Ikwe: Native Women and Their Path to Leadership." *Wicazo Sa Review* 26, 2 (2011): 57–82.

Lavell, Jeannette Corbiere, and Dawn Memee Lavell-Harvard. *"Until Our Hearts Are On The Ground": Aboriginal Mothering, Oppression, Resistance and Rebirth.* Madison: Demeter Press, 2006.

Lawrence, Bonita. "Gender, race, and regulation of native identity in Canada and the United States: An overview." *Hypatia: A Journal of Feminist Philosophy* 18, 2 (2003): 3–25.

———. *"Real" Indians and Others: Mixed-Blood Urban Native Peoples and Indigenous Nationhood.* Vancouver: UBC Press, 2004.

Lucashenko, Melissa. "Violence Against Indigenous Women: Public and Private Dimensions." *Violence Against Women* 19, 3 (1996): 378–90.

Luther, Emily. "Whose 'Distinctive Culture'?" *Indigenous Law Journal* 8, 1 (2010): 27–53.

Mankiller, Wilma P. *Every Day is a Good Day: Reflections by Contemporary Indigenous Women.* Colorado: Fulcrum Publishing, 2004.

Maracle, Lee. *I am Woman: A Native Perspective on Sociology and Feminism.* Vancouver: Press Gang Publishers, 1999 [1996].

Martin, Karen, and Booran Mirraboopa. "Ways of Knowing, Being and Doing: A Theoretical Framework and Methods for Indigenous and Indigenist Research." *Journal of Australian Studies* 76, 27 (2003): 203–14.

McIsaac, Elizabeth. "Oral Narratives as a Site of Resistance: Indigenous Knowledge, Colonialism, and Western Discourse." *Indigenous Knowledges in Global Contexts: Multiple Readings of our World.* Ed. George J. Sefa Dei, Budd L. Hall, and Dorothy Goldin Rosenberg. Toronto: University of Tornoto Press Inc, 2000. 89–100.

Mihesuah, Devon A. "Commonality of Difference: American Indian Women and History." *American Indian Quarterly* 20.1 (1996): 15–27.

Mihesuah, Devon Abbott. *Indigenous American Women: Decolonization, Empowerment, Activism.* Lincoln: University of Nebraska Press, 2003.

Mithlo, Nancy Marie. "'A Real Feminine Journey': Locating Indigenous Feminisms in the Arts." *Meridians: Feminism, Race, Transnationalism* 9, 2 (2009): 1–30.

Moreton-Robinson, Aileen. *Talkin' up to the White Woman: Indigenous Women and Feminism.* Queensland: University of Queensland Press, 2000.

Ohmagari, Kayo. "Transmission of Indigenous Knowledge and Bush Skills Among the Western James Bay Cree Women of Subarctic Canada." *Human Ecology* 25, 2 (1997).

Palmer, Farah R., Tina Masters. "Maori Feminism and Sport Leadership: Exploring Maori Women's Experiences." *Sport Management Review* 13, 4 (2010): 341–4.

Radcliffe, Sarah A., Nina Laurie, and Robert Andolina. "The Transnationalization of Gender and Reimagining Andean Indigenous Development." *Signs: Journal of Women in Culture and Society* 29, 2 (2004): 387–416.

Seligmann, Linda J. "To Be In Between: The Cholas as Market Women." *Comparative Studies in Society and History* 31, 4 (1989): 694–721.

Simms, Muriel. "Impressions of Leadership Through a Native Woman's Eyes." *Urban Education* 35, 5 (2000): 637–44.

Smith, Andrea. *Conquest: Sexual Violence and American Indian Genocide*. Cambridge, MA: South End Press, 2005.

——. "Native American Feminism, Sovereignty, and Social Change." *Feminist Studies* 31, 1 (2005): 116–32.

Smith, Carol A. "The Symbolics of Blood: Mestizaje in the Americas." *Identities: Global Studies in Culture and Power* 3, 4 (1997): 495–521.

Sneider, Leah. "Gender, Literacy, and Sovereignty in Winnemucca's Life Among the Piutes." *American Indian Quarterly* 36, 3 (2012): 257–87.

Thomas, Robina, and Jacquie Green. "A Way of Life: Indigenous Perspectives on Anti-Oppressive Living." *First Peoples Child and Family Review* 3, 1 (2007): 91–104.

Tohe, Laura. "There is No Word for Feminism in My Language." *Wicazo Sa Review* 15, 2 (2000): 103–10.

Voyageur, Cora. *Firekeepers of the Twenty-First Century: First Nations Women Chiefs*. Montreal: McGill-Queen's University Press, 2008.

Whall, Helena, and Meena Shivdas. *Indigenous Women's Rights: Challenging Social and Gender Hierarchies*. Commonwealth Secretariat: 2007.

Williams, Carol. *Indigenous Women and Work: From Labour to Activism*. Illinois: University of Illinois Press, 2012.

Wilson, Kathi. "Ecofeminism and First Nations People in Canada: Linking Culture, Gender, and Nature." *Gender, Place, and Culture: A Journal of Feminist Geography* 12, 3 (2005): 333–55.

Yasaitis, Kelly E. "Native American Women: Where Are They Today?" *Gender Issues* 21, 4 (2003): 71–80.

3. QUEER INDIGENOUS AND TWO-SPIRIT THEORY

Adams, Heather, and Layli Phillips. "Ethnic Related Variations from the Cass Model of Homosexual Identity Formation: The Experiences of Two-Spirit, Lesbian and Gay Native Americans." *Journal of Homosexuality* 56, 7 (2009): 959–76.

——. "Experiences of Two-Spirit Lesbian and Gay Native Americans: An Argument for Standpoint Theory in Identity Research." *Identity: An International Journal of Theory and Research* 6, 3 (2006): 273–91.

Balestrery, Jean E. "Intersecting Discourses on Race and Sexuality: Compounded Colonization Among LGBTTQ American Indians/Alaska Natives." *Journal of Homosexuality* 59, 5 (2012): 633–55.

Bowers, Randolph. "Diversity in Creation: Identity, Race, Sexuality, and Indigenous Creativity." *International Journal of Diversity in Organizations, Communities, and Nations* 7, 1 (2007): 80–9.

Driskill, Qwo-Li. "Call Me Brother: Two-Spirit-edness, the Erotic, and Mixedblood Identity as Sites of Sovereignty and Resistance in Gregory Scofield's Poetry." In *Speak to Me Words: Essays on Contemporary American Indian Poetry*, ed. Dean Rader and Janice Gould. Tucson: University of Arizona Press, 2003.

——. "Doubleweaving Two-Spirit Critiques." *GLQ: A Journal of Lesbian and Gay Studies* 16, 2 (2010): 69–92.

——. "Mothertongue: Incorporating Theatre of the Oppressed into Language Restoration Movements." In *Nurturing Native Languages*, ed. Jon Reyhner, Octaviana Trujillo, Roberto Luis Carrasco, and Louise Lockard. Flagstaff: Northern Arizona University, 2003.

——. "Stolen From Our Bodies: First Nations Two-Spirits/Queers and the Journey to a Sovereign Erotic." *SAIL* 16, 2 (2004): 50–64.

———. "Theatre as Suture: Grassroots Performace, Decolonization and Healing." In *Aboriginal Oral Traditions: Theory, Practice, Ethics*, ed. Renée Hulan and Renate Eigenbrod. Winnipeg: Fernwood Publishing, 2008.

Driskill, Qwo-Li, Chris Finley, Brian Joseph Gilley, and Scott Lauria Morgensen, Eds. *Queer Indigenous Studies: Critical Interventions in Theory, Politics, and Literature*. Tucson: University of Arizona Press, 2011.

Evans-Campbell, Teresa, Karen Fredriksen-Goldsen, Karina U. Walters, and Antony Stately. "Caregiving Experiences Among American Indian Two-Spirit Men and Women: Contemporary and Historical Roles." *Journal of Gay and Lesbian Social Services* 18, 3 (2005): 75–92.

Gilley, Brian Joseph. *Becoming Two-Spirit: Gay Identity and Social Acceptance in Indian Country*. Lincoln: University of Nebraska Press, 2005.

———. "Making Traditional Spaces: Cultural Compromise at Two-Spirit Gatherings in Oklahoma." *American Indian Culture and Research Journal* 28, 2 (2004): 81–95.

———. "Two-Spirit Men's Sexual Survivance against the Inequality of Desire." In *Queer Indigenous Studies: Critical Interventions in Theory, Politics, and Literature*, ed. Qwo-Li Driskill, Chris Finley, Brian Joseph Gilley, and Scott Lauria Morgensen. Tucson: University of Arizona Press, 2011. 123–31.

Jacobs, Sue-Ellen, Wesley Thomas, and Sabine Lang. *Two-Spirit People: Native American Gender Identity*. Illinois: Board of Trustees of the University of Illinois, 1997.

Jamieson, Sara. "Ayahkwe Songs: AIDS and Mourning in Gregory Scofield's 'Urban Rez' Poems." *Canadian Poetry: Studies, Documents, Reviews* 57 (2005): 52–64.

Justice, Daniel Heath. "Notes Toward a Theory of Anomaly." *GLQ: A Journal of Lesbian and Gay Studies* 16, 1-2 (2010): 207-42.

Justice, Daniel Heath, and James H. Cox. "Queering Native Literature, Indigenizing Queer Theory." *Studies In American Indian Literatures* 20, 1 (2008): xiii-xiv.

Labelle, Diane, and Fiona Meyer-Cook. "Namaji: Two-Spirit Organizing in Montreal, Canada."

Journal of Gay and Lesbian Social Servies 16,1 (2003): 29–51.

Lang, Sabine. "Transformations of Gender in Native American Cultures." *Litteraria Pragensia* 21, 42 (2011): 70–81.

Morgensen, Scott Lauria. "Settler Homonationalism: Theorizing Settler Colonialism within Queer Modernities." *GLQ: A Journal of Lesbian and Gay Studies* 16, 1-2 (2010): 105Tohe, Laura. "There is No Word for Feminism in My Language." *Wicazo Sa Review* 15, 2 (2000): 103–10.31.

———. *Spaces Between Us: Queer Settler Colonialism and Indigenous Decolonization*. Minnesota: University of Minnesota Press, 2011.

Rifkin, Mark. *The Erotics of Sovereignty: Queer Native Writing in the Era of Self-Determination*. Minneapolis: University of Minnesota Press, 2012.

———. "Romancing Kinship: A Queer Reading of Indian Education and Zitkala-Ša's *American Indian Stories*." *GLQ: A Journal of Lesbian and Gay Studies* 12, 1 (2006): 27–59.

———. *When Did Indians Become Straight? Kinship, the History of Sexuality, and Native Sovereignty*. New York: Oxford University Press, 2011.

Ristock, Janice, Art Zoccole, and Lisa Passante. "Migration, Mobility and the Health and Well-Being of Aboriginal Two-Spirit/LGBTQ People: Findings from a Winnipeg Project." *Canadian Journal of Aboriginal Community-Based HIV/AIDS Research* 4 (2011): 5–30.

Scudeler, June. "'This Song I am Singing': Gregory Scofield's Interweavings of Métis, Gay, and Jewish Selfhoods." *Studies in Canadian Literature* 31, 1 (2006): 129–45.

Smith, Andrea. "Queer Theory and Native Studies: The Heteronormativity of Settler Colonialism." *GLQ: A Journal of Lesbian and Gay Studies* 16, 1Tohe, Laura. "There is No Word for Feminism in My Language." *Wicazo Sa Review* 15, 2 (2000): 103–10.2 (2010): 42–68.

Wilson, Alex. "How We Find Ourselves: Identity Development and Two-Spirit People." *Harvard Education Review* 66, 2 (2010): 303–18.

Wood, John C. *When Men Are Women; Manhood Among Gabra Nomads of East Africa*. Wisconsin: University of Wisconsin Press, 1999.

ACKNOWLEDGEMENTS

Sincere thanks are first due those whose wisdom appears within these pages. I feel fortunate for the time I was able to spend with each of you while conducting these interviews, and I am profoundly grateful for the gift of your words. The goal of this collection is to honour your knowledge, imagination, humour, and strength by allowing your words to enliven further discussions about Indigenous masculinities and gender. To Daniel Heath Justice, Niigaanwewidam James Sinclair, and Richard Van Camp—with whom I've been discussing masculinity for nearly a decade—thank you for modelling the contours of compassionate brotherhood. To Kim Anderson, Kateri Akiwenzie-Damm, Kristina Bidwell, Renate Eigenbrod, Brendan Hokowhitu, Rob Innes, Randy Jackson, Keavy Martin, Rick Monture, Scott Morgensen, Deanna Reder, Armand Garnet Ruffo, Jon Swift, and Ty Tengan, thank you for your fearless questioning, your critical sophistication, your inspiration, and your ethics. To the late Tommy Thrasher, thank you for your wisdom, generosity, and kindness; I'm tracking your footprints and remembering commitments. To my father and my brother—Ian and Sean McKegney—to my grandfathers—Lowry McKegney and Walter Lindhorst—and to Alan MacInnis, Chris McNeil, Tim Weis, and Tony Weis, all of whom have informed my understanding of non-dominative masculinity, I am happily indebted. To my most meaningful teachers—Sherrie, Caitlyn, Kyara, and Bubbles McKegney—I am endlessly grateful.

The travel required to conduct these interviews was made possible by two grants from the Social Sciences and Humanities Research Council. I was the primary researcher on one and a collaborator on the other, which was led by Dylan Robinson and Keavy Martin. I would like to thank SSHRC for its financial support, and I would like to thank Dylan, Keavy, and our colleagues Naomi Angel, Jonathan Dewar, Bev Diamond, Byron Dueck, David Garneau, Helen Gilbert, Elizabeth Kalbfleisch, Peter Morin, Niigaan Sinclair, and Pauline Wakeham for helpful critical perspectives on matters germane to this collection. To Jo-Ann Episkenew, who insisted that these interviews be published when she heard I was conducting them as part of a research project on Indigenous masculinities, I am most thankful. The collection was also made possible by the inspired efforts of Cara Fabre and Jennifer Hardwick, who worked with me as research assistants. I thank you for your professionalism, for your work ethic, and for the stellar critical insights you brought to the project; *Masculindians* is unquestionably enriched by your efforts. I wish to thank Glenn Bergen, David Carr, and Ariel Gordon at the University of Manitoba Press for your enthusiasm for this collection, your commitment to seeing it completed effectively and ethically, and your efforts to ensure that it reaches many readers. To Glenn I'd like to give special thanks for suggesting Dana Claxton's "Daddy's Gotta New Ride" from her *Mustang Suite* for the book's cover image. And to Dana Claxton, thank you for your creative brilliance and for the critical insight you share through the medium of the image.

INDEX

hunting, 2, 18, 25, 53, 63, 67, 115, 116, 132, 135, 137–38, 162, 164, 187, 230, 235

I

identity, 2–3, 5, 44, 81, 86, 90–91, 113, 117, 127–29, 131, 134, 149, 150–53, 158, 168, 173, 179, 225, 227, 228, 236

imperialism, 120–21, 123

incarceration, 6n2, 19, 29, 63, 66, 81–82, 132, 168, 171, 181, 203, 209, 231

Indian Act, 2, 18, 62, 77–78, 89, 93, 100, 205

Indigenous cultural traditions, 3–6, 7, 16–19, 57, 62–63, 77–78, 80–83, 85–86, 92, 97, 99, 108, 110, 114–19, 121, 123, 130, 133, 151–52, 154, 157, 163–64, 168, 179–80, 187, 190–91, 207, 210, 211, 212, 226–28, 230

Indigenous governance, 3, 7, 77, 89–91, 93, 94

initiation, 36, 90, 118, 187–88, 204, 226–27

Inuit, 42n1, 66, 68, 121, 131n3

Iroquois people and culture, 4, 10, 44, 57, 62, 77. *See also* Haudenosaunee people and culture

J

Jesuits, 42–43

Johnston, Basil H., 7, 9, 41–47, 224

Justice, Daniel Heath, 5, 6, 134–45, 181, 224

K

kinship, 5, 34, 61, 91, 93, 96, 132, 138, 192

L

land, 3, 10, 31, 68–69, 77, 82, 89, 91, 93, 112–14, 119, 121, 134, 204, 219–20, 225–27, 235–36

language, 6, 21–22, 24, 35–36, 43, 46–47, 58, 62–63, 84, 86, 97, 106, 121–23, 165, 203, 205–07, 210–11, 224, 237

lateral violence, 8, 54, 123

law, 3, 19, 43, 53, 57, 81, 110, 113, 119, 133, 121, 187, 237

Lawrence, Bonita, 6, 10, 49, 93, 97, 152

leaders, 18, 20, 67–68, 80, 89, 96, 99, 100, 103, 110, 112–13, 121, 162, 197, 204, 206, 231

literature, 7, 10, 29, 34, 46, 49, 55, 63, 78, 91, 108, 127, 143–45, 170, 178, 185–86, 199, 208, 224, 231, 232

longhouse, 19, 34, 77

M

manhood, 2, 5–6, 8–9, 19, 95, 114, 123, 126–27, 161, 188, 194, 199, 201, 215, 226–28, 233–34, 236

Māori people and culture, 6–7, 98–108

Maoli people and culture, 6–7, 109–10, 112, 115

Maracle, Lee, 6, 30–40, 176, 223, 227, 230, 233

masculinity, 1–11, 21–22, 29, 41, 57, 62, 78–79, 91, 92, 98–103, 107–08, 110–11, 114, 116, 121, 123–24, 127–33, 136, 161–62, 166–68, 170–71, 173, 180–81, 186, 200, 205, 211–212, 214–18, 211, 214, 225, 227–28, 230–237; hypermasculinity, 1, 4, 7, 60, 78, 145, 236; Indigenous masculinities, 3–9, 21, 62, 91–92, 92, 99, 101, 108, 121, 124, 228, 231–33, 235–36; settler masculinities, 8, 235–36

McLeod, Neal, 4, 63 n.3, 203–12, 224

media, 3, 7, 62, 78, 106, 113–14, 158, 177–78

medicine, 20, 29, 38, 67, 88, 96–97, 119, 152, 153, 184–86, 189, 191, 220

menstruation, 28, 49, 51, 152, 153

Métis people and culture, 89, 93, 127–28, 131, 144, 203–04, 212

midwifery, 119, 121–22, 124, 201

military, 25, 96, 106, 110–11, 114–15, 155, 166–68

misogyny, 8, 97, 99, 113, 137, 218

missing women, 181–82

modernity, 67–68, 99–100, 104, 167

monotheism, 22, 24–29

Moses, Daniel David, 56–64, 223, 224

motherhood, 8, 17–18, 20, 25, 26, 31, 34, 37, 45–46, 48–51, 53, 57, 60, 61, 63, 65, 70–71, 88, 94, 133, 135, 137, 143, 152–54, 157, 166, 168, 173, 192, 194, 196–99, 202, 204–06, 212, 215–17

N

nationhood, 1, 3, 18, 32, 47, 89, 93, 110–12, 119, 121, 134, 225–27, 232, 234–35, 237

New Zealand, 7, 98–107, 119, 236

noble savage, 1, 78, 112, 125

O

Ojibway people and culture, 17, 24, 156, 167, 168, 230. *See also* Anishnaabe people and culture

oppression, 8, 30, 104, 113, 123, 178, 202, 218, 233

orality, 58, 206–07

P

Pan-Indian, 156, 235,

pantheism, 22, 24, 26, 27, 29

pathologization, 102, 108, 113, 115

patriarchy, 2–4, 7–9, 11, 57, 77, 88–89, 91–95, 99–100, 102, 121, 133, 218, 225

performance and performativity, 29, 100, 126–27, 157–58, 200, 207, 234, 236

poetry and poetics, 5, 10, 25, 34, 39, 48–50, 53–55, 58–60, 94, 178, 180, 195, 200, 204–05, 207–09, 215–16, 219–21, 237

politics, 5, 9, 18, 77, 79–81, 84, 86, 88–89, 93–94, 102, 109–10, 126–27, 134, 215, 218, 231

polytheism, 22–23

popular culture, 1, 6–7, 62, 78, 99, 102, 107, 111–12, 139–40, 224, 236

poverty, 88, 102, 185, 200, 231, 234, 237

power, 2, 6–8, 23–26, 28, 49–50, 52, 61, 67, 77, 79,
    84, 90–92, 94–95, 100, 103, 126, 130, 133, 141,
    144, 152, 157, 162, 167–69, 171, 178, 180, 182,
    187, 189, 190, 193, 197, 204–05, 214
prison, 29, 63, 81–82, 203, 209, 231. *See also*
    incarceration
protectorship, 18, 30–31, 64, 88, 96, 114, 123,
    158–59, 163–64, 167–68, 174, 182–83, 185,
    187, 190, 193, 214, 216, 224–27, 228
puberty, 17, 89 90, 226

Q

quarantine, 36, 38, 40
queerness, 3, 7–10, 144–45, 150–51, 218, 236. *See
    also* Two Spirit people and theory

R

race, 2, 3, 128, 139–40, 234
reconciliation, 44, 137, 209, 216–17
reserves, 2, 45, 47, 51, 52, 55, 83, 89–90, 158, 161,
    162, 186–87, 209, 234
residential schooling, 4, 17, 31, 41–44, 46–47,
    52–53, 66–67, 71, 73, 77–78, 93, 119, 121–22,
    150, 155–56, 166–69, 174, 176, 179, 181, 204,
    205, 225–26
resilience, 5, 88, 229
resistance, 3, 88, 99, 103, 113, 123, 203–04, 231, 237
respect, 17, 19, 40, 49–51, 54–55, 62, 66–67, 85–87,
    90, 94, 105, 113, 144, 152, 155, 158–59, 168,
    173, 187, 190, 198, 200, 202, 210, 229, 231, 232
responsibilities, 3, 6, 7, 16–20, 25, 34, 35, 39, 45, 46,
    54, 56, 60, 64, 76, 79, 81, 82, 84–86, 90, 96, 104,
    108, 116, 123, 134–35, 138, 164, 183, 188, 196,
    206–08, 2011–12, 221, 224, 227–31, 233–34,
    236–37
Rifkin, Mark, 2–3
rites of passage, 5, 19, 122, 150, 188
roles, 3, 4, 7, 17–18, 42, 57, 61, 62, 77, 86, 90, 92, 93,
    108, 110, 116, 121–24, 131, 133, 150, 170, 180,
    182, 215, 225, 228–29
Roman Catholicism, 72, 133, 176, 191, 197, 200
rugby, 101, 103–07

S

Scofield, Gregory, 48, 213–21, 223
settlers, 1, 3, 5, 7–9, 57, 77, 99, 111–12, 114, 119,
    193, 196, 208, 235, 236
sexuality, 10, 19, 23, 28, 49–53, 118–22, 139–40,
    144–45, 149–51, 153, 157, 161–62, 166,
    176–79, 182, 188–90, 190, 197–98, 202,
    214–15, 220, 223–26, 230–31
sexual violence, 8, 19, 26–27, 42, 95, 120, 121, 144,
    231, 235
shame, 10, 30, 50, 52–53, 93, 95, 112–14, 119, 122,
    145, 155, 176–77, 188–89, 192, 196–97, 198
Smith, Andrea, 6, 8, 179

social justice, 87, 118–19, 121–22, 124, 236
sovereignty, 87–89, 118–19, 122
spirituality, 27, 49, 61, 63–64, 76–77, 82–84, 105,
    115, 189, 191, 197, 211, 214, 220
sport, 6–7, 73, 101–07, 110, 158, 174–75, 207, 218,
    224, 236
stereotypes, 1, 3, 78–79, 93, 103, 105, 112, 140–41,
    158, 162–64, 180–81, 186
Stimson, Adrian, 148–59, 224
suicide, 6n2, 55, 69, 171, 191–92
sweat lodges, 43, 49, 152–53, 156–57, 169, 192,
    219–220

T

talk-story, 116–17
Tengan, Ty P. Kāwika, 3, 6–7, 109–17, 223
theatre, 25, 29, 58–61
Thrasher, Thomas Kimeksun, 65–73, 224
Tlicho (Dogrib) people and culture, 5, 186, 190–92,
    231
trauma, 8, 25, 32, 44, 53, 95, 106, 200, 201, 208
Trickster, 3–4, 46, 57, 164
Two Spirit people and theory, 3, 7–10, 34, 122, 124,
    150–51, 153–54, 158, 161, 166, 200, 218. *See
    also* queerness

U

urban, 18, 62, 80, 90, 104, 107–08, 111, 129,
    162–64, 168, 200, 214, 234

V

Van Camp, Richard, 3, 5–6, 9, 177, 184–93, 224,
    226, 230–31
violence, 4, 6, 8, 10, 19, 28, 44–45, 52–55, 60, 62, 79,
    81, 88–90, 94–95, 102, 109, 113m 116, 120–21,
    123, 127–29, 131–33, 144, 162, 181–82,
    187–88, 192, 195, 197–98, 200, 204, 209, 215,
    223, 231; colonial violence, 4, 120, 121, 123,
    127, 131; gender-based violence, 8, 94–95, 123.
    See also sexual violence
Vizenor, Gerald, 2, 3, 210

W

warriorhood, 1, 32, 34, 41, 45, 55, 62, 63, 76,
    78–79, 83–86, 93, 95–96, 102–03, 105–06, 109,
    112–14, 130, 142–45, 149, 151, 181, 185–88,
    193, 210–11, 223–26
Womack, Craig S., 3, 63, 237
weetigo/windigo/wîhtikow, 169, 207–08

Y

youth, 11, 36, 41, 46, 56, 79, 80, 94, 101, 104, 114,
    120, 122, 129, 160, 188–89, 226, 237